Collins

AQA GCSE 9-1
French

Revision Guide

Vanessa Salter and Karine Harrington

About this Revision & Practice book

Revise

These pages provide a recap of everything you need to know for each topic.

HT Higher Tier content is highlighted with this icon.

You should read through all the information before taking the Quick Test at the end. This will test whether you can recall the key facts.

> **Quick Test**
>
> 1. How do you say in French...? before; now; in the future.
> 2. What is the difference between **je joue au foot** and **je jouais au foot**?
> 3. Translate into English: **J'allais au club des jeunes.**
> 4. Translate into French: I used to go swimming.
> 5. Translate into English: **Je voudrais essayer les sports d'hiver.**

Practise

These topic-based questions appear shortly after the revision pages for each topic and will test whether you have understood the topic. If you get any of the questions wrong, make sure you read the correct answer carefully.

Review

These topic-based questions appear later in the book, allowing you to revisit the topic and test how well you have remembered the information. If you get any of the questions wrong, make sure you read the correct answer carefully.

Mix it Up

These pages feature a mix of questions from the different topics. They will make sure you can recall the relevant information to answer a question without being told which topic it relates to.

Workbook & Audio

This section features even more topic-based questions as well as practice exam papers, providing two further practice opportunities for each topic to guarantee the best results.

Visit our website at **www.collins.co.uk/collinsGCSErevision** to download listening tracks to accompany the listening exam paper. You will also find lots more information about the advantages of spaced practice and how to plan for it.

ebook

To access the ebook revision guide visit
collins.co.uk/ebooks
and follow the step-by-step instructions.

QR Codes

Found throughout the book, the QR codes can be scanned on your smartphone for extra practice and explanations.

A QR code in the Revise section links to a Quick Recall Quiz and / or the Key Sounds on that topic.

A QR code in the Practise and Review sections links to audio content to be used with the question indicated by the 🔊 icon.

A QR code in the Workbook section links to one or both of the following:
*   a video working through the solution to one of the questions on that topic, indicated by the ▶ icon
*   audio content to be used with a question, indicated by the 🔊 icon.

Acknowledgements

The authors and publisher are grateful to the copyright holders for permission to use quoted materials and images.

All images © Shutterstock.com

Every effort has been made to trace copyright holders and obtain their permission for the use of copyright material. The authors and publisher will gladly receive information enabling them to rectify any error or omission in subsequent editions. All facts are correct at time of going to press.

Published by Collins
An imprint of HarperCollins*Publishers* Ltd
1 London Bridge Street
London SE1 9GF

HarperCollins*Publishers*
Macken House, 39/40 Mayor Street Upper,
Dublin 1, D01 C9W8, Ireland

© HarperCollins*Publishers* Limited 2024

ISBN 9780008664206

10 9 8 7 6 5 4 3 2 1

British Library Cataloguing in Publication Data.

A CIP record of this book is available from the British Library.

Authors: Vanessa Salter, Karine Harrington and Stuart Glover
Publishers: Sara Bennett and Clare Souza
Project editor: Chantal Addy
Cover Design: Sarah Duxbury and Kevin Robbins
Inside Concept Design: Sarah Duxbury and Paul Oates
Text Design and Layout: Jouve India Private Limited
Production: Bethany Brohm
Printed in India by Multivista Global Pvt.Ltd

This book contains FSC™ certified paper and other controlled sources to ensure responsible forest management.

For more information visit: www.harpercollins.co.uk/green

Contents

Contents

Review Questions

Key Concepts

1   Copy out the words below into the correct space in the three lists.

juillet	hiver	dimanche	printemps	août
mardi	avril	vendredi	mercredi	janvier

| **Les jours de la semaine**
(days of the week)

lundi

‥‥‥‥‥‥‥

‥‥‥‥‥‥‥

jeudi

‥‥‥‥‥‥‥

samedi

‥‥‥‥‥‥‥ | **Les mois**
(months)

‥‥‥‥‥‥‥   ‥‥‥‥‥‥‥

février

mars   **septembre**

‥‥‥‥‥‥‥   **octobre**

mai   **novembre**

juin   **décembre** | **Les saisons**
(seasons)

le ‥‥‥‥‥‥‥

l'été

l'automne

l' ‥‥‥‥‥‥‥ |

[10 marks]

2   Complete the following to make true sentences about yourself.

    a)   Je m'appelle ‥‥‥‥‥‥‥‥‥‥‥‥‥   My name is ‥‥‥‥‥‥‥‥‥‥‥‥‥

    b)   **J'ai (treize / quatorze / quinze / seize) ans.**   I am (13 / 14 / 15 / 16) years old.

    c)   **Je suis né(e) en (2010 / 2011 / 2012 / ‥‥‥‥).**   I was born in (2010 / 2011 / 2012 / ‥‥‥‥).

    d)   **Je ressemble à (ma mère / mon père / ‥‥‥‥‥‥).**   I look like (my mother / my father / ‥‥‥‥).

[4 marks]

3   Answer these questions in French.

    a)   **Où habites-tu?**

    b)   **As-tu des frères et sœurs?**

    c)   **As-tu un animal à la maison?**

    d)   **Quelle est la date de ton anniversaire?**   [4 marks]

4 Copy each group of numbers, changing the words into numerals.

a) dix, deux, douze

b) quatre, quarante, quatorze

c) quinze, cinquante-cinq, cinq

d) trente, treize, trois

e) soixante, soixante-dix, seize

f) vingt-quatre, quatre-vingts, quatre-vingt-dix   [6 marks]

5 Write these numerals as French words.

a) 32

b) 53

c) 46

d) 65

e) 74

f) 93

g) 82   [7 marks]

6 Draw lines to match the time to the correct sentence.

a) 8.00

b) 8.10

c) 8.15

d) 8.25

e) 8.30

f) 8.45

g) 8.50

Il est huit heures et demie.

Il est neuf heures moins dix.

Il est huit heures.

Il est huit heures et quart.

Il est neuf heures moins le quart.

Il est huit heures vingt-cinq.

Il est huit heures dix.   [7 marks]

7 Draw lines to match the weather phrases.

a) il fait beau

b) il pleut

c) il fait du soleil

d) il neige

e) il fait du brouillard

it's foggy

it's snowing

it's fine

it's sunny

it's raining   [5 marks]

My Family and Me

Quick Recall Quiz

Key Sounds

You must be able to:

- Talk and write about (your family's) appearance and personality
- Say how well you get on with family members
- Make adjectives agree correctly.

Family Members

mon (demi-) frère	my (step / half-) brother
mon (beau-) père	my (step-) father
mon oncle	my uncle
mon grand-père	my grandfather
mon cousin (m) / **ma cousine** (f)	my cousin
ma (demi-) sœur	my (step / half-) sister
ma (belle-) mère	my (step-) mother
ma tante	my aunt
ma grand-mère	my grandmother
mes (grands-) parents	my (grand) parents

Key Point

There are three words for 'my' and three words for 'your':

Masc. singular	**mon**	**ton**
Fem. singular	**ma**	**ta**
Plural	**mes**	**tes**

Introducing People and Describing Appearance

voici	here is / are	**voilà**	there is / are
il s'appelle	his name is	**elle s'appelle**	her name is
il est	he is	**elle est**	she is
ils sont	they are	**elles sont**	they (f) are
assez	quite	**très**	very
trop	too	**un peu**	a bit

HT **Je (te) présente...**	I introduce… (to you)
HT **Décris ta famille!**	Describe your family!

Key Verbs

il est	he is
elle est	she is
ils sont	they are
elles sont	they are

- Adjectives describe people and things. They must agree with the noun they describe.
- **Regular** adjectives add **–e** in the feminine singular, **–s** in the masculine plural and **–es** in the feminine plural. If the adjective already ends in **–e** (e.g. **jeune**) it stays the same in the feminine. Notice that some adjectives, like **vieux** and **beau**, are irregular.

	masculine singular	feminine singular	masculine plural	feminine plural
big / tall	**grand**	**grande**	**grands**	**grandes**
small	**petit**	**petite**	**petits**	**petites**
pretty	**joli**	**jolie**	**jolis**	**jolies**
young	**jeune**	**jeune**	**jeunes**	**jeunes**
old	**vieux**	**vieille**	**vieux**	**vieilles**
beautiful / good looking	**beau**	**belle**	**beaux**	**belles**

Key Sounds

Open **eu / œu** sound. Listen and repeat: **sœur**

- **Voici mon père. Il s'appelle Tom. Il est très grand et assez jeune.**
  Here is my father. His name is Tom. He is very tall and quite young.
  Voilà mes sœurs, Belle et Sophie. Elles sont très grandes et assez jeunes.
  There are my sisters, Belle and Sophie. They are very tall and quite young.
  Ma mère est assez belle mais un peu vieille!
  My mother is quite beautiful but a bit old!

Relationships

Je m'entends bien avec…	I get on well with…
Je ne m'entends pas très bien avec…	I don't get on very well with…
Je me dispute avec…	I argue with…
On se dispute toujours.	We argue all the time. / We're always arguing.

Describing Personality

- Here are some **regular** adjectives that follow the rules given on page 8:

amusant	funny	**agréable**	nice
bavard	talkative	**calme**	quiet
content	happy	**drôle**	funny
embêtant	annoying	**sympa(thique)**	kind / pleasant
fort	loud / strong	**terrible**	awful
intelligent	clever	**timide**	shy
		triste	sad

HT **sensible**	sensitive

- Some adjectives have slightly different patterns:

généreux / généreuse	generous
travailleur / travailleuse	hard-working
gentil /gentille	kind
fier / fière	proud
actif / active	active

Je m'entends bien avec mes cousines, car elles sont toujours très gentilles et vraiment patientes.
I get on well with my cousins because they are always very kind and really patient.
Par contre, je me dispute souvent avec mon frère parce qu'il est vraiment embêtant.
On the other hand, I often argue with my brother, because he is really annoying.

Key Point

Some 'relationship' verbs are reflexive – remember to use a reflexive pronoun (**me**, **te**, **se**, etc.) with the verb:
Je me dispute avec…
I argue with…
Elle s'entend bien avec…
She gets on well with…

Key Sounds

-ill- / -ille sound:
famill**e** (family), **vie**ill**e** (old), **gent**ill**e** (kind)
Practise saying these words out loud.

Key Point

To describe relationships in more detail, use expressions of frequency:

toujours	always
souvent	often
parfois	sometimes
généralement	generally
normalement	usually
vraiment	really / truly
presque	almost
surtout	above all

Quick Test

1. Give two ways of introducing someone in French.
2. Choose the correct word:
   mon / ma / mes sœur; mon / ma / mes parents; mon / ma / mes père.
3. Write these adjectives in the feminine form:
   grand, joli, jeune, petit, beau, vieux, gentil.
4. Translate into English:
   Je m'entends très bien avec mon oncle. Il est assez vieux, mais il est toujours heureux et agréable.
5. Translate into French:
   I don't get on very well with my sister. She is very loud and annoying. We're always arguing.

My Friends and Me

You must be able to:

- Describe a friend's appearance and personality
- Explain why you are friends
- Use **on** and **nous** correctly.

My Friends and Me

mon ami (m) **/ mon amie** (f)	my friend
mon copain (m) **/ ma copine** (f)	my friend / mate
mon meilleur ami / copain	my best friend (male)…
ma meilleure amie / copine	my best friend (female)…
il a	he has
elle a	she has
l'œil	eye
les yeux	eyes
les cheveux	hair
les yeux bleus	blue eyes
les cheveux longs et bruns	long, brown hair
Il a quatorze ans.	He is 14 years old.
Elle est plus grande que moi.	She is taller than me.
Il est moins grand que moi.	He is smaller (less tall) than me.
Elle est de taille moyenne.	She is of medium height.

Mon meilleur ami s'appelle Lucas. Il a les yeux bruns et les cheveux courts et noirs.
My best friend is called Lucas. He has brown eyes and short, black hair.
Ma meilleure copine s'appelle Chloé. Elle est un peu plus grande que moi.
My best friend is called Chloe. She is a bit taller than me.

Why We are Good Friends

il est	he is
il n'est pas	he isn't
il n'est jamais	he is never
elle est	she is
elle n'est pas	she isn't
elle n'est jamais	she is never
on est / nous sommes	we are
en colère	angry / cross

Il est toujours amusant et (il) n'est jamais en colère.
He is always funny and (he) is never angry.
Elle est très bavarde, mais elle n'est pas affreuse.
She is very talkative, but she isn't awful.
On est très actifs et sportifs.
We are very active and sporty.

j'aime...	I like...
j'adore...	I love...
HT j'apprécie...	I like... / appreciate...
sa confiance	his / her confidence
son indépendance	his / her independence
ses compétences	his / her abilities
HT son attitude	his / her attitude
HT son soutien	his / her support
HT ses qualités	his / her qualities

Mon meilleur ami est vraiment sympa; j'adore sa confiance.
My best friend is really nice; I love his confidence.

HT **Ma meilleure copine est souvent vive et j'apprécie son attitude positive.**
My best mate is often lively and I like her positive attitude.

Our Interests

nous avons / on a...	we have...
les mêmes intérêts / passe-temps	the same interests / hobbies
nous aimons / on aime...	we like...
la même musique	the same music
la même équipe de foot	the same football team
les mêmes sports	the same sports
les mêmes émissions de télé	the same TV programmes
nous faisons / on fait...	we do...
beaucoup de choses ensemble	lots of things together

- **On** and **nous** can both be used to mean 'we'. Take care to use the correct verb ending with each one. In the present tense: **on** uses the **il / elle** (3rd person singular) verb form. Most verbs end in **-ons** in the **nous** form.

On sort / Nous sortons tous les week-ends.
We go out every weekend.

On rit / Nous rions toujours.
We always laugh / we're always laughing.

On s'amuse bien / Nous nous amusons bien.
We have a good time.

On va / Nous allons au cinéma.
We go to the cinema.

On joue / Nous jouons à des jeux vidéo ensemble.
We play video games together.

On écoute / Nous écoutons de la musique ensemble.
We listen to music together.

Key Point

The possessive adjectives **son**, **sa** and **ses** can mean 'his', 'her' or 'its'. The gender of the noun determines which of the three words to use – so a masculine noun uses **son**: **son soutien** can mean both 'his support' and 'her support'. A feminine noun uses **sa**: **sa confiance** can mean both 'his confidence' and 'her confidence'. Listen to or read the rest of the sentence to decide the correct English translation.

Key Point

même (same) is an important little word.
To say 'the same':
le même (followed by a masculine singular noun)
la même (followed by a feminine singular noun)
les mêmes (followed by a plural noun)

Key Verbs

nous avons / on a
we have
nous sommes / on est
we are
nous aimons / on aime
we like
nous faisons / on fait
we do
nous allons / on va
we go

Quick Test

1. Find the odd word out and explain why:
   active / inquiète / positif / sportive / généreuse
2. Choose the correct words, then translate the sentence:
   Nous aimons le / la / les même / mêmes musique et le / la / les même / mêmes sports.
3. Change the following to **on** + verb:
   nous avons, nous allons, nous aimons, nous faisons.
4. Write a sentence with each of the verbs in **3**.

Marriage and Relationships

Quick Recall Quiz

Key Sounds

You must be able to:

- Describe people's marital status
- Give your opinions on marriage and future relationships
- **HT** Use **depuis** with the present tense.

Relationships

le garçon	boy	**la fille**	girl
le fils (unique)	(only) son	**la fille (unique)**	(only) daughter
l'homme	man	**la dame**	lady
le mari	husband	**la femme**	woman / wife
l'adulte	adult	**l'enfant**	child
l'adolescent	adolescent / teenager	**le couple**	couple
le / la partenaire	partner	**la personne**	person

Je suis fils / fille unique. — I am an only child.
Ce garçon est le fils de mon oncle. — This boy is my uncle's son.
Cette dame est la femme de mon fils. — This lady is my son's wife.
Cet homme est le frère de mon père. — This man is my father's brother.

Marital Status

célibataire	single (i.e. not married)
(être) marié(e)	(to be) married
(être) séparé(e)	(to be) separated
habiter seul	to live alone
habiter ensemble	to live together
se marier	to get married
se séparer	to separate

HT **Ma sœur est mariée depuis six mois.**
My sister has been married for six months.

HT **Mes parents sont séparés depuis deux ans.**
My parents have been separated for two years.

- Use the reflexive verb **se marier** when talking about getting married.
  Ma cousine va se marier en juin.
  My cousin **is going to get married** in June.
  Mon frère s'est marié la semaine dernière.
  My brother **got married** last week.

In the Future

Tu voudrais te marier?	Do you want to get married?
Je désire...	I want to...
J'espère...	I hope (to)...
Je préfère...	I prefer (to)...
Je voudrais...	I would like to...
Je ne voudrais pas...	I wouldn't like to...
J'ai l'intention de...	I intend to...
Je ne sais pas (encore)...	I don't know (yet)...

Key Point

In French, the word 'this' must agree with the noun to which it refers. Use **ce** for a masculine singular noun, **cet** for a masculine noun beginning with a vowel or silent **h** and **cette** for a feminine singular noun. In the plural, use **ces**.

Key Sound

Soft **c** and **ç**: when **c** is followed by **e** or **i** it has a soft sound and is pronounced as **s** (e.g. **c**e (this), **c**ette (this), **c**inéma (cinema)). If it is followed by **a**, **o** or **u** it has a harsh sound and is pronounced as **k** (e.g. **c**ouple (couple)), but we use **ç** to make it soft (e.g. gar**ç**on (boy)).

Key Point

To express your opinions about future relationships, use these phrases with an infinitive, e.g. **J'espère trouver l'amour.** I hope to find love.

Ça m'est égal.	I'm not bothered.		
HT **J'aimerais...**	I would like to...		
HT **Il vaut mieux...**	It's better (to)...		
changer	to change	**choisir**	to choose
rencontrer	to meet	**trouver**	to find

J'espère rencontrer mon partenaire idéal. I hope to meet my ideal partner.
Je désire avoir des enfants. I want to have children.
Je voudrais me marier. I would like to get married.
J'ai l'intention de rester célibataire. I intend to stay single.
Je préfère vivre en couple. I prefer to live together as a couple.

For or Against Marriage?

Que penses-tu du mariage?	What do you think about marriage?
À mon avis,…	In my opinion,…
Pour moi,…	For me,…
Personnellement,…	Personally,…

l'amour	love	**l'avenir**	future
le choix	choice	**le mariage**	marriage / wedding
le mariage du même sexe	same sex marriage		
le PACS	civil partnership		
la foi	faith	**le sentiment**	feeling
la société	society	**la tradition**	tradition
la vie	life	**HT** **l'enfance**	childhood

Personnellement, je suis pour le mariage car c'est important pour ma foi et c'est mieux pour les enfants.
Personally, I am for marriage because it's important for my faith and it's better for children.

Je suis contre le mariage. Pour moi, vivre ensemble est plus pratique et plus moderne.
I'm against marriage. For me, living together is more practical and more modern.

À mon avis, c'est un choix personnel. Le mariage change la vie et l'amour est plus important que la tradition.
In my opinion, it's a personal choice. Marriage changes your life and love is more important than tradition.

Key Sound

ce and **se** sound exactly the same. **ce** means 'this' whereas **se** is part of a reflexive verb. When you are writing, think about the grammar and the context to ensure you have the correct spelling. In the same way, think carefully about **c'est** (it is) and **s'est** (reflexive form)!

Key Point

 Depuis means 'since'. Use it with the present tense to say how long something has been going on, e.g. **Mon oncle est marié depuis trois semaines!** My uncle has been married for three weeks!

Key Sound

-er verbs in the infinitive form, e.g. **chang**er (to change), **rest**er (to stay), **se mari**er (to marry) and words ending in **é**, e.g. **sépar**é (separated), **mari**é (married) sound the same.

Key Point

Use **plus** or **moins** with adjectives to make the comparative, e.g. **C'est plus pratique.** It's more practical. **C'est moins traditionnel.** It's less traditional. **C'est mieux.** It's better. **C'est pire.** It's worse.

Quick Test

1. Choose **ce, cet, cette** or **ces** to fill the blanks and explain why.
   _____ dame _____ couple _____ filles _____ enfant
2. Translate into English:
   a) **Mon frère est marié depuis trois ans.**
   b) **Ma sœur s'est mariée le week-end dernier.**
3. Translate into French:
   a) My parents have been married for twenty years.
   b) I would like to stay single (unmarried).
4. Put these verbs into the negative form:
   je désire   tu voudrais   j'ai l'intention de   tu penses

Practice Questions

Identity and Relationships with Others

1 Choose the correct underlined words to complete each sentence.

   a) Ma tante est assez <u>jeune</u> / <u>jeunes</u> et très <u>joli</u> / <u>jolie</u>, mais un peu <u>bavard</u> / <u>bavarde</u>.

   b) Mon beau-père est trop <u>vieux</u> / <u>vieille</u> et assez <u>paresseux</u> / <u>paresseuse</u>.

   c) Mes frères sont <u>petit</u> / <u>petits</u>, <u>beau</u> / <u>beaux</u> et très <u>amusants</u> / <u>amusantes</u>.

   d) Ma sœur est assez <u>belle</u> / <u>belles</u> et un peu plus <u>grand</u> / <u>grande</u> que moi.　　[10 marks]

2 Fill in the blanks with the correct words from the box below.

cheveux	faisons	meilleure	heureuse	jamais
depuis	s'entend	moins	verts	son

Ma _____ copine s'appelle Yasmine. Elle a les yeux _____ et les bruns et longs. Elle est un peu _____ grande que moi. Je la connais _____ six ans. On _____ très bien et on ne se dispute _____. Nous _____ beaucoup de choses ensemble. J'aime _____ attitude positive – Yasmine est toujours _____.

[10 marks]

3 Unscramble the sentences.

   a) Mon ville allons meilleur les copain moi week-ends en tous et

   b) amusante mère Ma heureuse et toujours est

   c) les et yeux et cheveux J'ai courts bleus noirs les

   d) généreux gentil embêtante plutôt Mon est et frère mais sœur est ma　　[4 marks]

4 Fill in the blanks using the correct word in the brackets.

   a) Nous _____ (sont, sommes, est) de bons amis.

   b) Elles _____ (a, avons, ont) les cheveux longs.

   c) Il _____ (vont, va, vais) en ville.

   d) Je _____ (m'entends, m'entend, m'entendre) bien avec mon frère.

   e) Elle n'_____ pas (es, s'est, est) mariée.　　[5 marks]

5 Read the sentences. Write **P** for a positive opinion, **N** for a negative opinion or **P+N** for a positive and negative opinion.

a) Je me dispute souvent avec mon frère car il est toujours en colère. ....

b) Nous sortons tous les week-ends et nous nous amusons bien ensemble. ....

c) Je m'entends bien avec mon père – il n'est jamais embêtant. ....

d) J'adore sa confiance, mais elle peut parfois être un peu paresseuse. .... [4 marks]

6 Correct the mistake in the underlined words.

a) On <u>faisons</u> beaucoup de choses ensemble.

b) Nous <u>aime</u> la même équipe de foot.

c) <u>On</u> avons les mêmes intérêts.

d) On <u>aimons</u> les mêmes émissions de télé.

e) <u>Nous</u> va au cinéma ensemble.

f) On <u>écoutons</u> de la musique ensemble. [6 marks]

7 Read the sentences aloud.

a) Mon meilleur copain s'appelle Lucas.

b) Je préfère rester célibataire.

c) J'ai une grande famille.

d) Mon oncle est assez vieux.

e) Elle a les yeux bleus.

f) Ma sœur n'est pas mariée. [6 marks]

8 Complete the sentences, using your own ideas.

a) Je m'entends bien avec .... parce qu'il / elle ....

b) Je me dispute souvent avec .... car ....

c) Mon meilleur copain / Ma meilleure copine a les yeux .... et les cheveux ....

d) Mon meilleur ami / Ma meilleure amie est toujours .... Il / Elle n'est jamais ....

e) Nous avons .... On aime .... On .... ensemble.

[11 marks]

Food and Drink

Quick Recall Quiz

Key Sounds

You must be able to:

- Discuss food and drink, including likes and preferences
- Talk and write about mealtimes and eating out
- Use the perfect tense with **avoir** to talk about what you have eaten or drunk.

Food and Drink

J'ai faim!	I'm hungry!	**J'ai soif!**	I'm thirsty!

J'ai faim – passe-moi le pain, s'il te plaît!
I'm hungry – pass me the bread, please!
J'ai soif – où est le lait, s'il vous plaît? I'm thirsty – where is the milk, please?

la boisson	drink / beverage	**l'alcool**	alcohol
les courses	food shopping	**la cuisine**	cooking / cookery
le goût	taste	**le fast-food**	fast food
le produit	product	**la nourriture**	food
HT **le régime**	diet	**la recette**	recipe

Key Point

Some common phrases use the verb **avoir** in French when we use the verb 'to be' in English. For example, **J'ai faim** (literally I have hunger) I'm hungry, **j'ai soif** I'm thirsty.

Types of Cuisine

frais (m) / **fraîche** (f)	fresh	**local**	local
régional	regional	**spécial**	special
naturel	natural	**simple**	simple
traditionnel	traditional	**végan**	vegan
végétarien	vegetarian		

J'aime manger des produits locaux. I like eating local produce / products.
Mes parents préfèrent la cuisine indienne.
My parents prefer Indian cookery / cuisine.
Ma tante prépare des recettes végétariennes.
My aunt prepares vegetarian recipes.

- Adjectives ending in **-el** and **-en** (e.g. **traditionnel**, **végétarien**) double the consonant in the feminine form, e.g.

  la cuisine traditionnelle traditional cuisine
  les recettes végétariennes vegetarian recipes

Key Point

Adjectives ending in **-al** (e.g. **local**, **régional**, **spécial**) change to **-aux** in the masculine plural form, e.g.

des produits locaux
local products
des vins régionaux
regional wines
des repas spéciaux
special meals

Mealtimes

le petit-déjeuner	breakfast	**le déjeuner**	lunch
le dîner	dinner	**le repas**	meal

manger (to eat)	**je mange**	**on mange**	**nous mangeons**
boire (to drink)	**je bois**	**on boit**	**nous buvons**
prendre (to take, have)	**je prends**	**on prend**	**nous prenons**

Pour le petit-déjeuner, je ne prends rien.
For breakfast, I don't eat anything.
Ma sœur ne mange jamais de poulet parce qu'elle n'aime pas le goût.
My sister never eats chicken because she doesn't like the taste.

HT **Elles ne boivent plus d'alcool.** They no longer drink alcohol.

HT **Nous ne mangeons ni viande ni poisson car nous sommes végans.**
We eat neither meat nor fish because we are vegan.

Key Sounds

-al; **aux**. Listen and repeat: **loc**al, **loc**aux; **région**al, **région**aux; **spéci**al, **spéci**aux
Remember some nouns make a similar change: **animal**, **animaux**; **journal**, **journaux**

HT **Ils ne mangent que des produits frais.**
They only eat fresh produce / products.

Eating in a Restaurant

la carte	menu	**l'addition**	bill	
les entrées	starters	**le service**	service	

le plat (principal) (main) course / dish

- To describe an event in the past, use the perfect tense.
- Regular **-er** verbs follow this pattern:

j'ai mangé	I ate (I have eaten)
on a mangé	one / we ate (have eaten)
nous avons mangé	we ate (have eaten)
ils ont mangé	they ate (have eaten)

commander	to order	**visiter**	to visit
réserver	to reserve	**commencer**	to start
coûter	to cost	**payer**	to pay for

- Regular **-ir** verbs follow this pattern:

j'ai choisi	I chose (I have chosen)
on a choisi	one / we chose (have chosen)
nous avons choisi	we chose (have chosen)
ils ont choisi	they chose (have chosen)

servir	to serve	**finir**	to finish

- Some past participles are irregular and need to be learnt by heart:

j'ai bu	I drank (have drunk)
j'ai pris	I had / took (have taken)

- To express an opinion in the past, use the imperfect tense:

c'était parfait	it was perfect

Récemment, nous avons mangé dans un restaurant français célèbre où nous avons commandé des plats traditionnels.
Recently, we ate in a famous French restaurant where we ordered traditional dishes.
Comme entrée, j'ai choisi un plat végétarien.
As a starter, I chose a vegetarian dish.
Comme plat principal, ma mère a pris du poisson avec des légumes frais.
As a main course, my mother had fish with fresh vegetables.
Nous avons bu de l'eau et du vin local.
We drank water and local wine.
Après, on a mangé du fromage et des glaces et on a bu du café.
After(wards), we ate cheese and ice creams and drank coffee.
La nourriture était délicieuse et le service était excellent.
The food was delicious and the service was excellent.
C'est mon oncle qui a payé l'addition!
(It is) my uncle (who) paid the bill!

Quick Test

1. **a)** Put these adjectives into their feminine form:
   traditionnel, **végétarien**, **frais**
   b) Put these into the masculine plural form: **local**, **régional**
2. Translate into English: **Je ne prends rien pour le petit-déjeuner et je ne bois jamais d'alcool.**
3. Translate into French:
   My family ate in a famous restaurant and the meal was perfect.

Revise

Key Point

Translating a negative phrase into English requires thought to ensure a 'good' translation, for example **je ne bois rien** translates as 'I drink nothing' but 'I don't drink anything' sounds more natural. Important negative phrases include:

ne...pas	not
ne...jamais	never (not ever)
ne....rien	nothing (not anything)

Key Verbs

je mange	I eat
j'ai mangé	I ate
je bois	I drink
j'ai bu	I drank
c'était	it was

Key Sounds

There is a very important distinction between **je** (meaning 'I') and **j'ai** (meaning 'I have'). Make sure that you pronounce these two words accurately and use them in the correct context. Practise saying **je mange**, **j'ai mangé** (I eat, I ate), then try **je visite**, **j'ai visité** (I visit, I visited) and **je commence**, **j'ai commencé** (I start, I started).

Routines

You must be able to:

- Talk and write about your daily routine and weekend activities
- Use reflexive verbs with confidence
- Explain how you spent your time last week.

Daily Routine

se lever	to wake up	**se laver**	to (have a) wash
se coucher	to go to bed		
s'organiser	to organise oneself / get organised		
la routine	routine	**l'activité**	activity
quotidien	daily	**en semaine**	during the week
le week-end	at the weekend		

How Often?

tous les jours	every day	**chaque jour**	every day
normalement	normally	**généralement**	usually
souvent	often	**parfois**	sometimes
toujours	always		
le lundi	on Mondays	**tous les samedis**	every Saturday
une fois par semaine		once a week	

Normalement, je me lève à sept heures du matin.
Normally I get up at 7 o'clock in the morning.

Tu te laves et tu prends ton petit-déjeuner.
You get washed and have your breakfast.

Il s'organise et se prépare pour la journée scolaire.
He gets organised and gets ready for the school day.

Elle se couche vers vingt-deux heures tous les jours car elle est fatiguée.
She goes to bed at 10pm every day because she is tired.

Je vais toujours au collège à pied mais je rentre souvent chez moi en voiture.
I always walk to school but I often go home by car.

Tu te couches à quelle heure en semaine?
What time do you go to bed during the week?

Il fait des activités sportives trois fois par semaine.
He does some sport three times a week.

Généralement, le soir, elle regarde la télé mais parfois elle sort avec des amis.
Generally in the evening she watches TV but sometimes she goes out with friends.

At the Weekend

Le week-end, c'est différent.	At the weekend it's different.
Le samedi, je me lève plus tard.	On Saturdays, I get up later.
Le dimanche, je passe plus de temps chez moi.	On Sundays, I spend more time at home.
Je fais moins de travail.	I do less work.

Key Verbs

je me lève	I get up
je me couche	I go to bed

Key Point

Use time phrases to enhance your spoken or written work and to provide more detail.

Key Sound

ou sound – listen and repeat: **se coucher** (to go to bed), **souvent** (often), **toujours** (always), **tous les jours** (every day)

Last Week

tôt	early
tard	late
le matin	(in) the morning
le soir	(in) the evening
à sept heures du matin	at 7 o'clock in the morning
à midi	at noon / at lunchtime

Lundi dernier, à midi, je suis allé(e) au club de musique au collège.
Last Monday lunchtime, I went to music club at school.
Mercredi dernier, après le collège, nous sommes allé(e)s au club de foot.
After school last Wednesday, we went to football club.
Jeudi dernier, je me suis levé(e) très tôt le matin.
Last Thursday, I got up very early in the morning.
Vendredi dernier, je me suis couché(e) très tard le soir.
Last Friday, I went to bed very late in the evening.

Last Weekend

Samedi matin, je suis resté(e) à la maison.
On Saturday morning, I stayed at home.
J'ai joué à des jeux vidéo avec mon frère.
I played computer games with my brother.
Samedi après-midi, je suis allé(e) à la piscine.
On Saturday afternoon, I went to the swimming pool.
J'ai rencontré mes amis.   I met my friends.
Samedi soir, je suis rentré(e) chez moi.
On Saturday evening, I went back home.
J'ai regardé un film à la télé.   I watched a film on TV.
Dimanche dernier, je suis sorti(e) avec ma famille.
Last Sunday I went out with my family.
Nous sommes parti(e)s au bord de la mer en voiture.
We left for the coast by car.
Nous sommes arrivé(e)s vers onze heures.
We arrived around 11 o'clock.
Nous avons passé toute la journée à la plage.
We spent all day at the beach.

Key Verbs

je suis allé(e)   I went
je suis resté(e) I stayed
je suis sorti(e) I went out
je me suis levé(e) I got up
je me suis couché(e)
I went to bed
nous sommes allé(e)s
we went

Key Point

Remember when you use verbs that take **être** (to be) in the perfect tense, you must make the past participle agree with the subject, e.g. **il est allé** (he went) but **elle est allée** (she went).

Quick Test

1. What do these words mean in English?
   souvent, parfois, toujours, tôt, tard
2. How do you say in French...?
   in the morning, on Saturdays, at the weekend, at lunchtime
3. Translate into English:
   Normalement, je me couche vers vingt-deux heures en semaine.
4. Translate into French: Last Saturday, I went into town with my friends.

To Be Healthy

You must be able to:

- Discuss all the elements of a healthy lifestyle
- Talk and write about health and illness
- Use different ways of saying how you might improve your health or lifestyle.

Fitness and Health

être en bonne / mauvaise santé	to be in good / bad health
C'est bon / mauvais pour la santé.	It's good / bad for your health.
Es-tu en forme?	Are you fit? (in good shape?)
Je (ne) suis (pas) en forme.	I'm (not) in good shape.
J'ai de bonnes / mauvaises habitudes.	I have good / bad habits.
Je fais beaucoup d'exercice.	I do a lot of exercise.
Je bois assez d'eau tous les jours.	I drink enough water every day.
Je ne mange pas trop de fast-food.	I don't eat too much fast food.
Je bois moins de café.	I drink less coffee.
Je dors plus de huit heures par nuit.	

I sleep for more than eight hours per night.

Accidents and Illness

Tu vas bien? / Vas-tu bien?	Are you well?
Je (ne) vais (pas) bien.	I (don't) feel well.
Je suis malade.	I am ill.
J'ai mal au dos / au bras.	I have backache / my arm hurts.
J'ai mal à la tête / jambe.	I have a headache / my leg hurts.
J'ai mal à l'oreille / aux yeux.	I have earache / my eyes hurt.

l'accident	accident	l'hôpital	hospital
l'urgence	emergency	le médecin	doctor
le médicament	medicine / drug	la maladie	illness
le rendez-vous	appointment	le soin	care
le traitement	treatment	souffrir (de)	to suffer (from)
inquiétant	worrying / disturbing	grave	serious

J'ai eu un accident.	I had an accident.
Je suis allé(e) à l'hôpital.	I went to hospital.
Ce n'est pas grave.	It's not serious.

J'ai un rendez-vous chez le médecin demain.
I have an appointment with the doctor tomorrow.

HT **Je me suis cassé le bras.**	I broke my arm.
HT **Il souffre d'une maladie rare qui peut être traitée par de nouveaux médicaments.**	

He's suffering from a rare illness that can be treated with new drugs.

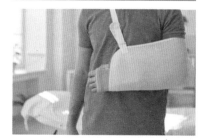

To Improve Your Health

le cœur	heart	**équilibré**	balanced
arrêter	to stop		
dormir	to sleep	**éviter**	to avoid
fumer	to smoke	**se relaxer**	to relax
tuer	to kill	**vapoter**	to vape

HT	**le sang**	blood
HT	**la peau**	skin
HT	**diminuer**	to lower / decrease
HT	**réduire**	to reduce
HT	**garder la forme**	to stay in shape
HT	**se sentir**	to feel

- To talk about health and fitness, we can start sentences in different ways. For example, we can use modal verbs such as **je veux** (I want to), **on peut** (you / we can), **on doit** (you / we must) or **il faut** (it's necessary to / we must). Each of these are followed by the infinitive of the verb to complete the sentence:

  Je veux faire des promenades plus souvent.
  I want to go for walks more often.
  On peut faire du sport régulièrement. One / we can do sport regularly.
  On doit manger assez de fruits et de légumes.
  We must eat enough fruit and vegetables.
  Il faut éviter les cigarettes et la drogue.
  We must avoid cigarettes and drugs.

  - HT **Il vaut mieux aller (au collège) à pied.**
    It's better to walk (to school).
  - HT **Cela vaut la peine de se relaxer avant de se coucher.**
    It's worth relaxing before going to bed.

- We can use other verbs to say what we are doing, are going to do or have done to improve our health and why:

  J'essaie de manger équilibré parce que c'est bon / meilleur pour le corps et l'esprit.
  I try to eat a balanced diet because it is good / better for your body and your mind.
  Je vais me coucher plus tôt car je veux être moins fatigué le matin.
  I'm going to go to bed earlier because I want to be less tired in the morning.
  J'ai décidé d'arrêter de fumer / vapoter parce que, selon les experts, le tabac peut tuer.
  I've decided to stop smoking / vaping because according to experts, tobacco can kill.
  J'ai choisi de changer ma routine quotidienne pour avoir plus d'énergie.
  I've chosen to change my daily routine so that I have more energy.
  J'ai commencé à mener une vie saine et je me sens mieux dans ma peau.
  I've started to lead a healthy lifestyle and I feel better about myself.
  J'ai réussi à regarder moins de télévision avant d'aller au lit et je dors mieux.
  I've succeeded in watching less TV before going to bed and I sleep better.

Quick Test

1. Translate into English: **J'ai mal à la tête et j'ai mal aux yeux.**
2. Translate into French:
   I don't do enough exercise. I want to go for walks more often.

Key Sounds

au / **eau** / closed **o** / **ô**: sounds like 'oh', e.g. m**au**vais (bad), p**eau** (skin), l'**eau** (water), se rep**o**ser (to rest), l'h**ô**pital (hospital). Try saying: **Il v**au**ut mieux se rep**o**ser à l'h**ô**pital!** It's better to rest in the hospital!

Key Point

Some verbs are followed by prepositions. Learn these carefully:

essayer de	to try to
décider de	to decide to
choisir de	to choose to
commencer à	to start / begin to
réussir à	to succeed (in)

Key Point

Think carefully about translating the word 'better' in English. In French, there are two different words: **bon** (good) becomes **meilleur** but **bien** (well) becomes **mieux**. **C'est bon / meilleur pour la santé.** It's good / better for your health. **Je vais bien / mieux.** I feel well / better.

Healthy Living and Lifestyle

1 Choose the correct underlined words to complete the sentences.

a) **Nous aimons manger des produits <u>locales / locaux</u> parce qu'ils sont plus <u>frais / fraîches</u> et <u>naturels / naturelles</u>.**

b) **Ma famille préfère la cuisine <u>régionale / régionaux</u> avec des plats <u>traditionnels / traditionnelles</u>.**

c) **Je prépare des recettes <u>végétariens / végétariennes</u> pour être en <u>bon / bonne</u> santé.**

d) **On peut réduire ses <u>mauvais / mauvaises</u> habitudes et mener une vie plus <u>sain / saine</u>.** [9 marks]

2 Read the following sentences aloud.

a) **Nous préparons des repas spéciaux.**

b) **Elle ne boit jamais d'alcool.**

c) **Je ne mange plus de viande.**

d) **Elle se couche tôt tous les soirs.**

e) **Il fait régulièrement de l'exercice.**

f) **J'ai mangé un plat régional dans un restaurant local.**

[6 marks]

3 Unscramble the sentences.

a) **heures Je semaine à lève sept me en**

b) **d'aller moi Je chez avant au prends collège petit-déjeuner le**

c) **pendant du Nous sport faire la aimons récré**

d) **beaucoup couche Le je plus me tard week-end** [4 marks]

4 Draw lines to complete the sentences.

a) **Nous avons**   couche de bonne heure.

b) **Je n'ai**   éviter le fast-food.

c) **Il faut**   de manger équilibré.

d) **Je me**   mangé dans un restaurant.

e) **On doit essayer**   pas bu d'alcool. [5 marks]

5 Translate the sentences into English.

a) Je n'aime pas trop les légumes.

b) Je ne prends rien pour le petit-déjeuner.

c) Je ne bois pas assez d'eau.

d) Il ne fait plus d'exercice.

e) Elle ne mange jamais de viande.

f) Nous ne mangeons que des produits frais. [6 marks]

6 Fill in the blanks by choosing the correct word from the brackets to complete the sentences.

a) Lundi dernier, ... resté(e) chez moi. (j'ai / je suis)

b) J'ai .... aux jeux vidéo avec mes copains. (jouer / joué)

c) Nous .... mangé en ville. (sommes / avons)

d) Nous .... allés au cinéma. (sommes / avons)

e) Ma sœur a .... de l'eau minérale. (bu / boit) [5 marks]

7 Read the sentences. Write **P** for a positive attitude towards healthy living, **N** for a negative attitude or **P+N** for a positive and negative attitude.

a) J'essaie de manger équilibré mais je ne fais pas beaucoup d'exercice. ....

b) J'ai commencé à me coucher plus tôt et je suis moins fatigué le matin. ....

c) Je ne bois que de l'eau fraîche et je ne mange jamais de fast-food. ....

d) Je ne peux pas arrêter de fumer car c'est trop difficile! ....

[4 marks]

8 Complete the sentences using your own ideas.

a) **Généralement, je me lève** .... **et puis** ....

b) **Avant d'aller au collège, je** .... **ou** ....

c) **Souvent, le soir, je mange** .... **et je bois** ....

d) **Je n'aime pas** .... **; je préfère** ....

e) **Pour rester en forme, j'essaie de** ....

f) **J'ai décidé de** ....

[10 marks]

Review Questions

Identity and Relationships with Others

1 Choose the correct verb from the box below to complete the sentences.

m'entends	suis	avons	s'appelle
est	a	va	sont

a) Mon frère .... Bruno.

b) Mes sœurs .... plus grandes que moi.

c) Je .... bien avec mon père.

d) Nous .... les mêmes intérêts.

e) On .... souvent au cinéma.

f) Je .... pour le mariage.

g) Mon meilleur copain .... toujours sympa.

h) Elle .... les yeux bleus et les cheveux longs.   [8 marks]

2 Use the vocabulary list on the AQA website to find and write down the feminine form of these adjectives.

a) **blanc** – white   c) **fou** – crazy   e) **nouveau** – new

b) **bon** – good   d) **long** – long   [5 marks]

3 Find and write down four more adjectives that decline in the same way as the adjectives below. Write the four adjectives out in full using masculine singular, feminine singular, masculine plural and feminine plural.

a) **généreux / généreuse**   b) **actif / active**   c) **fier / fière**   [3 marks]

4 Listen to the pronunciations. Write **1**, **2** or **3** for the correct pronunciation and explain why.

a) **Ma sœur a les yeux verts et les cheveux courts et bruns.**   ....

b) **Mes parents sont mariés depuis longtemps.**   ....

c) **Cette fille est un membre de ma famille!**   ....

d) **Mon copain Luc, un bon garçon, va rester célibataire.**   ....

[8 marks]

5 Read the sentences. Write **P** for past events, **N** for current events (now) or **F** for future events. Then translate them into English.

a) Je sors souvent avec mes amis. ....

b) Ma cousine s'est mariée au mois de mai. ....

c) On se dispute toujours. ....

d) J'espère trouver mon partenaire idéal un de ces jours! ....

e) J'ai l'intention d'avoir des enfants. ....

f) Nous nous amusons bien. ....

[12 marks]

6 Tick the sentences that give a positive opinion about getting married.

a) C'est important pour moi de me marier. ☐

b) Je préfère mon indépendance. ☐

c) Ce n'est pas pour moi. ☐

d) Le mariage est mieux pour les enfants. ☐

e) L'amour est plus important que la tradition. ☐

f) Je ne voudrais pas habiter avec mon partenaire. ☐ [2 marks]

7 Complete this passage about a best friend by inserting the correct form of **son / sa / ses**.

J'aime bien .... cheveux longs et .... yeux bleus. Mais ce n'est pas .... apparence qui est importante pour moi. Il est toujours sympa et j'adore .... confiance. Il est très sportif et .... sport préféré est le foot. .... sœur joue souvent avec nous et j'apprécie .... compétences. [7 marks]

At School

Quick Recall Quiz

Key Sound

You must be able to:

- Discuss school subjects, your likes, dislikes and preferences
- Talk and write about your school, its buildings and your day
- Use **-er** and **-ir** verbs confidently in the present tense.

School Subjects

l'allemand (m)	German	**l'anglais** (m)	English
l'espagnol (m)	Spanish	**le cours**	lesson
la géographie	geography	**le français**	French
l'informatique (f)	IT	**l'histoire**	history
la matière	school subject	**les langues** (f)	languages
la physique	physics	**la musique**	music
la politique	politics	**la religion**	RE
les sciences (f)	science	**le sport**	sport / PE
la technologie	technology	**le théâtre**	drama
les math(ématique)s (f)	math(ematic)s		

HT **le commerce** business

J'étudie l'anglais et l'histoire.	I study English and history.
Je fais de l'informatique le lundi.	I do IT on a Monday.
J'ai choisi le théâtre et l'espagnol.	I have chosen drama and Spanish.

My Preferences

J'aime (bien)...	I (quite) like...	**J'adore...**	I love...
Je n'aime pas... (du tout)	I don't like... (at all)		
Je déteste...	I hate...	**Je préfère...**	I prefer...
Je trouve...	I find...		
Ma matière préférée, c'est...	My favourite subject is...		
être fort(e) en	to be good at	**être faible en**	to be weak in
être nul en	to be rubbish at	**capable**	able / capable
amusant	funny	**difficile**	difficult
dur	hard	**facile**	easy
génial	great / brilliant	**intéressant**	interesting
inutile	useless	**pratique**	practical
super	super	**terrible**	terrible
utile	useful	HT **divers**	varied / diverse

J'aime les sciences parce que les cours sont intéressants.
I like science because the lessons are interesting.

Je trouve les maths utiles mais je préfère la géographie.
I find maths useful but I prefer geography.

Ma matière préférée, c'est la technologie car c'est pratique et j'adore travailler avec mes mains.
My favourite subject is technology because it's practical and I love working with my hands.

Ma sœur est très forte en français mais assez faible en physique.
My sister is very good at French but quite weak in physics.

> ### Key Verbs
>
> | | |
> |---|---|
> | **J'étudie...** | I study... |
> | **Je fais de...** | I do... |
> | **J'ai choisi...** | I chose / I have chosen... |

> ### Key Sound
>
> There is an important difference in pronunciation of the verb **je préfère** (I prefer) and the adjective **préféré** (favourite). Make sure you use the correct part of speech in your written and spoken work so that you say and spell these words correctly.

> ### Key Point
>
> When you are saying you are good or weak in a subject, the definite article is not used. Therefore, **j'aime l'anglais et je suis fort(e) en anglais** (I like English and I am strong in English); **j'adore la religion mais je suis faible en religion** I love RE but I am weak in RE.

My School

le collège	secondary school	**le lycée**	sixth form college / grammar school
l'école (primaire)	(primary) school	**le directeur**	the headteacher
l'élève	pupil	**en seconde**	in Year 11
le prof(esseur)	teacher	**en quatrième**	in Year 9
en troisième	in Year 10		

Je vais au collège. I go to secondary school.
Je suis en troisième. I'm in Year 10.
Il y a 1 200 élèves et 100 professeurs.
There are 1,200 pupils and 100 teachers.

le bâtiment	building	**la bibliothèque**	library
le bureau	office	**la cour**	playground
la piscine	swimming pool	**HT la réception**	reception
la salle (de classe)	(class)room		
le terrain (de sport)	the (sports)field		

Les bâtiments au lycée sont très vieux.
The buildings at school are very old.
On a beaucoup de place dans la cour.
We have a lot of space in the playground.
Nous avons une nouvelle bibliothèque et un grand terrain de sport.
We have a new library and a big sports field.

The School Day

arriver	to arrive	**commencer**	to start
durer	to last	**finir**	to finish
manger	to eat	**quitter**	to leave
le club	club	**le cours / la leçon**	lesson
la récré(ation)	break	**à midi**	at lunch time
HT la rentrée	return to school (in September)		

J'arrive au collège de bonne heure. I arrive at school early.
On commence (les cours commencent) à huit heures et demie.
We start (lessons start) at half past eight.
Il y a cinq cours par jour. There are five lessons per day.
Chaque leçon dure une heure. Each lesson lasts for one hour.
Il y a une récré à onze heures qui dure vingt minutes.
There is a break at 11 o'clock that lasts 20 minutes.
À midi, je vais au club de sciences ou je joue au foot.
At lunchtime, I go to science club or I play football.
Nous commençons / nous finissons la dernière leçon à deux heures dix.
We start / we finish the last lesson at ten past two.
On finit (les cours finissent) à trois heures et quart.
We finish (lessons finish) at quarter past three.

> ### Key Point
>
> **il y a** is a very useful phrase which means 'there is' or 'there are', e.g. **Il y a un terrain de sport**. There is a sports field. **Il y a 60 salles.** There are 60 rooms.

> ### Key Point
>
> Do not confuse these two nouns!
>
> | | |
> |---|---|
> | **le cours** | lesson |
> | **la cour** | playground |

> ### Key Point
>
> **-er** verbs and **-ir** verbs decline differently. Make sure you know how to use them correctly, e.g.
>
> **commencer** (to start) = **il commence**, **nous commençons**, **les cours commencent**
> **finir** (to finish) = **il finit**, **nous finissons**, **les cours finissent**

Quick Test

1. Give the French for the following subjects: history, IT, science, maths, RE
2. Complete these sentences: **Je vais** ....;
   Je suis ....; **Il y a** .... **élèves**.
3. Change these verbs to the 'nous' form: **j'arrive, je quitte, je finis**
4. Change these verbs to the 'ils' form: **on commence, on finit, il dure**

School Life

You must be able to:

- Talk and write about life at school
- Understand **-re** verbs in the present tense
- Discuss homework, exams, uniform and rules
- Use modal verbs and imperatives confidently in the present tense.

Quick Recall Quiz

Key Sounds

School Work

l'éducation	education	**l'enseignement**	education / teaching
le travail (scolaire)	(school) work		
les devoirs	homework	**l'examen**	exam
la note	mark	**le résultat**	result
HT **le contrôle**	test	HT **l'échec**	failure
améliorer	to improve	**apprendre**	to learn
comprendre	to understand	**corriger**	to correct
demander	to ask	**dire**	to say
discuter	to discuss	**écrire**	to write
lire	to read	**organiser**	to organise
parler	to talk	**penser**	to think
préparer	to prepare	**réfléchir**	to reflect on
réussir à	to succeed in	**répondre**	to reply
suivre	to follow	**réussir un examen**	to pass an exam
traduire	to translate		
HT **enseigner**	to teach	HT **obtenir**	to obtain / get

-re verbs

- The verb **répondre** (to reply) follows the pattern of the verb **entendre** (to hear): **j'entends, tu entends, il / elle entend, nous entendons, vous entendez, ils / elles entendent.**
- **-re** verbs such as **apprendre** (to learn) and **comprendre** (to understand) follow the pattern of the verb **prendre** (to take): **je prends, tu prends, il / elle prend, nous prenons, vous prenez, ils / elles prennent.**
- The verbs **dire** (to say) and **lire** (to read) follow the pattern of the verb **traduire** (to translate): **je traduis, tu traduis, il / elle traduit, nous traduisons, vous traduisez, ils / elles traduisent.**
- **Je réponds aux questions et j'écris des réponses.**
  I reply to questions and write answers.

En classe de français, nous apprenons des mots et nous traduisons des textes.
In French (classes), we learn new words and translate texts.

Souvent, en classe, on pense et puis on discute des idées ensemble.
Often in class we think and then we discuss ideas together.

Nous préparons les examens.
We prepare/ we are preparing for (the) exams.

Si on ne comprend pas, on peut demander au prof.
If you don't understand, you can ask the teacher.

Quand le prof corrige un exercice, on peut améliorer son travail / sa note.
When the teacher corrects a written exercise, you can improve your work / your mark.

Key Point

The three main types of French verbs (**-er, -ir, -re**) follow specific patterns (declensions) and have different endings. Make sure you know how to decline them.

Key Sound

é (pronounced 'ay') is a key sound in French. **-er** and **-ez** also sound the same, e.g. **réponse** (answer), **demander** (to ask), **répétez!** (repeat!)

Key Point

on peut (you / we can) is followed by another verb in the infinitive form, e.g.:

on peut demander
you can ask
on peut finir
you can finish
on peut dire
you can say

Equipment

le livre	book	**l'ordinateur**	computer
le portable	mobile / laptop	**le sac**	bag
le stylo	pen	**le tableau**	board
HT **le dictionnaire**		dictionary	
HT **les études**		studies	

Regarde le tableau! Regardez le tableau!	Look at the board!
Écoute! Écoutez!	Listen!
Répète, s'il te plaît! Répétez, s'il vous plaît!	Repeat, please!
Prend ton stylo! Prenez vos stylos!	Take your pen(s)!
Fais de ton mieux! / Faites de votre mieux!	Do your best!
Ne parle pas! Ne parlez pas!	Don't talk!

Revise

Key Point

The imperative is used to give instructions. In French, there is a different way to instruct one person (**regarde!** (look!)) and a group of people (**regardez!** (look!)).

School Rules

la règle		rule	
l'uniforme scolaire		(school) uniform	
porter	to wear	**apporter**	to bring
interdit	forbidden	**en retard**	late
il faut		we (you) must / it is necessary	
on doit		we (you) must / have to	
on ne doit pas		we (you) must not	
on ne peut pas		we (you) can't	
HT **on n'a pas le droit de**		we're (you're) not allowed to	
HT **le comportement**		behaviour	
HT **le droit**	right	HT **le règlement**	school rules
HT **obliger à**	to force / oblige	HT **permettre (à)**	to allow, permit
HT **être permis / interdit de**		to be allowed / forbidden	

- **Il faut suivre les règles.** We must follow the rules.
  Il faut porter l'uniforme scolaire. It's necessary to wear school uniform.
  Il faut apporter l'équipement nécessaire.
  You must bring the necessary equipment.
- **On doit faire les devoirs.** We must do our homework.
  On ne doit pas arriver en retard. You must not arrive late.
  On ne peut pas manger en classe. We can't eat in class.
  Fumer est interdit. Smoking is forbidden.

Key Sound

è examples: **règle** (rule), **collège** (school), **élève** (pupil)

Key Point

on doit and **il faut** are useful phrases for saying 'you **must** or **have to** do something'. They are followed by the infinitive of the verb, e.g.

On doit écouter.
You must listen.
Il faut faire les devoirs.
You have to (it is necessary to) do homework.

Quick Test

1. Give the French for: homework, exam, mark, result, school work
2. Put these phrases into the negative:
   on peut discuter, on doit parler, il faut manger
3. Use the appropriate form of the verb:
   nous _____ **beaucoup en classe (apprendre); je** _____ **les textes (lire); on** _____ **aux questions (répondre)**
4. Translate into English:
   Au collège, on travaille dur pour réussir les examens.

Post-16 Study and Work

You must be able to:

- Talk and write about your plans for study and work
- Say what you would like to do, or intend to do
- Discuss jobs and employment
- Use a future time frame to give information about your future.

After School

continuer	to continue	**quitter**	to leave
rentrer	to return	**terminer**	to finish
progresser	to progress		

le baccalauréat (le bac)	A-Level(s) equivalent
en première	in Year 12
un apprentissage	apprenticeship
un stage	work experience
l'université	university
HT **l'entretien**	interview
HT **une année sabbatique**	a gap year

L'année prochaine, je veux continuer mes études.
Next year I want to continue my studies.
Après le bac, j'espère aller à l'université.
After A-Levels, I hope to go to university.
L'année prochaine, je vais quitter l'école.
Next year I am going to leave school.
Je voudrais commencer un apprentissage.
I would like to start an apprenticeship.

In the Future

le boulot	job	**la carrière**	career
l'emploi	work / job	**le métier**	job / occupation
le travail	work	**le bénévole**	volunteer
le candidat	applicant	**l'employé(e)**	employee
le patron	boss	**le collègue**	colleague
le chômage	unemployment	**le choix**	choice
le rêve	dream	**le salaire**	salary
l'espoir	hope	**l'usine**	factory
HT **l'étudiant(e)**	student		

Comme métier, je veux travailler avec des enfants.
As an occupation, I want to work with children.
Je ne veux pas travailler dans une usine.
I don't want to work in a factory.
Je voudrais devenir médecin. I would like to become a doctor.
Je ne voudrais pas être au chômage. I wouldn't want to be unemployed.
J'ai l'intention d'avoir un boulot varié. I intend to have a varied job.
Je rêve de trouver un emploi idéal. Ça vaut la peine d'essayer!
I dream of finding an ideal job. It's worth trying!
Je n'ai aucune idée de ce que je veux faire.
I have no idea what I want to do.

Key Point

The following time phrases are useful when talking about the future:

l'année prochaine	
next year	
bientôt	soon
puis	then
à l'avenir	in the future
plus tard (dans la vie)	
later (in life)	
après (l'université)	
after (university)	
dans dix ans	
in 10 years' time	

Key Sound

-tion: notice how the **t** is pronounced, e.g. **l'inten**tion (intention), **la nata**tion (swimming), **la na**tion (nation)

Key Point

Use these phrases followed by a verb in the infinitive to vary how you talk about your future plans:

je (ne) veux (pas)	
I (don't) want to	
je (ne) voudrais (pas)	
I would (not) like to	
j'espère	I hope to
j'ai l'intention de	
I intend to	
je rêve de	I dream of
HT **j'aimerais**	I would love to

Jobs and Professions

l'acteur / l'actrice	actor	**l'aidant(e)**		carer
le facteur / la factrice	post person			
l'artiste	artist	**l'auteur**		author
l'écrivain / l'écrivaine	writer			
l'influenceur / l'influenceuse	influencer			
le / la journaliste	journalist			
le médecin	doctor	**le / la secrétaire**		secretary
le chanteur / la chanteuse	singer			
le policier / la policière	police officer			
le serveur / la serveuse	waiter			
le chef	chef / boss			

HT **la cheffe**	chef / boss	HT **l'avocat**	lawyer
HT **le chercheur**	researcher	HT **le scientifique**	scientist
HT **le soldat**	soldier		

Je voudrais devenir journaliste.   I would like to become a journalist.
Ma sœur est écrivaine.   My sister is a writer.

Talking in the Future

Que vas-tu faire à l'avenir?	What are you going to do in the future?
HT **Que feras-tu à l'avenir?**	What will you do in the future?

- There are two main ways to talk about the future in French. You can use the correct form of the verb **aller** + an infinitive, e.g. **je vais devenir influenceur**. This is translated as 'I am going to become an influencer'.

  HT The other way is to use the future tense. To form the future tense, take the full infinitive of the verb and add these endings:
  je -ai; **tu -as**; **il / elle / on -a**; **nous -ons**; **vous -ez**; **ils / elles -ont**. For example, **je commencerai un apprentissage**. This is translated as 'I will start / I will be starting an apprenticeship'. Some verbs are irregular – notice the four main ones in the sentences below.

- **Je vais avoir / J'aurai un métier intéressant.**
  I'm going to have / I will have an interesting job.
  Je vais aller / J'irai à l'étranger.   I'm going to go / I will go abroad.
  Je vais être / Je serai célèbre.   I'm going to be / I will be famous.
  Je vais faire / Je ferai du travail bénévole.
  I'm going to do / I will do voluntary work.
  Je vais voyager / Je voyagerai partout dans le monde.
  I'm going to / I will travel all over the world.
  Je vais gagner / Je gagnerai un bon salaire.
  I'm going to earn / I will earn a good salary.

Quick Test

1. Translate into English:
   L'année prochaine, je voudrais commencer un apprentissage.
2. What is the French for...? in the future; later (in life); in five years' time
3. Translate into French:
   I intend to become a scientist. I'm going to be (I will be) famous.
4. Change to the **il / elle** form:
   je vais aller; je vais voyager; je vais faire; je vais travailler
5. HT Put the verbs in 4. into the future tense.

Education and Work

1 Unscramble the sentences and translate them into English.

a) l'histoire préfère la J'aime mais je géographie bien

b) mais Je en suis informatique j'adore faible ça! assez

c) préférée en Ma fort parce mathématiques matière je c'est les que suis maths!

d) l'allemand j'adore les l'espagnol J'ai et car langues choisi

e) beaucoup je la n'aime car la trouve Je un peu technologie difficile pas [10 marks]

2 Read the sentences aloud.

a) Je vais au collège et je suis en troisième.

b) Il y a mille élèves et cent professeurs.

c) J'étudie huit matières.

d) Ma matière préférée, c'est l'anglais.

e) J'ai cinq cours par jour.

f) Après les examens, je veux faire un apprentissage.

[6 marks]

3 Complete the sentences using the verbs from the box below. There are some verbs that you will not need.

finissent	finit	dure	durent	commencent	commence	apprenons
apprend	réponds	répondons	avons	ont	écris	écrit

a) Les cours .... à huit heures et demie.

b) Nous .... une récré à onze heures qui .... vingt minutes.

c) En classe, nous .... beaucoup.

d) Je .... aux questions et j' .... les réponses.

e) La journée scolaire .... à trois heures et quart. [7 marks]

4 Translate the sentences into English.

a) Ma mère est professeur.

b) J'ai l'intention de continuer mes études.

c) Je rêve d'avoir un boulot varié.

d) Je voudrais devenir artiste.

[4 marks]

5 Translate the sentences into French.

a) My father is a postman.

b) I'm going to be a doctor.

c) My sister wants to become a policewoman.

d) I intend to work abroad. [4 marks]

6 Read the sentences. Write **P** for a positive opinion, **N** for a negative opinion or **P+N** for a positive and negative opinion.

a) J'aime bien mon métier car je le trouve varié et intéressant. ....

b) J'apprécie le salaire. Travailler la nuit est moins agréable. ....

c) Je ne peux pas supporter mon boulot, surtout en été. ....

d) J'ai toujours voulu faire ce métier et je ne regrette pas mon choix. .... [4 marks]

7 Rewrite the sentences.

a) **Faites les devoirs!** On doit ....

b) **Écoutez en classe!** Il faut ....

c) **N'arrivez pas en retard!** Il ne faut pas ....

d) **Ne mangez pas en classe!** On ne peut pas ....

e) **Portez l'uniforme scolaire!** ....

f) **Suivez les règles!** ....

g) **Ne parlez pas!** .... [7 marks]

8 Complete the sentences, using your own ideas.

a) **L'année prochaine,** ....

b) **Je voudrais** .... **mais je ne voudrais pas** ....

c) **Comme métier,** ....

d) **Plus tard dans la vie, j'espère** ....

e) **Dans dix ans,** ....

[6 marks]

Review Questions

Healthy Living and Lifestyle

1 Draw lines to match the French and the English phrases.

j'ai faim	I'm 15

j'ai soif	I'm cold

j'ai chaud	I'm hungry

j'ai froid	I'm hot

j'ai peur	I'm thirsty

j'ai quinze ans	I'm frightened

[6 marks]

2 Fill in the blanks with the correct words from the box below:

avons   sommes   spéciaux   choisi   dernier   arrivés   fêter   indien   nourriture

Le week-end ...., nous sommes allés en ville pour .... l'anniversaire de ma sœur.

Nous .... mangé dans un restaurant .... où on peut choisir des plats .... des

différentes régions. Nous sommes .... de bonne heure et ma mère a .... une table

près de la fenêtre. La .... était délicieuse et nous nous .... très bien amusés!

[9 marks]

3 Put these sentences into the past (using the perfect tense) by changing the underlined verb. The first one has been done for you.

a) <u>Je commande</u> le poulet. = J'ai commandé le poulet.

b) <u>Je mange</u> équilibré. ....

c) <u>Nous mangeons</u> beaucoup de fruits. ....

d) <u>Je choisis</u> de faire du sport. ....

e) <u>Il boit</u> assez d'eau. ....

f) <u>Je vais</u> à la piscine. ....

[5 marks]

4 Complete the sentences using the correct form of **au**, **à la**, **à l'** or **aux**.

a) J'ai mal .... tête et j'ai mal .... oreille!

b) Je suis allé .... hôpital parce que je suis tombé et que j'avais très mal .... dos et
.... jambe.

c) Je reste .... maison et je joue .... jeux vidéo.

d) Le vendredi, je vais .... piscine mais mon frère joue .... foot.   [9 marks]

5 Read the email. Write **P** for an event in the past, **N** for an event now or **F** for an event in the future.

> **Salut Sam,**
>
> **Tu as demandé si je suis en forme. Alors oui, dans ma famille, on mange bien. Par exemple,
> on mange des légumes frais et on boit de l'eau minérale. Mes parents ont arrêté de fumer au
> mois de janvier et mon père a dit qu'il va faire un régime. Il va faire plus d'exercice en faisant
> des promenades avec ma mère! Moi, je dors bien et je continue de jouer au foot trois fois par
> semaine, mais malheureusement je ne vais plus à la piscine parce que j'ai trop de devoirs à faire!**
>
> **À bientôt,**
>
> **Éric**

a) eating fresh vegetables ....   d) sleeping well ....

b) smoking ....   e) going to the swimming pool ....

c) going on a diet ....   [5 marks]

6 Use the email in question **5** to answer the following questions in English.

a) What does Éric's family do to stay healthy?

....

b) How is Éric's father going to get more exercise?

....

c) How often does Éric play football?

....

[3 marks]

Sport and Sporting Activities

You must be able to:

- Talk and write about sport and sporting activities
- Discuss which sports and activities you used to do
- Compare past and present activities
- Talk about activities you would like to try in the future.

Sport and Sporting Activities

jouer	to play
le foot(ball)	football
Je joue au foot.	I play football.
faire	to do
l'exercice (m)	exercise
la natation	swimming
le vélo	bike
Je fais du vélo.	I ride my bike.
aller	to go
le centre sportif	sports centre
le club des jeunes	youth club
la montagne	mountain
le parc	park
la piscine	swimming pool
la plage	beach
le stade	stadium
Je vais au stade.	I go to the stadium.

- To say <u>what you used to do</u>, use the <u>imperfect</u> tense:
  Quand j'étais plus jeune, je jouais au foot tous les jours.
  When I was younger, I used to play football every day.
  Je faisais du vélo tous les week-ends.
  I used to ride my bike every weekend.

- To say <u>where you used to go</u>, use the <u>imperfect</u> tense:
  Quand j'avais onze ans, j'allais à la piscine trois fois par semaine.
  When I was 11, I used to go to the swimming pool three times a week.

Opinions

actif (m) / active (f)		active
sportif (m) / sportive (f)		sporty
Il est actif / Elle est active.		He / She is active.
C'est…		It is…
amusant	fun(ny)	**bon**	good
dangereux	dangerous	**difficile**	difficult
dur	hard	**facile**	easy
passionnant	exciting	**populaire**	popular
J'aime / je n'aime pas…		I like / I do not like…
le danger	the danger	**le défi**	the challenge
la participation	the participation	**le succès**	the success
HT le risque	the risk	HT la vitesse	the speed

> **Key Verbs**
>
> | | |
> |---|---|
> | jouer | to play |
> | faire | to do |
> | aller | to go |

> **Key Point**
>
> **jouer à** + sport = to play a sport – **jouer au foot** (to play football)
>
> **faire de** = to do an activity – **faire du vélo** (m) (to ride a bike), **faire de l'exercice** (to do exercise), **faire de la natation** (f) (to swim)
>
> **aller à** + place = to go to – **aller au parc** (to go to the park), **aller à la plage** (to go to the beach)

> **Key Sounds**
>
> gn – **montagne** (mountain), **campagne** (countryside), **champagne** (champagne)
> q – **quand** (when), **équipe** (team), **pratiquer** (to practise)

> **Key Verbs**
>
> | | |
> |---|---|
> | je jouais | I used to play |
> | je faisais | I used to do |
> | j'étais | I was |
> | j'avais | I had (but 'I was' when talking about your age) |
> | j'allais | I used to go |

Comparing Now and Then – Useful Verbs

arrêter de	to stop	**avoir envie de**	to want to
avoir peur de	to be frightened of	**commencer à**	to start
courir	to run	**danser**	to dance
espérer	to hope to	**essayer de**	to try
gagner	to win	**participer à**	to take part in
préférer	to prefer	**s'intéresser à**	to be interested in
HT **blesser**	to injure	**mener**	to lead
HT **pratiquer**	to practise / do	**profiter de**	to make the most of

Useful Connectives and Phrases

avant	before	**quand**	when
maintenant	now	**mais**	but
il y a … ans	…years ago	**cependant**	however
en ce moment	at the moment	**donc**	therefore
quand j'avais…ans	when I was…	**même si**	even if
de nos jours	nowadays	**puis**	then
à l'avenir	in the future	**malgré**	despite

Avant, je dansais tout le temps, mais maintenant je préfère courir.
Before, I used to dance all the time, but now I prefer running / to run.
Il y a cinq ans, j'avais peur (du danger), cependant de nos jours je m'intéresse vraiment aux sports extrêmes.
Five years ago I was afraid (of the danger), however nowadays I'm really interested in extreme sports.

Types of Sports to Try in Future

les sports d'équipe	team sports
les sports d'hiver	winter sports
les sports individuels	individual sports

À l'avenir, je vais essayer d'autres sports.
In the future, I'm going to try (out) other sports.
J'ai envie de pratiquer les sports d'hiver.
I want to do winter sports.
Je voudrais participer au Tour de France.
I would like to take part in the Tour de France.

Key Sounds

The word **intention** (intention) has three key sounds – **intention**. Practise saying it out loud until you perfect each syllable. Then try **cependant** (however) and **en ce moment** (at the moment).

Key Verbs

J'ai envie de	I want to
Je voudrais	I would like to

Quick Test

1. How do you say in French…? before; now; in the future.
2. What is the difference between **je joue au foot** and **je jouais au foot**?
3. Translate into English: **J'allais au club des jeunes.**
4. Translate into French: I used to go swimming.
5. Translate into English: **Je voudrais essayer les sports d'hiver.**

Music

Quick Recall Quiz

Key Sounds

You must be able to:

- Discuss music and your opinions
- Talk and write about your favourite singer or group
- Use superlatives like 'the best', 'the worst' and 'the most'.

Music

la musique	music
l'artiste (m,f)	artist
le chanteur	(male) singer
la chanteuse	(female) singer
le groupe	group
la chanson	song
chanter	to sing
écouter	to listen (to)
jouer (d'un instrument musical)	to play (a musical instrument)
s'intéresser à	to be interested in
télécharger	to download

Je m'intéresse beaucoup à la musique.
I'm very interested in music.

Je télécharge des chansons et j'écoute de la musique sur mon portable.
I download songs and listen to music on my phone.

> **HT** **La musique, c'est ma passion!**   Music is my passion!

My Favourites

As-tu un chanteur ou une chanteuse préféré(e)?
Do you have a favourite singer?

Mon chanteur préféré s'appelle…	My favourite (male) singer is (called)…
Ma chanteuse préférée est…	My favourite (female) singer is…
Mon groupe préféré est…	My favourite group…
C'est le meilleur groupe du monde.	They're the best group in the world.
C'est la chanteuse la plus populaire.	She's the most popular singer.
C'est l'artiste le plus sympa.	He is the kindest / nicest artist.

> **HT** **Le chanteur que j'aime le plus, c'est….**
> The singer I like best is…

> **HT** **La chanteuse que j'aime le moins, s'appelle…**
> The singer I like least is…

Key Point

le meilleur	the best (m)
la meilleure	the best (f)
les meilleur(e)s	
the best (pl)	
le pire	the worst (m)
la pire	the worst (f)
les pires	the worst (pl)

My Likes and Dislikes

Je l'aime	I like him / her / it
Je les aime	I like them
Je ne l'aime pas	I don't like him / her / it
Je ne les aime pas	I don't like them

Key Point

car	because
parce que	because
à cause de	because of

la chanson	song
les paroles	lyrics
HT le rythme	rhythm

Je l'aime car il est si original.
I like him because he is so original.

Je l'adore parce que j'aime chanter toutes ses chansons.
I love him / her because I like singing all his / her songs.

J'adore ses chansons à cause des paroles.
I love his / her songs because of the lyrics.

HT **Le rythme me relaxe et je me sens heureux / heureuse.**
The rhythm relaxes me and I feel happy.

Opinions Using the Perfect Tense

J'ai toujours écouté ses chansons même si mes copains ne les aiment pas.
I've always listened to his / her songs even is my friends don't like them.

Je n'ai jamais écouté la musique de X parce que je n'aime pas les paroles.
I've never listened to X's music because I don't like the lyrics.

C'est le meilleur / pire groupe du monde!
They're the best / worst group in the world!

Comme leurs chansons sont intéressantes, ils ont eu beaucoup de succès!
As their songs are interesting, they were very successful!

Music Performances

le concert	concert
les émissions de musique	music programmes
le festival (de musique)	(music) festival

L'année dernière, je suis allé(e) au festival de Glastonbury où j'ai vu beaucoup de chanteurs et groupes que j'adore.
Last year I went to Glastonbury festival, where I saw lots of singers and groups that I love.

Samedi prochain, je vais voir mon groupe préféré en concert à Paris.
Next Saturday I'm going to see my favourite group in concert in Paris.

Key Verbs

Je l'aime.
I like him / her / it.
Je les aime.   I like them.
Je ne l'aime pas.
I don't like him / her / it.
Je ne les aime pas.
I don't like them.

Key Sounds

As **je** and **j** are used so often in your speaking, it is important that you get the sound right. Practise these: **j'aime** (I like), **je l'aime** (I like him / her / it), **je chante** (I sing), **j'écoute** (I listen)

Quick Test

1. How do you say in French...?
   a) I like her.
   b) I don't like them.
2. Change to the feminine form: **le pire, le meilleur, le plus populaire**
3. Translate into English:
   J'adore ses chansons car les paroles sont extraordinaires.
4. Translate into French: He's the best singer in the world.

Film, TV and Cinema

Quick Recall Quiz

Key Sounds

You must be able to:

- Talk and write about film, TV and cinema
- Use comparatives to debate an issue and express an opinion
- Express preferences.

Film, TV and Cinema

le film d'action / de guerre	action / war film		
l'acteur	(male) actor	**l'actrice**	(female) actor
Internet	the internet	**l'ordinateur**	computer
le théâtre	theatre	**l'écran**	screen
à la télé	on TV	**le jeu (télévisé)**	game (show)
le jeu vidéo	computer game	**la télé-réalité**	reality TV
une émission de sport / de musique	a sports / music programme		
une histoire	a story		
HT **une série**	a series		

Le film commence à vingt heures. The film starts at 8pm.
L'émission a fini à neuf heures et demie.
The programme finished at half past nine.

Using qui and que

- **qui** and **que** can both be translated as 'that' in English. To help you use the correct word, remember that **qui** (also meaning 'who' or 'which') is used for the subject of the sentence whilst **que** is used for the direct object of the sentence.
  C'est l'histoire d'un ado qui sauve la planète.
  It's the story of a teenager who saves the planet.
  C'est l'histoire d'une fille qui recherche sa famille.
  It's the story of a girl who is looking for her family.
  Ce sont toujours mes parents qui paient les billets.
  It's always my parents who pay for the tickets.
  Le dernier film que j'ai vu s'appelle…
  The last film (that) I saw is called…
  Le meilleur film que j'ai regardé, c'est…
  The best film (that) I've watched is…
  La dernière fois que je suis allé(e) au cinéma…
  The last time (that) I went to the cinema…

> **Key Point**
>
> **C'est un film qui est très populaire.**
> It's a film that is very popular.
> **C'est un film que j'aime beaucoup.**
> It's a film that I really like.

Using Comparatives to Debate an Issue

- Comparatives translate 'more' or 'less'. In English, the comparative is often formed by adding **-er** to the adjective. In French, we use **plus** and **moins** with all adjectives and adverbs, apart from **meilleur, mieux** (better) and **pire** (worse).

plus grand	bigger
moins grand / plus petit	smaller
plus cher	more expensive
moins passionnant	less exciting
plus rapidement	more quickly
moins facilement	less easily

Go to the Cinema or Watch Films at Home?

On est plus confortable chez soi.
You're more comfortable at home.

Mais c'est moins passionnant qu'une visite au cinéma.
But it's less exciting than a visit to the cinema.

Les billets de cinéma deviennent de plus en plus chers.
Cinema tickets are becoming more and more expensive.

Cependant, les films sont meilleurs sur grand écran.
However, films are better on the big screen.

On a de moins en moins de temps pour sortir.
We have less and less time to go out.

Donc une visite au cinéma est plus spéciale.
So a visit to the cinema is more special.

Je peux me relaxer plus facilement à la maison.
I can relax more easily at home.

On peut voir les nouveaux films immédiatement au cinéma.
We can see new films immediately at the cinema.

Selon ma mère, il vaut mieux rester chez nous parce qu'on peut regarder le film quand on veut. Si on va au cinéma, on doit payer les billets et on ne sait pas où on va s'asseoir.
According to my mother, it's better to stay at home because you can watch the film whenever you want. If you go to the cinema, you have to pay for tickets and you don't know where you'll be sitting.

Preferences

Quelle sorte de film / émission est-ce que tu préfères?
What sort of film / programme do you prefer?

Je préfère les émissions de musique.
I prefer music programmes.

Ma famille préfère les films d'action et la télé-réalité.
My family prefers action films and reality TV.

Nous préférons télécharger toute la série et regarder les émissions tout de suite. Mes parents préfèrent regarder des films en ligne.
We prefer to download a complete series and watch the programmes straight away. My parents prefer to watch films on line.

J'aime mieux regarder les matchs de mon équipe de foot préférée à la télé.
I prefer to watch the matches of my favourite football team on TV.

> **HT** **Si j'avais le choix, je préférerais jouer aux jeux vidéo avec mes copains.**
> If I had the choice, I would prefer to play computer games with my friends.
>
> **HT** **Si j'avais l'occasion, j'aimerais mieux aller à la première du film.**
> If I had the opportunity, I would prefer to go to the film premiere.
>
> **HT** **Ce serait tellement mieux de regarder le film avec tous les acteurs présents!**
> It would be so much better to watch the film with all the actors being there!

Key Point

Use **plus** and **moins** with adjectives and adverbs to form the comparative.

plus	more
moins	less
de plus en plus	
more and more	
de moins en moins	
less and less	

Key Verbs

je peux	I can
on peut	
one / you / we can	
nous pouvons	we can
ils peuvent	they can
je préfère	I prefer
elle préfère	she prefers
nous préférons	we prefer
ils préfèrent	they prefer

Key Sounds

on / om – listen and repeat: c**on**fortable (comfortable), d**on**c (therefore), émissi**on** (programme), t**om**ber (to fall)

> ### Quick Test
>
> 1. Change these verbs to the 'nous' form: **je préfère, je peux, je regarde**
> 2. Translate into French: more and more expensive; less and less popular
> 3. Translate into French: It's the story of a boy who saves the planet.

Free-time Activities

1 Fill in the blanks with **préfère** or **préfèrent** to complete the sentences.

    a) Mes parents .... les films de guerre, mais ma sœur .... la télé-réalité.

    b) Je .... les sports individuels, mais mes copains .... les sports d'équipe.

    c) Ma famille .... écouter de la musique moderne.

    [5 marks]

2 Draw lines to match the phrases to make sentences.

Je m'intéresse	allé au festival de musique.
Je préfère	joué au foot.
J'ai toujours	aux jeux vidéo.
Je suis	regarder des émissions de sport.

    [4 marks]

3 Read the following sentences aloud.

    a) Je peux jouer au foot.

    b) Elle allait à la montagne.

    c) Quand j'étais plus jeune, j'aimais le sport.

    d) C'est un film qui m'intéresse.

    e) Je préfère les émissions de musique.

    f) On est plus confortable chez soi.

    [6 marks]

4 Read the sentences. Write **P** for a sentence about the past, **N** for now or **F** for future.

    a) À l'avenir, je voudrais aller en France.. ....

    b) Avant, je regardais la télé tous les soirs. ....

    c) Maintenant, je préfère sortir. ....

    d) Quand j'étais plus jeune, j'aimais les films d'action. ....

    e) Il y a cinq ans, elle jouait d'un instrument. ....

    f) Tous les jours, je télécharge de la musique. ....

    g) Je n'ai jamais écouté ses chansons. ....

    h) Je vais aller au concert en ville demain. ....

    [8 marks]

5 Choose the correct word to complete each sentence.

    a) C'est une chanson (qui / que) j'aime beaucoup.

    b) C'est le dernier film (qui / que) j'ai vu.

    c) C'est l'histoire d'une famille (qui / que) est en danger.

    d) C'est un groupe (qui / que) est très populaire.

    e) Ce sont les paroles (qui / que) j'aime le plus.

    f) Ce sont des acteurs (qui / que) sont très célèbres.   [6 marks]

6 Translate these sentences into English.

    a) C'est le meilleur groupe du monde.

    b) Les films sont meilleurs sur grand écran.

    c) Faire du sport, c'est plus amusant.

    d) Regarder la télé, c'est moins passionnant.

    e) C'était la chanson la plus populaire de l'année.

    f) Les billets deviennent de plus en plus chers.   [6 marks]

7 Change the sentences in question **6** to say the opposite. The first one has been done as an example.

    a) C'est le pire groupe du monde!

    b) ....

    c) ....

    d) ....

    e) ....

    f) ....   [5 marks]

8 Complete the sentences using your own ideas about your free time.

    a) Le week-end ou le soir, j'aime ....

    b) Je n'aime pas .... mais je préfère ....

    c) Quand j'étais plus jeune, je ....

    d) Pour moi, le sport, c'est .... et je ....

    e) En ce qui concerne la musique, j'adore ....

    f) Mon groupe / chanteur préféré ....

    g) À la télé, je regarde ....

    h) À l'avenir, je voudrais ....

    [10 marks]

Education and Work

1 Match the adjectives in the box below to the sentence in which they are mentioned. Write the letters alongside the sentences.

A happy	**B** funny	**C** young	**D** great	**E** boring
F kind	**G** useful	**H** modern	**I** easy	

a) **Mon prof d'anglais est très gentil.** ....

b) **À mon avis, la technologie est vraiment utile.** ....

c) **J'adore les mathématiques parce que c'est amusant!** ....

d) **J'aime bien la religion mais c'est assez facile.** ....

e) **Mon prof de français est assez jeune et moderne.** ....

f) **L'informatique? Oui, c'est génial!** ....

g) **Je n'aime pas la politique parce que c'est trop ennuyeux.** ....

h) **Notre prof de sciences est toujours heureux.** .... [9 marks]

2 Translate the sentences into French.

a) My sister is good at history.

b) I am quite weak in science.

c) I have chosen German and sport (PE).

d) I like reading and writing (to read and write) in class. [4 marks]

3 Translate the sentences into English.

a) **Je préfère les matières pratiques comme la musique et le théâtre.**

b) **Au collège, je suis en seconde.**

c) **Il faut suivre les règles et travailler dur.**

d) **Il y a cinq cours par jour et chaque cours dure une heure.** [4 marks]

4 Without looking back at the revise spread, complete these infinitives in French.

a) a .... – to improve

b) c .... – to correct

c) d .... – to discuss

d) p .... – to talk

e) p .... – to think

f) p .... – to prepare

g) r .... – to succeed in

h) r .... – to pass an exam

i) a .... – to learn

j) c .... – to understand

k) d .... – to say

l) é .... – to write

m) l .... – to read

n) r .... – to reply

o) s ....– to follow

p) t .... – to translate   [16 marks]

5 Listen to the pronunciations. Write **1**, **2** or **3** for the correct pronunciation for each sentence and explain why.

a) **Je préfère les sciences parce que les cours sont intéressants.** ....

b) **Les cours finissent à trois heures et quart.** ....

c) **Il faut suivre les règles et on doit porter l'uniforme scolaire.** ....

d) **J'ai l'intention d'avoir un boulot varié et intéressant.** ....

[8 marks]

6 Read the text. Fill in the blanks using the infinitives in the box below.

passer	continuer	voyager	aller	quitter	faire	décider

L'année prochaine, je vais .... mes examens et donc je dois .... quoi faire. Moi, je n'ai pas l'intention de .... l'école parce que je veux .... mes études et puis .... à l'université. Avant d'y aller, je vais .... une année sabbatique. Je vais .... en Asie parce que j'adore la culture asiatique.   [7 marks]

7 Translate the underlined text into English.

<u>Je vais y aller</u> avec un ami. <u>J'ai envie de devenir</u> ingénieur parce que <u>je voudrais avoir</u> un boulot intéressant et varié. Et bien sûr, <u>je rêve de gagner</u> un bon salaire!   [4 marks]

Festivals and Public Holidays

Quick Recall Quiz

Key Sounds

You must be able to:

- Describe how you spend public holidays
- Use times of the day accurately
- Explain different opinions about traditions and customs.

Festivals

la fête nationale / le quatorze juillet	Bastille Day / the 14th July
la fête des Mères	Mother's Day
la fête de la Musique	World Music Day
la Saint-Valentin	St Valentine's Day
le jour férié	public holiday
le défilé	procession
le festival	festival
HT **le feu d'artifice**	firework display
la tradition	tradition
traditionnel / traditionnelle	traditional
célébrer	to celebrate
fêter	to celebrate
passer	to spend (time)
en famille	with family
avec des amis	with friends
HT **garder**	to keep

Comment passes-tu la fête nationale / le quatorze juillet?
How do you spend Bastille Day / the 14th July?

On passe la journée à manger, à chanter et à danser.
We spend the day eating, singing and dancing.

L'après-midi, il y a des défilés dans les rues.
In the afternoon, there are processions in the street(s).

Le soir, nous regardons un spectacle ou un feu d'artifice.
In the evening we watch a show or a firework display.

National, Regional and Local Festivals

Chaque région de France a des fêtes annuelles.
Each region of France has annual festivals.

Elles célèbrent la nourriture et la culture locales.
They celebrate local food and culture.

On célèbre la diversité et la différence.
They celebrate diversity and difference.

Souvent, il y a de la musique régionale.
Often, there is regional music.

Les gens portent des vêtements divers ou extraordinaires et dansent dans les rues.
People wear varied or extraordinary clothes and dance in the streets.

Il y a beaucoup de bruit, de couleurs et de joie!
There's lots of noise, colour and joy!

> ### Key Point
>
> Spending time doing something is translated with **à** + the infinitive in French, e.g. **On passe son temps à danser.** (We spend time dancing.)

> ### Key Sound
>
> **oi / oy**. Listen and repeat: **le soir** (evening), **moi** (me), **l'histoire** (history)
>
> **oy** has the same sound: **moyen** (medium), **voyage** (journey), **joyeuse** (joyful)

> ### Key Point
>
> Learn how to translate the times of day carefully: **le matin** (in the morning(s)), **l'après-midi** (in the afternoon(s)), **le soir** (in the evening(s)), **la journée** (day(time)), **la soirée** (evening(time)). This rule applies to days of the week, too, e.g. **le samedi** (on Saturdays).

Are Traditional Festivals Important?

à mon avis…	in my opinion…
pour moi…	for me…
pour les touristes / les jeunes…	for tourists / young people…
pour eux…	for them…
pour ceux qui…	for those who…
personnellement…	personally…
selon eux…	according to them…
selon certains…	according to some…
certains disent que…	some say that…
beaucoup de gens pensent que…	lots of people think that…
d'autres notent / remarquent que…	others note / remark that…
HT **il est important de…**	it is important to…
HT **il n'est pas essentiel de…**	it is not necessary to…

À mon avis, les fêtes traditionnelles sont passionnantes parce que je m'intéresse à l'histoire.
In my opinion, traditional festivals are exciting because I'm interested in history.

C'est un bon spectacle pour les touristes.
It's a great sight for tourists.

Pour ceux qui aiment les fêtes traditionnelles, il est important de préserver la culture régionale.
For those who like traditional festivals, it is important to preserve regional culture.

Selon certains, les fêtes traditionnelles peuvent unir les générations.
According to some, traditional festivals can unite generations.

Certains disent qu'elles ne sont plus nécessaires.
Some say that they are no longer necessary.

D'autres soulignent l'importance de la vie moderne et la diversité de notre société actuelle.
Others underline the importance of modern life and the diversity of our current society.

Key Point

When giving the opinions of other people, use the 3rd person plural of the verb, e.g. **ils aiment** (they like), **ils sont** (they are), **ils pensent** (they think), **ils peuvent** (they can). Use words such as **selon** (according to) or **pour** (for) to add complexity to your sentence structure.

Key Sound

Do not pronounce the **-nt** at the end of 3rd person plural verb forms. Listen and repeat: **ils pensent** (they think), **ils peuvent** (they can), **ils disent** (they say), **ils choisissent** (they choose). Notice the liaison with verbs beginning with a vowel, e.g. **ils aiment** (they like), **elles adorent** (they love).

Quick Test

1. Find the three errors in this sentence and correct them:
   Dans le matin, on passons notre temps en préparer la musique pour le concert.
2. Put these verbs into the 3rd person plural, e.g. **on passe = ils passent: on aime, on pense, on est, on peut**
3. Translate into English: **Pour ceux qui aiment l'histoire, les fêtes traditionnelles sont importantes.**
4. Translate into French:
   According to some, it is not necessary to preserve regional culture.

Religious Festivals

You must be able to:

- Talk and write about religious festivals and how you celebrate them
- Discuss past and future celebrations
- Use different time frames confidently.

Religious Festivals

Noël	Christmas
Pâques	Easter
l'Aïd	Eïd
bouddhiste	Buddhist
chrétien / chrétienne	Christian
juif / juive	Jewish
musulman(e)	Muslim
HT **catholique**	Catholic

C'est une fête bouddhiste célébrée au mois de mars.
It's a Buddhist festival celebrated in March.

la religion	religion
religieux / religieuse	religious
l'église (f)	church
la mosquée	mosque
la synagogue	synagogue
le temple	temple

Pour toutes les fêtes religieuses, on va à la mosquée.
For all religious festivals, we go to the mosque.

Celebrating Religious Festivals

aller à l'église / à la mosquée / à la synagogue
to go to church / mosque / synagogue

donner / ouvrir les cadeaux	to give / open presents
chanter des chansons (de Noël)	to sing songs (carols)
jouer à des jeux	to play games
préparer des plats	to prepare meals / dishes
manger un repas spécial	to eat a special meal
chercher des œufs en chocolat	to look for chocolate eggs
aider des personnes dans le besoin	to help people in need

Time Phrases

l'an dernier	last year
l'année dernière	last year
il y a deux ans	two years ago
l'an prochain	next year
l'année prochaine	next year
dans deux ans	in two years' time

Key Point

Chez literally means 'at the house of'.

chez moi	at my house / at home
chez toi	at your house
chez nous	at our house / at home

chez ma tante
at my aunt's house

Key Sound

ch – this is a soft 'sh' sound in French and is pronounced very differently from the hard-sounding English 'ch'. Listen and repeat: **ch**anter (to sing), **ch**anson (song), **ch**er**ch**er (to look for), nous **ch**er**ch**ons (we look for), pro**ch**ain (next)

Using Time Frames Confidently

- To say what you usually do, use the present tense:

  Qu'est-ce que tu fais pour fêter Pâques?

  What do you do to celebrate Easter?

  Normalement, on passe la journée en famille. Nous cherchons les œufs en chocolat dans le jardin avant de les manger!

  Usually, we spend the day with the family. We look for chocolate eggs in the garden before eating them!

- To say what you did in the past, use the perfect tense:

  Qu'est-ce que tu as fait pour célébrer Noël l'année dernière?

  What did you do to celebrate Christmas last year?

  Je suis allé(e) à l'église où nous avons chanté des chansons de Noël. Après ça, nous sommes rentrés chez nous pour donner et ouvrir nos cadeaux.

  I went to church where we sang carols. After that, we went home to give and open our presents.

- To say what you are going to do in the future, use the future time frame:

  Qu'est-ce que tu vas faire pour célébrer l'Aïd l'année prochaine?

  What are you going to do for Eid next year?

  Je vais préparer des plats spéciaux avec Maman et puis nous allons les manger. Nous allons fêter l'Aïd avec toute la famille et je vais jouer à des jeux avec mes cousins.

  I'm going to prepare some special dishes with Mum and then we're going to eat them. We're going to celebrate Eid with the whole family and I'm going to play games with my cousins.

  HT Qu'est-ce que tu feras pour célébrer l'Aïd l'année prochaine?

  What will you do for Eid next year?

  HT Je mangerai des plats spéciaux après les avoir préparés avec Maman. Nous fêterons ça avec toute la famille et je jouerai à des jeux avec mes cousins.

  I will eat some special dishes after having prepared them with Mum. We will celebrate with the whole family and I will play games with my cousins.

- To say what you would like to do, use the conditional tense:

  Qu'est-ce que tu voudrais faire à Noël?

  What would you like to do at Christmas?

  Je voudrais aller chez mon oncle et aider des gens qui vivent dans la pauvreté.

  I would like to go to my uncle's house and help people who live in poverty.

  HT J'aimerais voyager à l'étranger et célébrer Noël dans un pays froid où il y aurait beaucoup de neige.

  I would like to travel abroad and celebrate Christmas in a cold country where there would be lots of snow.

Key Point

You may want to talk or write about past or future celebrations. Ensure you put the verbs into the correct tense:

j'ai passé	I spent
je passe	I spend
je vais passer	I'm going to spend
je suis resté(e)	I stayed
je reste	I stay
je vais rester	I'm going to stay

Key Sounds

è / ê / ai all have the same sound in French. Listen and repeat: **après** (after), **fêter** (to celebrate), **je vais** (I go)

Quick Test

1. Give **two** ways of saying 'at home' in French, using **chez**.
2. What is the difference in meaning between **il y a deux ans** and **dans deux ans**?
3. Put these sentences into the past tense: **Je passe la journée avec ma famille. Nous mangeons beaucoup et donnons des cadeaux.**
4. Translate into French: I'm going to celebrate Easter with my friends. We're going to eat lots of chocolate eggs!

Celebrating with Friends and Family

You must be able to:

- Talk about birthday and wedding celebrations
- Ask and answer questions about special occasions
- Explain your preferences and why you enjoy these days.

Celebrating with Friends and Family

inviter	to invite
recevoir	to receive
l'événement	event
la naissance	birth
le mariage	wedding / marriage
la fête d'anniversaire	birthday party
Félicitations!	Congratulations!
Bon anniversaire!	Happy birthday!
Joyeux anniversaire!	Happy birthday!
Bonne chance!	Good luck!
HT **féliciter**	to congratulate

J'ai organisé une fête d'anniversaire surprise pour ma sœur.
I've organised a surprise birthday party for my sister.

Je vais inviter tous ses amis. I'm going to invite all her friends.

Key Sounds

The letters **s**, **t**, **n** and **x** are pronounced at the end of a word when the following word begins with a vowel. This is called a liaison and the two words 'join together' in sound. Listen to these examples and repeat: **nous sommes allés** (we went), **je vais inviter** (I am going to invite), **c'était un événement** (it was an event), **ton anniversaire** (your birthday), **Joyeux anniversaire** (Happy birthday)

Question Words

qui?	who?	**comment?**	how?
que?	what?	**combien?**	how much / many?
quel(le)(s)?	which?	**où?**	where?
quand?	when?	**pourquoi?**	why?

Quelle est la date de ton anniversaire?
When is your birthday?

Mon anniversaire, c'est le treize juillet.
My birthday is on the thirteenth of July.

Quelle est ta fête préférée?
What (which) is your favourite celebration?

Ma fête préférée, c'est mon anniversaire.
My favourite celebration is my birthday.

Comment aimes-tu fêter ton anniversaire?
How do you like celebrating your birthday?

J'aime bien inviter toute la famille chez moi.
I like inviting all my family to my house.

Cependant, j'adore aussi sortir en ville avec mes copains.
However, I also love going out in town with my friends.

Pourquoi? Why?

car je peux voir tous les membres de ma famille.
because I can see all my family.

HT **parce que ça me permet de voir tous mes copains.**
because I can see all my friends.

Conjunctions

car	because	**donc**	so, therefore
parce que	because	**comme**	as
cependant	however	**et**	and
mais	but	**ou**	or

HT	**par contre**	on the other hand
HT	**ça me permet de**	I can (it allows me to)

Describing a Family Event

- To talk or write about something **in the past** in French, we use the perfect tense for 'events' and the imperfect tense for 'description':

  Au mois de juillet, je suis allé(e) au mariage de ma cousine.

  In July, I went to my cousin's wedding.

  C'était une grande fête et l'occasion de voir tous les membres de la famille.

  It was a big celebration and an opportunity to see all the members of the family.

  D'abord, nous sommes allés à l'église pour le mariage religieux.

  First of all, we went to the church for the official marriage service.

  Ensuite, il y avait une grande réception avec un repas spécial.

  Then, there was a big reception with a special meal.

  Plus tard, il y avait de la musique et nous avons dansé jusqu'à minuit!

  Later, there was music and we danced until midnight!

  Tout le monde était heureux et joyeux.

  Everyone was happy and joyful.

  C'était vraiment fantastique et le meilleur jour de l'année!

  It was really fantastic and the best day of the year!

- To talk or write about something in the future in French, we can use the near future or the future tense:

  Je vais célébrer mes seize ans avec tous mes amis.

  I'm going to celebrate my sixteenth birthday with all my friends.

  Premièrement, on va manger au restaurant en ville.

  First of all, we're going to eat in a restaurant in town.

  Il y aura un grand gâteau d'anniversaire pour moi.

  There will be a big birthday cake for me.

  Après, nous allons voir notre groupe préféré en concert.

  Afterwards, we are going to see our favourite group in concert.

  Ce sera (ça va être) excellent – quel bon cadeau!

  It will be (it's going to be) excellent – what a great present!

Key Verbs

il y avait	there was / there were
c'était	it was
il y aura	there will be
ce sera	it will be

Key Point

Use adverbs to provide more detail and complexity:

premièrement	firstly
d'abord	first of all
puis	then
ensuite	then
après	after(wards)
plus tard	later
enfin	finally
finalement	in the end, after all

Quick Test

1. What do these question words mean in English?
   qui?, quand?, comment?, où?, pourquoi?
2. Give the French for: first of all, later, afterwards, then, finally
3. Put this account into the past by changing the verbs:
   Je vais aller au mariage de mon frère. On va manger et danser.
   Ce sera formidable!

Customs, Festivals and Celebrations

1 Draw lines to match the English and French question words.

a) qui?	i) when?
b) comment?	ii) why?
c) quand?	iii) which?
d) où?	iv) who?
e) pourquoi?	v) how?
f) quel(le)s?	vi) where?

[6 marks]

2 Read the sentences. Write **P** for past, **N** for present (now) or **F** for future.

a) **Nous cherchons les œufs en chocolat dans le jardin.** ....

b) **Je vais célébrer mon anniversaire avec mes cousins.** ....

c) **On passe la journée en famille.** ....

d) **Nous avons chanté des chansons traditionnelles.** ....

e) **Je suis allé(e) au mariage de ma sœur.** ....

f) **Nous allons voir notre groupe préféré en concert.** ....

g) **Je suis resté chez moi.** .... [7 marks]

3 Choose a suitable time phrase from the list below to add to each of the sentences in question **2**.

la semaine dernière   à Pâques   l'an dernier   l'année prochaine   normalement
d'habitude   il y a deux ans   le week-end prochain   dans deux ans   à l'Aïd

[7 marks]

4 Read these sentences aloud.

a) **Le soir, nous regardons un spectacle.**

b) **Pour ceux qui aiment les fêtes traditionnelles, c'est amusant.**

c) **Beaucoup de gens pensent que Noël est la fête la plus importante.**

d) Chez nous, on chante des chansons intéressantes.

e) Après le mariage, je vais faire la fête avec ma famille.

f) Nous sommes allés en ville pour mon anniversaire. [6 marks]

5 Match up the halves of the sentences below and then translate them into English.

a) Les touristes regardent	i) à chanter des chansons traditionnelles.
b) Beaucoup de gens mangent	ii) danse dans les rues.
c) Tout le monde aime donner	iii) le défilé et le feu d'artifice.
d) On passe la journée	iv) et recevoir des cadeaux.
e) En fin de soirée, on	v) des plats spéciaux. [10 marks]

6 Put these sentences into the 3rd person plural by using the **ils / elles** form of the verb.
An example has been done for you.

Example: **On mange des gâteaux. = Ils mangent des gâteaux.**

a) On danse dans les rues.

b) On fête l'anniversaire de ma mère.

c) Je pense que c'est important.

d) On dit que c'est nécessaire.

e) Je peux manger toute la journée!

f) On choisit de célébrer l'événement en famille. [6 marks]

7 Complete the sentences, using your own ideas about festivals and celebrations.

a) Ma fête préférée, c'est .... parce que ....

b) J'aime surtout .... et ....

c) L'an dernier, pour Noël / l'Aïd, nous ....

d) Pour mon anniversaire, je préfère ....

e) L'année prochaine, je voudrais ....

f) En ce qui concerne les fêtes traditionnelles, j'adore .... [8 marks]

Review Questions

Free-time Activities

1 Write the correct endings for these verbs in the present tense.

a) **Nous ador**................... We adore

b) **Elle écout**................... She listens to

c) **Ils télécharg**................... They download

d) **Nous chant**................... We sing

e) **Elles s'intéress** .... **à** They are interested in

f) **Quelle sorte de musique aim**...................**-tu?** What sort of music do you like?

g) **Quelle sorte de films préfér**...................**-vous?** What sort of films do you prefer? [7 marks]

2 Choose the correct verb from the box below to complete the sentences.

| je vais | je fais | je faisais | j'allais |

a) **Il y a deux ans,** .... **au club des jeunes.**

b) **En ce moment,** .... **souvent des promenades à la campagne.**

c) **Maintenant,** .... **au centre sportif tous les samedis.**

d) **Quand j'étais plus jeune,** .... **de la natation trois fois par semaine.**

[4 marks]

3 Read the sentences and decide whether they are about watching the television, going to the cinema or both. Write **T** for television, **C** for cinema or **B** for both.

a) **Les effets spéciaux sont meilleurs sur le grand écran.** ....

b) **Les places deviennent de plus en plus chères.** ....

c) **On peut appuyer sur 'pause' et continuer quand on veut.** ....

d) **On n'a pas besion de regarder toutes les publicités.** ....

e) **On peut parler un peu si on veut.** ....

f) **Tout le monde aime acheter du pop-corn et du chocolat au magasin!** ....

g) **Pour moi, l'essentiel est le confort et on peut se relaxer où on veut.** .... [7 marks]

4 Translate the sentences in question **3** into English.

a) ....

b) ....

c) ....

d) ....

e) ....

f) ....

g) .... [7 marks]

5 Unscramble the sentences.

a) **Quand onze semaine ans, j'allais j'avais à la trois fois par piscine**

b) **Ils beaucoup avec ont leur succès eu musique de**

c) **Samedi groupe je vais voir prochain mon en concert préféré à Paris**

d) **J'ai chansons écouté ses toujours si mes même ne les aiment copains pas**

e) **J'aime matchs mieux les de mon équipe regarder de foot à la télé préférée** [5 marks]

6 Change the sentences by replacing the underlined noun with the correct pronoun – **le, la** or **les**. An example has been done for you.

Example: **Il préfère <u>les films d'action.</u> = Il les préfère.**

a) **Il préfère <u>la télé-réalité.</u>**

b) **Nous regardons <u>le match</u> en ligne.**

c) **Elle adore <u>ses films.</u>**

d) **Je n'aime pas <u>les paroles.</u>** [4 marks]

Celebrities

You must be able to:

- Discuss the lives and lifestyles of celebrities
- Talk and write about their careers and personal life.

Quick Recall Quiz

Key Sounds

Celebrity Lifestyle

la célébrité	celebrity
la personnalité	personality
la star	star / celebrity
célèbre	famous
connu(e)	well-known

Il y a beaucoup de célébrités dans le monde du cinéma, du sport, de la musique et de la télévision.
There are lots of celebrities in the world of film, sport, music and TV.

Les stars ont une popularité / réputation nationale et internationale.
Stars have a national and international popularity / reputation.

Quelques personnalités sont connues à cause de la télé-réalité.
Some personalities are known because of reality TV (shows).

Elles deviennent célèbres à cause des médias.
They become famous because of the media.

Elles sont très riches et ont beaucoup d'argent.
They are very rich and have lots of money.

HT **Les célébrités mènent une vie très différente de la nôtre.**
Celebrities lead a very different life to ours (our own).

les médias	the media
le journal	newspaper
les journaux	newspapers
HT **la presse**	the press

On suit leur mode de vie dans les journaux.
We follow their lifestyle in the newspapers.

On lit les entretiens dans la presse et en ligne.
We read interviews in the press and on line.

On s'intéresse à une façon de vivre différente.
We are interested in a different way of living.

On aime voir leurs grandes maisons et leurs voitures rapides.
We like to see their big houses and their fast cars.

On discute de leurs carrière(s) ou leur vie personnelle.
We discuss their career(s) or their personal life.

Key Sounds

Single vowel sounds – **a**, **e**, **i**, **o**, **u** and **y**. These are very common sounds that you know from very short words: **a** as in **la**, **e** as in **je**, **i** as in **il**, **o** as in **trop**, **u** as in **tu** and **y** as in **il y a**. Learn a word for each single vowel sound so that you can replicate the sound with all new words you come across.

Key Point

leur / **leurs** translate as 'their' in English. **Leur** is used for the singular and **leurs** is used for the plural: **leur façon de vivre** (their way of living), **leurs grandes maisons** (their big houses)

Describing the Career of a Celebrity

la carrière	career
le prix	prize
le tour	tour
HT **la tournée**	tour
HT **l'ouverture**	opening

J'ai toujours voulu devenir acteur / chanteuse.
I (have) always wanted to become an actor / singer.

Elle a toujours voulu devenir joueuse de foot professionnelle.
She (has) always wanted to become a professional footballer.

Quand j'étais enfant, je jouais / je faisais...
When I was a child I was playing / I was doing...

À l'âge de seize ans, il chantait dans un groupe.
At the age of 16, he was singing in a group.

J'ai commencé en 2015 comme...
I started in 2015 as...

Sa première équipe / chanson était...
His / her first team / song was...

Mon dernier rôle / personnage (à la télé) était...
My last role / character (on TV) was...

HT **Dans son nouveau film, il est le héros / elle est l'héroïne.**
In his / her new film, he is the hero / she is the heroine.

HT **Depuis mon enfance...**   Since my childhood...

Il a gagné un prix / un concours / le Tour de France.
He (has) won a prize / a competition / the Tour de France.

Elle a sorti son nouveau livre / sa nouvelle chanson.
She (has) released her new book / her new song.

Il a fait une tournée européenne / mondiale.
He went on a European / world tour.

HT **Elle a lancé une publicité.**   She (has) launched an advert.

HT **Il a diffusé sa nouvelle série.**   He (has) broadcast his new series.

Elle a annoncé qu'elle se séparait de son partenaire.
She announced that she was separating from her partner.

Il va se marier le mois prochain.
He's going to get married next month.

Elle habite à Paris / en France avec son partenaire / ses enfants.
She lives in Paris / in France with her partner / children.

Son mari / Sa femme / Sa famille est très fier / fière.
His / her husband / wife / family is very proud.

On attend le prochain film / chapitre / la prochaine saison avec intérêt.
We await the next film / chapter / season with interest.

HT **On dit qu'elle aura un brillant avenir.**
They say that she will have a bright future.

Key Point

You may need to read or listen to an account by a famous person where they are talking about themselves, or you may need to listen to or read an article written about them. Make sure you can use the first person (**je** form) and the third person (**il / elle** form) to discuss your favourite celebrities.

Quick Test

1. Choose the correct word: **leur / leurs maisons**; **leur / leurs amis**; **leur / leurs famille**
2. Give the French for: lifestyle; interviews; team; character; competition
3. Translate into English: **Il a annoncé qu'il se séparait de sa femme.**
4. Translate into French: She has always wanted to become a singer.

Online Influencers

You must be able to:

- Discuss different types of influencers
- Talk and write about their work
- Express your opinions regarding influencers.

Types of Influencers

les influenceurs	influencers
la mode	fashion
la santé	health
le mode de vie	lifestyle
la nourriture	food
les animaux	animals / pets
le sport	sport
la forme physique	fitness
les voyages	travel
la technologie	technology
les jeux vidéo	gaming / computer games

Il y a toutes sortes d'influenceurs en ce moment.
There are all sorts of influencers at the moment.

Les influenceurs sont de plus en plus nombreux.
There are more and more influencers. (Influencers are becoming more and more numerous.)

Ils ont de plus en plus d'influence.
They are having more and more influence.

Ils parlent de la mode / la santé.   They talk about fashion / health.

What Influencers Do

le site	site
le blog	blog
l'article	article
le selfie	selfie
les réseaux sociaux	social media
HT **le texte**	text
HT **le streaming**	streaming

Ils postent des blogs / des articles en ligne.
They post blogs / articles online.

Ils mettent des vidéos amusantes sur leur site.
They put funny videos on their site.

Ils communiquent sur les réseaux sociaux.
They communicate on social media.

Ils donnent des conseils / leur avis sur…
They give advice about / their opinion on…

Ils recommandent certains produits.
They recommend certain products.

Key Verbs

ils sont	they are / are being
ils font	they do / are doing
ils vont	they go / are going
ils ont	they have / are having

Key Point

The phrase **de plus en plus** (meaning 'more and more') is very useful when discussing trends. **De moins en moins** (meaning 'less and less') can be used in a similar way.

Ils ont des millions de fans.
They have millions of followers / fans.
Ils peuvent gagner beaucoup d'argent.
They can earn a lot of money.
HT Ils font de la publicité pour les marques.
They advertise brands.

Becoming Famous

Comment es-tu devenu(e) célèbre?   How did you become famous?
Elle a regardé une émission à la télé sur les influenceurs.
She saw a programme on TV about influencers.
Il a commencé à créer des vidéos.   He started to make videos.
Elle a décidé de poster des blogs en ligne.
She decided to post blogs online.
Il a pris des photos et a mis les images sur son site.
He took photos and put pictures on his site.
Elle a eu beaucoup de succès.   She was very successful.
Il est devenu très populaire.   He became very popular.
Elle est devenue une des influenceuses françaises les plus célèbres.
She became one of the most famous French (female) influencers.

Opinions on Influencers

suivre   to follow
suivi (par)   followed (by)
je suis   I follow

Je suis les influenceurs sur les réseaux sociaux.
I follow influencers on social media.
Je lis les articles.   I read articles.
J'aime lire des blogs sur les animaux.   I love reading blogs about animals.
J'adore regarder des photos sur la mode.
I love looking at photos about fashion.
Je préfère les influenceurs qui partagent leurs expériences.
I prefer influencers who share their experiences.
À mon avis, les influenceurs sont extraordinaires.
In my opinion, influencers are extraordinary.
Je n'aime pas trop les vidéos 'amusantes' avec de petits enfants.
I don't like 'amusing' videos with little children in them too much.
Les influenceurs me donnent beaucoup d'idées utiles.
Influencers give me lots of useful ideas.
Mon rêve, c'est de devenir influenceur / influenceuse (moi-même).
My dream is to become an influencer (myself).

Key Point

When part of the verb **suivre** (to follow), **je suis** means 'I follow'. Look carefully at the context to decide whether you need to translate **je suis** as 'I follow' or 'I am'!

Key Sounds

Notice the difference between the **in** sound and the **i** sound. Listen and repeat: **influenceur** (influencer), **influenceuse** (influencer), **l'influence** (influence) and compare with: **l'idée** (idea), **l'image** (image), **je lis** (I read)

Quick Test

1. How do you translate 'more and more' into French?
2. Translate these verbs into French:
   they are going; they are having; they are doing
3. Translate into English:
   Il a posté des vidéos en ligne et il est devenu très populaire.
4. Translate into French: I follow fashion influencers on social media.

Celebrities and Their Role in Society

You must be able to:

- Talk and write about their contribution to society
- Express opinions on the advantages and disadvantages of being famous
- Discuss your favourite celebrities.

Effects on Society

l'égalité	equality
la liberté	liberty / freedom
la vérité	truth
bi(sexuel)	bi(sexual)
handicapé	disabled
hétéro	straight / heterosexual
transgenre	trans
HT **la diversité**	diversity

Certaines célébrités parlent facilement de leur identité.
Some celebrities talk easily about their identity.
Ils / Elles parlent des différences et de la diversité dans notre société.
They talk about differences and diversity in our society.
On peut exprimer des opinions ou ouvrir une discussion sur l'égalité.
You can express opinions or open a discussion about equality.

la santé mentale	mental health
les soucis	worries
les erreurs	mistakes / errors
la faute	mistake / error / fault

D'autres célébrités discutent de leurs problèmes et des solutions possibles.
Other celebrities discuss their problems and possible solutions.
Elles expliquent leurs difficultés et comment elles ont réussi.
They explain their difficulties and how they have succeeded.
Elles peuvent inspirer une génération. They can inspire a generation.
Elle a été une inspiration pour les jeunes / les filles / les handicapés.
She has been an inspiration for young people / girls / the disabled.

la catastrophe	catastrophe / disaster
la crise	crisis
la menace	threat
HT **le scandale**	scandal

Des personnes célèbres complètent des défis pour soutenir des causes diverses…
Famous people complete challenges to support varied causes…
…pour améliorer la vie des autres / l'environnement.
…to improve the life of others / the environment.
…pour aider les victimes de la violence / de la pauvreté / du chômage.
…to help victims of violence / poverty / unemployment.
Ils / Elles participent à des actions politiques comme des manifestations ou des grèves.
They participate in political actions such as demonstrations or strikes.

> ### Key Point
>
> To describe the actions of others, use the 3rd person plural (**ils / elles** form) of the verb, e.g. **ils parlent de** (they talk about); **ils discutent** (they discuss); **ils expliquent** (they explain); **ils expriment leurs opinions** (they express their opinions)

> ### Key Point
>
> **Pour** + the infinitive of the verb is a useful construction to include in your speaking and writing. It means 'to' when you can substitute 'in order to' in English and the sentence still makes sense, e.g. **pour aider les autres** (to help others = in order to help others)

Advantages and Disadvantages of Fame

Quelques avantages	Some advantages
On est riche.	You are rich.
On peut acheter tout ce qu'on veut.	You can buy whatever you like.
On peut voyager partout.	You can travel everywhere.
On est puissant.	You are powerful.
L'argent donne de la sécurité.	Money gives (you) security.
HT **la richesse**	wealth
Quelques inconvénients	Some disadvantages
Tous les aspects de la vie sont publics.	
All aspects of your life are public.	
Leur vie n'est jamais secrète.	Their life is never secret.
On peut recevoir des menaces.	You can receive threats.
On peut perdre sa popularité.	You can lose your popularity.
HT **On risque des scandales**.	You risk scandals.
C'est bien d'être célèbre parce que…	It's good to be famous because…
Par contre, ce n'est pas si bien, car…	
On the other hand, it's not so good, because…	
Pour moi, l'argent n'a pas beaucoup d'importance.	
For me, money isn't that important.	
Personnellement, être heureux est plus important.	
Personally, being happy is more important.	

Your Favourite Celebrities

Ma célébrité préférée s'appelle…	My favourite celebrity is called…
Il / elle est connu(e) comme artiste / sportif / sportive.	
He / she is known as an artist / sportsperson.	
J'apprécie son caractère / sa personnalité /ses compétences.	
I admire his / her character / personality / abilities.	
Je voudrais le / la rencontrer.	I would like to meet him / her.
J'aimerais passer une journée avec lui / elle.	
I would like to spend a day with him / her.	
Je voudrais prendre des photos / des selfies.	
I would like to take photos / selfies.	
J'aimerais voir son bateau / sa maison / ses enfants.	
I would love to see his / her boat / house / children.	
HT **Si j'avais le choix, je préférerais aller en vacances avec lui / elle.**	
If I had the choice, I would prefer to go on holiday with him / her.	
HT **Ce serait vraiment super!**	
It would be really great!	

Quick Test

1. Give the French for: freedom, equality, truth, crisis, threat
2. What do these verbs mean in English?:
   ils expriment; **ils parlent de**; **ils discutent**
3. Translate into French:
   in order to help; in order to improve; in order to support
4. Translate into English:
   J'aimerais passer la journée avec lui et prendre des selfies.

Celebrity Culture

1 Unscramble the sentences and translate them into English.

a) **Les célèbres des deviennent à célébrités cause médias**

b) **nombreux ligne Les plus en sont de influenceurs plus en**

c) **pour Elle une handicapés inspiration les été a**

d) **rencontrer Je célébrité journée elle voudrais préférée et passer ma une avec** [8 marks]

2 Read the following sentences aloud.

a) **Ils sont très riches et ont beaucoup d'argent.**

b) **On suit leur mode de vie dans les journaux.**

c) **J'ai toujours voulu devenir acteur.**

d) **Il y a toutes sortes d'influenceurs.**

e) **Ils communiquent sur les réseaux sociaux.**

f) **Je préférerais le rencontrer.** [6 marks]

3 Rewrite these sentences using '**pour** + the infinitive'. An example has been done for you.

Example: **Il a aidé les pauvres = pour aider les pauvres**

a) **Elle a aidé les jeunes = pour** ....

b) **Nous avons exprimé nos opinions = pour** ....

c) **Cela a amélioré l'environnement = pour** ....

d) **On a discuté du problème = pour** ....

e) **Il a fini l'entretien = pour** ....

f) **J'ai pris des selfies = pour** .... [6 marks]

4 Choose the correct underlined word to complete each sentence.

a) **On aime voir <u>leur / leurs</u> grandes maisons.**

b) **J'apprécie <u>leur / leurs</u> compétences.**

c) **Nous discutons de <u>leur / leurs</u> vie personnelle.**

d) **Ils ont sorti <u>leur / leurs</u> nouvelle vidéo.** [4 marks]

5 Change these sentences to talk about celebrities. Use the 3rd person plural (**ils / elles**) form of the underlined verb. An example has been done for you.

Example: **Il a beaucoup de succès. = Ils ont beaucoup de succès.**

a) **J'ai beaucoup d'argent.**

b) **Il est très populaire.**

c) **Je fais de plus en plus de blogs.**

d) **Il va gagner le concours.**

e) **Je peux parler de la diversité.**

f) **On discute des différences.**   [6 marks]

6 Read the sentences. Write **P** for a positive opinion, **N** for a negative opinion or **P+N** for a positive and negative opinion.

a) **Les célébrités ont un mode de vie spectaculaire!** ....

b) **Elles peuvent voyager partout dans le monde et passer des vacances extraordinaires.** ....

c) **La presse parle mal de beaucoup de stars.** ....

d) **On peut avoir beaucoup de succès ou on peut perdre sa popularité.** ....

[4 marks]

7 Read the sentences. Write **P** for an event in the past, **N** for an event now or **F** for an event in the future.

a) **Elle a sorti sa nouvelle chanson.** ....

b) **On attend le prochain film avec intérêt.** ....

c) **Elle habite en France avec ses enfants.** ....

d) **Elles mettent les vidéos amusantes sur leur site.** ....

e) **Je voudrais la rencontrer à l'avenir.** ....

f) **Ils ont participé à une manifestation contre la guerre.** ....   [6 marks]

8 Complete the sentences, using your own ideas.

a) **Mon acteur préféré** ....

b) **Je l'aime bien parce qu'il** ....

c) **Pour moi, les influenceurs** ....

d) **Je préfère suivre** ....

e) **Je pense que les célébrités** ....

f) **À l'avenir, je voudrais rencontrer** ....

[6 marks]

Review Questions

Customs, Festivals and Celebrations

1 Use the verbs in the box below to complete this account.

je suis allé	voir	J'ai trouvé	a joué	nous avons dansé
il y avait	C'était	était	nous sommes allés	

**Au mois de juillet, ... au mariage de mon frère. ....
une grande fête et l'occasion de .... tous les membres de
la famille. D'abord, ... à l'église pour le mariage religieux.
Ensuite, ... une grande réception avec un repas spécial. Plus tard,
un groupe .... de la musique et .... jusqu'à minuit!
Tout le monde .... heureux et joyeux. .... l'événement
vraiment fantastique!**

[9 marks]

2 Listen to the pronunciations. Write **1**, **2** or **3** for each sentence and explain why.

a) **Le soir, nous regardons un spectacle joyeux.** ....

....

b) **Ils montrent la diversité de notre société actuelle.** ....

....

c) **Nous avons chanté des chansons traditionnelles.** ....

....

d) **Après ça, je vais fêter l'événement avec ma famille.** ....

....

[4 marks]

3 Use the vocabulary list on the AQA website to find, write down and learn:

a) All the different forms of the verb **faire** that are listed. (How many did you find?)

b) The different forms of the verb **voir** listed. (Take care – they are not all listed in the same place!)

c) Now find two more similar examples where different forms of the same verb are listed separately.

d) Why do you think this might be useful for you? [4 marks]

4 Write the following account as a future event by changing all the underlined verbs. You may use either the near future (**aller** + infinitive) or the future tense.

J'ai célébré mes seize ans avec tous mes copains. Premièrement, <u>on a mangé</u> au restaurant en ville. <u>Ma mère a préparé</u> un grand gâteau d'anniversaire pour moi. Après ça, <u>nous avons vu</u> notre groupe préféré en concert. <u>C'était</u> vraiment excellent – quel bon cadeau!

[5 marks]

5 Read the sentences. Write **P** for a positive opinion, **N** for a negative opinion or **P+N** for a positive and negative opinion.

a) **J'aime bien passer la journée à chanter et à danser.** ....

b) **Selon certains, les fêtes traditionnelles peuvent unir les générations.** ....

c) **C'est un bon spectacle pour les touristes mais il y a trop de monde.** ....

d) **Il faut plutôt se concentrer sur la vie moderne et la diversité de notre société actuelle.** ....

e) **Est-il si important de préserver la culture régionale?** ....

[5 marks]

6 Translate these sentences into English.

a) **L'après-midi de la fête nationale, il y a des défilés dans les rues.**

b) **Pour ceux qui s'intéressent à l'histoire, il est important de préserver les traditions.**

c) **Nous sommes rentrés chez nous pour manger un repas spécial.**

d) **Je vais passer le jour férié en famille.**

e) **Le mariage de ma sœur a été un événement inoubliable.** [5 marks]

7 Using the ideas, vocabulary and grammar structures in questions **1** and **4**, alongside your own ideas, write a paragraph about your favourite event of last year and / or an event you would like to happen in the future.

....

....

....

....

[5 marks]

Travelling Abroad

Quick Recall Quiz

Key Sound

You must be able to:

- Talk about countries and nationalities
- Give the main details about a holiday
- Use key verbs in the present, past and future.

Countries and Nationalities

Feminine Countries and Places

l'Angleterre	England	**anglais(e)**	English
la France	France	**français(e)**	French
la Belgique	Belgium	HT **belge**	Belgian
la Suisse	Switzerland	HT **suisse**	Swiss
la Réunion	Reunion Island		
HT **la Corse**	Corsica		
HT **la Tunisie**	Tunisia	HT **francophone**	French-speaking
HT **l'Afrique**	Africa	HT **africain(e)**	African
HT **l'Europe**	Europe	HT **européen(ne)**	European

Masculine Countries and Places

le Canada	Canada	**canadien(ne)**	Canadian
le Maroc	Morocco	HT **marocain**	Moroccan
le Sénégal	Senegal		

Généralement, nous passons nos vacances en Belgique parce que la famille de ma mère habite là-bas.

Normally we spend our holidays in Belgium, because my mother's family lives there.

L'année dernière, je suis allé(e) à Québec au Canada avec mon collège pour faire un échange.

Last year I went to Quebec in Canada with my school on an exchange trip.

À l'avenir, je voudrais partir en vacances aux États-Unis.

In the future I would like to go on holiday to the United States.

> ### Key Point
>
> To say 'in' or 'to' a country (or place), use **en** with feminine nouns, use **au** with masculine nouns and **aux** with plural nouns. Use **à** with the names of towns, cities and villages.

Useful Verbs

Verb	Present tense	Past tense	Future tense
passer (to spend)	**je passe** / **nous passons**	**j'ai passé** / **nous avons passé**	**je vais passer** / **nous allons passer**
visiter (to visit)	**je visite** / **nous visitons**	**j'ai visité** / **nous avons visité**	**je vais visiter** / **nous allons visiter**
voyager (to travel)	**je voyage** / **nous voyageons**	**j'ai voyagé** / **nous avons voyagé**	**je vais voyager** / **nous allons voyager**
aller (to go)	**je vais** / **nous allons**	**je suis allé(e)** / **nous sommes allé(e)s**	**je vais aller** / **nous allons aller**
partir (to go)	**je pars** / **nous partons**	**je suis parti(e)** / **nous sommes parti(e)s**	**je vais partir** / **nous allons partir**
rester (to stay)	**je reste** / **nous restons**	**je suis resté(e)** / **nous sommes resté(e)s**	**je vais rester** / **nous allons rester**

- **HT** You may need to use a **range of persons** in your work, so check the endings for 'he' or 'she' and 'they', for example if you want to talk about someone else's holiday. You may also want to include a **wider range of tenses**. Why not use the future tense (e.g. **je passerai**) instead of the near future? Or compare what you used to do when you were younger using the imperfect tense (e.g. **je passais**) or where you would go using the conditional tense (e.g. **je passerais**)?

Transport

la voiture	car
l'autobus	bus
le bateau	boat
l'avion	plane
l'aéroport	airport
la gare	train station

Quand nous allons en vacances, nous préférons voyager en train parce que c'est meilleur pour l'environnement.

When we go on holiday we prefer travelling by train because it's better for the environment.

HT **L'année prochaine, nous allons partir en vacances en France et nous y voyagerons en bateau.**

Next year we're going to go on holiday to France and we will go there by boat.

Types of Holidays

à la campagne	to / at the countryside
à la plage / au bord de la mer	to / at the beach / the seaside
à la montagne	to / in the mountains
à l'étranger	abroad
sur une île / la côte	on an island / at the coast
dans un hôtel	in a hotel
dans un camping	at a campsite
dans les Alpes / Pyrénées	in the Alps / Pyrenees

J'aime bien passer les vacances à la plage parce qu'on peut nager dans la mer ou se relaxer au soleil.

I love spending holidays at the beach because you can swim in the sea or relax in the sun.

Key Point

Use **en** for means of transport e.g. **Je suis allé(e) en vacances en avion**. I went on holiday by plane.

Notice that you do not need the definite article: **la voiture** (the car) = **en voiture** (by car).

At Higher Tier, you can use the pronoun **y** (which means 'there') – it goes before the verb e.g. **Nous y sommes allé(e)s en autobus**. We went there by bus.

Key Sound

eu versus **u** – listen carefully to these words: **eu**ropéen, l'**Eu**rope; and then to these: s**u**r, autob**u**s. Repeat and practise these two different sounds.

Quick Test

1. Use the correct prepositions to complete the sentences.

    à   au   en

    a) **Normalement, je passe mes vacances** .... **France,** .... **la campagne.**

    b) **L'année dernière, nous sommes allés** .... **Québec,** .... **Canada.**

2. Use the appropriate form of the verbs.

    a) **L'été dernier, nous** .... **chez nous. (rester)**

    b) **Je** .... **mes prochaines vacances en Suisse. (passer)**

Holidays

Quick Recall Quiz

Key Sounds

You must be able to:

- Describe your holiday activities
- Use the perfect and imperfect tenses
- Use **il y a** and **il fait**.

Weather and Seasons

il fait beau / chaud	the weather is nice / hot
il fait du brouillard / froid	it's foggy / cold
il y a du soleil / du vent	it's sunny / windy
il pleut	it's raining
il neige	it's snowing
au printemps	in the spring
en été	in summer
en automne	autumn
en hiver	winter
le climat	climate
HT **la météo**	weather forecast

Je préfère les vacances au printemps parce qu'il fait beau mais il n'y a pas trop de soleil.

I prefer holidays in the spring(time) because the weather is nice but it's not too sunny.

Holiday Activities

se lever	to get up			
faire du camping		to go camping		
se coucher tard		to go to bed late		
faire des promenades		to go for walks		
courir	to run	**se perdre**	to get lost
dormir	to sleep	**rencontrer**	to meet
marcher	to walk	**se relaxer**	to relax
nager	to swim	**sortir**	to go out
HT **bénéficier de**		to benefit from		
profiter de		to enjoy, make the most of		

En vacances, j'ai la chance de me lever tard et puis d'être dehors toute la journée.

On holiday I have the opportunity to get up late and then to be outside all day.

Mon activité préférée pendant les vacances, c'est faire du camping avec mes copains.

My favourite activity during the holidays is to go camping with my friends.

HT **Ce qui me plaît le plus pendant les vacances, c'est profiter des promenades avec ma famille et me perdre en pleine campagne!**

What I like most on holiday is enjoying walks with my family and getting lost in the middle of the countryside!

> **Key Point**

Most weather expressions use **il fait** when we say 'it is' in English. For example, **il fait froid** (it is cold); **il fait du soleil** (it is sunny).

> **Key Sounds**

ain, **in**, **aim**, **im** are all nasal sounds. Listen to the following words and repeat: cop**ain**, tr**ain**, mat**in**, pr**in**temps, f**aim**, **im**possible

> **Key Point**

Il y a has two different meanings – 'there is / are' and '...ago'.
Il y a une piscine.
There is a swimming pool.
Il y a deux ans.
Two years ago.

Describing a Past Holiday

- If you want to describe a holiday in the past, you will need to use the perfect and the imperfect tenses.

  L'année dernière, je suis allé(e) en vacances dans le sud de la France, au bord de la mer pendant deux semaines et je nageais tous les jours.

  Last year I went on holiday to the south of France at the seaside for two weeks and every day I would go swimming.

  L'an dernier, en vacances, pendant que mon frère restait au lit le matin, je faisais des promenades avec mon père.

  Last year, on holiday, while my brother stayed in bed in the mornings, I went walking with my father.

  Notre logement était très confortable et il y avait deux grands restaurants tout près.

  Our accommodation was very comfortable and there were two big restaurants close by.

  Pendant nos vacances, il y avait du soleil et il faisait très chaud. Le temps était merveilleux!

  On our holiday it was very sunny and very hot. The weather was marvellous!

  Il y a deux ans, l'hiver, nous avons passé nos vacances au Canada en hiver et il neigeait tous les jours.

  Two years ago, we spent our holidays in Canada in the winter and it snowed every day.

- **HT** To describe your holiday, use the following two structures: **après avoir / être** + past participle (after doing) and **avant de** + infinitive (before doing).

  Avant de me coucher, j'aime faire une promenade sur la plage.

  Before going to bed, I like going for a walk on the beach.

  Après être allé(e) à la plage et après avoir nagé, j'ai rencontré mes amis au club des jeunes.

  After going to the beach and (after) swimming, I met my friends at the youth club.

Describing a Future / Dream Holiday

- If you want to describe a future holiday you will need to use the near future or future tense. For a dream holiday, use the conditional tense.

  L'année prochaine, je vais aller (j'irai) en vacances au Maroc.

  Next year I am going to go (I will go) on holiday to Morocco.

  Mon rêve, c'est de partir en vacances à l'île de la Réunion. Je voudrais y passer trois semaines.

  My dream is to go on holiday to Reunion Island. I would like to spend three weeks there.

> ## Key Point
>
> When describing a holiday, try to give as much detail as possible (where / who with / for how long / when / how / day and evening activities / opinion). Use the perfect tense for what you did and the imperfect to describe things, what you were doing and activities you would regularly do.

Key Verbs

il y a	there is / there are
il y avait	there was / there were
il y aura	there will be
HT il y aurait	there would be

Quick Test

1. Translate into French:
   a) The weather was hot and sunny.
   b) On holiday I like going for walks.
   c) Three years ago, I spent two weeks in France.
   d) Our accommodation was very comfortable.
   e) I would like to visit Morocco.

Going Abroad

You must be able to:

- Organise your accommodation, travel and events
- Talk about needs and problems when staying abroad
- Discuss reasons for going abroad.

Accommodation

réserver son logement	to book your accommodation
Je voudrais réserver…	I would like to book…
Avez-vous / Est-ce que vous avez…?	Do you have…?
J'ai réservé / J'ai une réservation	I've booked / I have a reservation
Est-ce qu'il y a …?	Is there…?
Est-ce qu'on peut…?	Can we…?
Où est-ce qu'on peut…?	Where can we…?
À quelle heure est…?	At what time is…?
Où se trouve / se trouvent…?	Where is / are…?
Où est / sont…?	Where is / are…?
Ça coûte combien?	How much is that?

Bonjour, est-ce que vous avez une chambre pour deux personnes avec vue sur la mer pour cinq nuits, s'il vous plaît?
Hello, do you have a room for two people with a sea view for five nights, please?

Bonsoir monsieur, j'ai une réservation au nom de…
Good evening Sir, I have a booking in the name of …

> ### Key Point
>
> Remember that there are different ways to ask a question in French: you can add **est-ce que** in your question, change the word order (subject-verb) or raise your voice at the end to show it's a question.

Travel

l'arrêt	stop	le départ	departure
en retard	late	le vol	the flight
acheter son billet	to buy your ticket		
traverser la Manche	to cross the English Channel		
la Méditerranée	the Mediterranean		

Où est-ce qu'on peut acheter un billet pour traverser la Manche en bateau, s'il vous plaît?
Where can we buy a ticket to cross the English Channel by boat, please?

Attention! Le vol Paris – Londres LG2030 va partir!
Attention please! The Paris to London flight LG2030 is about to leave!

In Town

demander des informations	to ask for information		
la carte	map / card	gratuit	free (of charge)
l'entrée (f)	entrance	disponible	available
la sortie	exit		

Bonjour, je voudrais réserver deux places pour le spectacle de demain soir à vingt heures.
Hello, I would like to book two tickets for the show tomorrow evening at 8pm.

Bienvenue, madame! L'entrée au château est gratuite pour les moins de seize ans.
Welcome, madam! Entrance to the castle is free for under 16s.

Dealing with Problems

J'ai perdu…	I've lost…
J'ai oublié…	I've forgotten…
Je n'ai pas de…	I don't have…
j'ai besoin de…	I need…
on m'a volé…	my … has been stolen
il n'y a pas de…	there isn't / aren't any…
…ne marche pas / ne marchent pas	…doesn't / don't work
…est sale / sont sales	…is / are dirty
HT …est cassé(e) / sont cassé(e)s	…is / are broken
HT il manque…	…is missing

ma clé	my key	ma pièce d'identité	my ID
mon portable	my mobile phone	mon sac	my bag
mon appareil photo	my camera		
HT mon argent		my money	
HT mes bagages		my luggage	
HT ma valise		my case	

Ah non! Quel dommage! J'ai oublié mon appareil photo.
Oh no! What a shame! I've forgotten my camera.

Je suis désolé(e), mais j'ai perdu ma clé.   I'm sorry, but I've lost my key.

Excusez-moi… dans ma chambre la télé ne marche pas, les toilettes sont sales et il n'y a pas de lumière.
Excuse me… in my bedroom the TV is not working, the toilet is dirty and there is no light.

Quelle catastrophe! Je pense qu'on m'a volé mon portable!
What a disaster! I think that my mobile phone has been stolen!

Why Go Abroad?

pour améliorer / apprendre la langue to improve / learn the language
pour utiliser son français   to use your French
pour voyager / faire du travail (bénévole)
to travel / work (volunteer)
pour découvrir…   to discover…
HT **pour pratiquer son français**   to practise your French

Why Speak another Language?

On peut rencontrer / parler / discuter avec les habitants de la région.
You can meet / speak to / discuss with local people.
On peut expliquer les problèmes.   You can discuss / explain problems.
C'est amusant!   It's fun!

Key Point

If you want to describe what happened during your last holiday, use your verbs in the imperfect e.g.:

La télé ne marchait pas.
The TV didn't work.
La fenêtre était cassée.
The window was broken.
Je n'avais pas assez d'argent.
I didn't have enough money.

Key Sounds

c is a hard sound: **c**lé (key), **c**atastrophe (disaster), **c**assé (broken), whereas **ch** is a soft sound: **ch**ambre (bedroom), **la Manch**e (the English Channel), **march**er (to walk). Listen and repeat.

Quick Test

1. Translate into English:
   a) Bonsoir, j'ai une réservation pour une chambre pour six nuits.
   b) J'ai perdu ma clé.
   c) À quelle heure commence le spectacle ce soir, s'il vous plaît?
2. Translate into French:
   a) Hello, I would like to book a room for two people for two nights, please.
   b) I would like to improve my French.

Practice Questions

Travel and Tourism

1 Choose the correct preposition for each sentence and explain why. Then translate the sentences into English.

    a) L'année prochaine, je vais passer mes vacances <u>en / au</u> Maroc.

    b) J'aimerais bien aller en vacances <u>à / dans</u> les Pyrénées <u>en / à</u> France.

    c) Normalement, nous allons en vacances <u>en / par</u> voiture car mon père aime conduire.

    d) Il y a trois ans, nous avons passé les vacances <u>au / en</u> Belgique.   [9 marks]

2 Choose the correct verb for each sentence from the box below.

j'allais	je vais passer	je passais	j'ai passé	nous passons

    a) Tous les ans, ... nos vacances au bord de la mer en France.

    b) L'année dernière, pendant mes vacances, ... à la plage tous les jours.

    c) Il y a deux ans, ... quinze jours au Sénégal avec ma famille.

    d) Je pense que .... mes prochaines vacances dans un camping à la campagne.

    e) Quand j'étais petite, ... mes vacances à la montagne, chez ma tante qui habite dans les Alpes.   [5 marks]

3 Read the following sentences aloud.

    a) J'aime bien passer les vacances en Europe.

    b) Nous sommes allés à Québec au Canada.

    c) Nous préférons voyager en train.

    d) En automne, il fait froid à cause du vent.

    e) On peut traverser la Manche en bateau.

    f) Est-ce qu'il y a une réservation au nom de Smith?   [6 marks]

4 Unscramble the sentences.

a) À vacances voudrais l'avenir en Maroc je partir au

b) À relaxer la nager on plage la mer ou dans se peut

c) Mon préférée les pendant activité vacances, du c'est camping faire

d) Je sur personnes une vue pour mer deux voudrais avec la chambre   [4 marks]

5 Translate the sentences into French.

a) I spend my holidays in England. ....

b) Two years ago, we went to Belgium. ....

c) The weather was sunny and hot. ....

d) We travelled by boat and by car. ....

e) I would like to visit Reunion Island. .... [5 marks]

6 Translate the sentences into English.

a) **J'ai perdu mon sac à l'aéroport.** ....

b) **Il neigeait tous les jours.** ....

c) **Je voudrais réserver deux places pour le spectacle de demain soir.**

....

d) **Nous avons visité Paris au printemps.** .... [4 marks]

7 Complete the sentences, using your own ideas.

a) **Pendant les vacances, j'aime** ....

b) **L'année dernière, j'ai passé les vacances** ....

c) **Nous avons voyagé** .... **et nous avons dormi** ....

d) **Tous les jours,** ....

e) **En ce qui concerne le temps,** ....

f) **Plus tard dans la vie, je voudrais** .... [6 marks]

Celebrity Culture

1 Match the different types of online influencers in French and English.

Il y a des influenceurs...

a) **de mode**

i) travel

b) **de santé**

ii) gaming / computer games

c) **de mode de vie**

iii) animals / pets

d) **de nourriture**

iv) sport

e) **d'animaux**

v) technology

f) **de sport**

vi) fashion

g) **de forme physique**

vii) health

h) **de voyages**

viii) lifestyle

j) **de technologie**

ix) fitness

k) **de jeux vidéo**

x) food

[10 marks]

2 Choose the correct verb from the words in the box to complete the sentences.

| font | vont | donnent | sont | mettent | ont |

a) **Les influenceurs** .... **de plus en plus nombreux.**

b) **Ils** .... **de plus en plus d'influence.**

c) **Ils** .... **leur avis sur des produits.**

d) **Ils** .... **des choses amusantes et** .... **des vidéos en ligne.**

e) **À l'avenir, ils** .... **devenir encore plus populaires.**

[6 marks]

3 Translate the sentences in question **2** into English.

[5 marks]

4 Listen to the pronunciations. Write **1**, **2** or **3** for each sentence and explain why.

a) **Les célébrités sont très riches et ont beaucoup d'argent.** ....

b) **Je suis les influenceurs sur les réseaux sociaux.** ....

c) **Les personnalités célèbres peuvent inspirer une génération.** ....

d) **Je voudrais rencontrer ma célébrité préférée.** .... [8 marks]

5 Read the passage below about Sebastien's favourite film star.

> **Ma célébrité préférée s'appelle Bastien Bouillon. Il est connu comme star de films français mais il est populaire dans le monde entier.**
>
> **Il a commencé sa carrière en 2009 et a participé à plus de 30 films différents.**
>
> **Je l'aime bien parce qu'il est vraiment gentil et que j'adore sa confiance comme acteur.**
>
> **Dans mon film préféré, il joue le rôle du héros et il travaille comme policier dans un petit village à la montagne.**
>
> **J'aime aller au cinéma avec mes copains pour voir ses films sur le grand écran.**
>
> **J'attends son prochain film avec impatience! Je vais le regarder aussitôt* que possible!**
>
> **Je voudrais le rencontrer et passer du temps avec lui.**
>
> *as soon as

a) Find all the verbs in the passage and write them in the correct columns.

Talking About the Past	Talking About Now	Talking About the Future

[10 marks]

b) Answer the questions in English.

i) What does Sebastien say about Bastien Bouillon's career? Give **two** details.

ii) What does Sebastien say about the role Bastien played in his favourite film? Give **two** details.

iii) What would Sebastien like to do? Give **two** details. [6 marks]

6 Write a similar passage about your favourite film star and / or your favourite sportsperson. [8 marks]

Understanding the Media

You must be able to:

- Understand announcements, articles and headlines
- Talk about mobile apps and their use
- Discuss preferences.

Announcements

aux magasins	at the shops
au supermarché	at / in the supermarket
en ville	in town
à la gare	at the train station
à l'aéroport	at the airport

'Achetez deux boîtes de café et recevez un sac gratuit à la caisse.'
'Buy two boxes of coffee and receive a free bag at the checkout.'

'Le musée est ouvert tous les jours sauf le lundi en toute saison.'
'The museum is open every day except Mondays all year round.'

'Le prochain train pour Paris est en retard – il va arriver dans dix minutes.'
'The next train for Paris is late – it will arrive in ten minutes' time.'

Key Point

Sauf meaning 'except' is a very useful word to know in French. It is often used with days of the week, months, or times of the year, e.g.:

Ouvert tous les jours, sauf le dimanche.
Open every day except Sundays.

Articles and Headlines

les médias	the media	**quotidien**	daily
la politique	politics	**le gouvernement**	government
le président	president	**le vote**	vote
HT **la loi**		(the) law / legislation	
HT **le ministre**		minister	
HT **le parlement**		parliament	
HT **le / la porte-parole**		spokesperson (man / woman)	

Le gouvernement va voter une nouvelle loi sur l'environnement / l'économie.
The government is going to vote on a new law about the environment / the economy.

l'accident (m)	accident	**la grève**	strike
la guerre	war	**la manifestation**	demonstration
le vol	theft		
HT **l'attentat** (m)		attack / assassination attempt	

La grève des journalistes commence demain.
The journalists' strike starts tomorrow.

Deux blessés après l'accident en centre-ville.
Two injured after accident in town centre.

les problèmes (sociaux)		(social) problems	
le logement		accommodation / housing	
le chômage	unemployment	**la pauvreté**	poverty
augmenter	to increase		
diminuer	to decrease	**annuler**	to cancel
HT **défendre**		to defend	

Key Sound

Listen to these words and practise the **-ien** sound in French: **quotidien** (daily), **canadien** (Canadian), **chrétien** (Christian), **végétarien** (vegetarian) Remember to change your pronunciation once these adjectives become feminine: **quotidienne, canadienne, chrétienne, végétarienne**

La situation est de pire en pire.
The situation is getting worse and worse.

La pauvreté augmente. Poverty is increasing.

Le chômage chez les jeunes a diminué.
Youth unemployment has decreased.

Apps

une appli(cation)	an app	**local**	local
national	national	**international**	local international
HT **global**		global	
HT **mondial**		worldwide	

Quelles sont les applications les plus connues?
Which are the most well-known apps?

Instagram, TikTok, Facebook et WhatsApp sont parmi les applications les plus téléchargées au monde.
Instagram, TikTok, Facebook and WhatsApp are amongst the most downloaded apps in the world.

Quelles sont les applis préférées des jeunes en France?
Which are the favourite apps of young French people?

Instagram est le réseau social le plus utilisé par les 16–25 ans français, suivi des applis Snapchat, TikTok, Netflix et Spotify.
Instagram is the most used social network by French 16–25 year-olds, followed by Snapchat, TikTok, Netflix and Spotify apps.

Quelle est ton appli préférée? What is your favourite app?

Je préfère YouTube parce que je peux y trouver toutes sortes de vidéos (amusantes et éducatives).
I prefer YouTube because I can find all sorts of (funny and educational) videos there.

Quelles sortes d'applis trouves-tu utiles?
What sort of apps do you find useful?

Les applis pour l'éducation, pour la santé, pour les jeux, pour les voyages, pour la musique, pour le shopping, pour la nourriture et les boissons, pour tout!
Apps for education, for health, for games, for travelling, for music, for shopping, for food and drink, for everything!

Key Point

Useful phrases: **de plus en plus** (more and more); **de moins en moins** (less and less); **de mieux en mieux** (better and better); **de pire en pire** (worse and worse); **aussi … que** (as … as)

Key Point

To say 'the most…' or 'the …est' in French, use **le / la / les plus…** e.g.:

le réseau social le plus utilisé
the most used social network
les applis les plus faciles
the easiest apps

Quick Test

1. Give the French for:
   a) a strike   b) a demonstration
   c) poverty   d) unemployment
2. Choose the correct word, then translate the phrases into English.
   a) **la nourriture la plus frais / fraîche / fraîches**
   b) **les applis les plus locale / locaux / locales**
   c) **le voyage le plus intéressante / intéressant / intéressantes**
   d) **l'application la plus amusante / amusant / amusants**
3. Translate into French: The castle is open every day except Tuesdays.

Using Technology

You must be able to:

- Discuss the types of technology you use
- Talk and write about on-line activities
- Use some irregular verbs in the perfect tense.

Computers and Mobiles

l'écran	screen	**le mail / l'e-mail**	e-mail
le site	site	**Internet**	the internet
le portable	laptop / mobile	**les SMS**	texts
le réseau social	social network	**le streaming**	streaming
HT **numérique**		digital	
HT **technique**		technical	

Je passe beaucoup de temps en ligne. I spend a lot of time online.

Chaque jour, je vais sur mes sites préférés.
Every day I go onto my favourite sites.

Comment utilises-tu la technologie? How do you use technology?

J'utilise les ordinateurs au collège... I use the computers at school...

pendant les cours d'informatique during IT lessons

pour faire des recherches to do research

pour écrire des réponses to write answers

J'utilise mon portable chez moi... I use my mobile at home...

pour communiquer avec mes copains / copines
for communicating with my friends

J'utilise les réseaux sociaux pour suivre les influenceurs et les célébrités.
I use social networks to follow influencers and celebrities.

J'utilise les applications (applis) pour regarder des vidéos et des émissions.
I use apps to watch videos and programmes.

Online Activities

acheter	to buy	**chercher**	to look for
découvrir	to discover	**enregistrer**	to record
fabriquer	to make / produce	**partager**	to share

Que fais-tu en ligne? What do you do online?

Je (t)chatte avec mes copains / copines.
I chat to my friends.

Je joue à des jeux vidéo. I play computer games.

Je poste des blogs. I post blogs.

Je télécharge des applis et de la musique.
I download apps and music.

Je prends des photos / des selfies et je les partage en ligne.
I take photos / selfies and share them online.

J'envoie et je reçois des SMS et des e-mails.
I send and receive texts and e-mails.

Je fais du shopping en ligne. I shop online.

Key Verbs

Some verbs are irregular in the present tense – learn them thoroughly:

je vais	I go
j'envoie	I send
je reçois	I receive
je fais	I do
je lis	I read
je suis	I follow

| **Je lis mes messages.** | I read my messages. |
| **Je suis mes personnalités préférées.** | I follow my favourite personalities. |

Discussing Recent Activities

hier	yesterday
le week-end dernier	last weekend
la semaine dernière	last week
le lendemain	the next / following day
récemment	recently

Useful Verbs

- The past participles of these verbs are irregular – learn them thoroughly so you can use them to talk and write about what you did in the past, using the perfect tense.

Infinitive	First person singular / plural	Third person singular / plural
avoir (to have)	**j'ai eu** (I had / have had)	**il a eu** (he had / has had)
écrire (to write)	**j'ai écrit** (I wrote / have written)	**elle a écrit** (she wrote / has written)
faire (to do)	**j'ai fait** (I did / have done)	**on a fait** (we / they did / have done)
lire (to read)	**nous avons lu** (we read / have read)	**ils ont lu** (they read / have read)
mettre (to put)	**nous avons mis** (we put / have put)	**ils ont mis** (they put / have put)
voir (to see)	**nous avons vu** (we saw / have seen)	**elles ont vu** (they saw / have seen)

Key Verbs	
j'ai eu	I had
j'ai écrit	I wrote
j'ai fait	I did
j'ai lu	I read
j'ai mis	I put
j'ai reçu	I received
j'ai suivi	I followed
j'ai vu	I saw

Hier soir, j'ai eu une conversation en ligne avec mon ami en Suisse.
Last night I had a conversation online with my friend in Switzerland.
Samedi dernier, j'ai écrit un blog sur ma région.
Last Saturday, I wrote a blog about my area.
Récemment, nous avons lu un article sur la santé des animaux en danger.
Recently we read an article about the health of animals in danger.
Ma mère a mis des photos de nos vacances avec ma tante et sa famille en ligne et le lendemain elle a reçu une invitation au mariage de ma cousine!
My mother put photos of our holiday with my aunt and her family online and the following day she received an invitation to my cousin's wedding!
Pour la première fois, mon père a fait des courses en ligne!
For the first time my father did the food shopping online!

Quick Test

1. How do you say in French?
   a) I chat   **b)** I download   **c)** I send   **d)** I receive
2. Translate into French:
   I use a computer at school and my mobile at home every day.
3. Translate into English: **Récemment, nous avons fait des recherches sur l'influence des réseaux sociaux sur les ados.**

Giving Opinions About Technology

Quick Recall Quiz

Key Sounds

You must be able to:

- Give your opinions on the technology you use
- Talk and write about advantages and disadvantages of technology
- Discuss how to stay safe online.

Giving Opinions About Technology

à mon avis, c'est…	in my opinion it's…
je trouve ça…	I find it…
je pense que…	I think (that)…
pour moi, la meilleure chose, c'est…	for me, the best thing is…
le pire, c'est…	the worst is…

Positive		Negative	
disponible	available	**trop cher**	too expensive
essentiel	essential	**affreux**	awful
facile	easy	**dangereux**	dangerous
gratuit	free	**inquiétant**	worrying
populaire	popular	**pas sûr**	not safe
rapide	quick	HT **trop puissant**	too powerful

À mon avis, c'est dangereux et inquiétant.
In my opinion, it's dangerous and worrying.

Pour moi, c'est un outil nécessaire dans le monde moderne / pour la vie actuelle.
For me, it's a necessary tool in the modern world / for current (daily) life.

Je pense que c'est beaucoup plus facile de faire les devoirs si on utilise toutes les ressources disponibles en ligne.
I think it's much easier to do homework if you use all the available resources online.

Je télécharge de la musique sur mon portable parce que je trouve ça rapide et moins cher.
I download music on my mobile because I find it fast and less expensive.

La meilleure chose, c'est qu'on peut vite communiquer.
The best thing is that you can communicate quickly.

HT **Le pire, c'est le vol d'identité.**
The worst is identity theft.

Advantages of Modern Technology

on peut…	you can…
je ne peux pas…	I can't…
c'est facile de…	it's easy to…
c'est utile pour…	it's useful for (…ing)…
HT **ce serait impossible de…**	it would be impossible to…

…communiquer avec des gens partout dans le monde.
…communicate with people all over the world.

…contacter quelqu'un en cas d'urgence.
…contact someone in an emergency.

Key Point

Try to think of both sides of an argument, so that you can give both positive and negative opinions on any subject.

Key Sounds

Words ending in '-ible' and '-able' are pronounced differently in French.
Listen, repeat and practise:
disponible (available), **imposs**ible (impossible), **terr**ible (terrible), **agré**able (pleasant), **cap**able (able)

…trouver rapidement des informations.
…find information quickly.
…organiser des sorties et des rendez-vous.
…organise outings and meetings.
…vivre sans la technologie.
…live without technology.

Disadvantages of Technology

il y a…	there is…
il n'y a pas de…	there isn't…
Parfois, il n'y a pas de réseau.	Sometimes, there is no network.

La nouvelle technologie change trop vite / coûte trop cher.
New technology changes too fast / costs too much.
On peut recevoir des menaces en ligne.
You can receive threats online.
Certains ados passent trop de temps devant leurs écrans.
Some teenagers spend too much time in front of their screens.

HT	**harceler**	to bully / harass
HT	**souffrir**	to suffer
HT	**Quelquefois, des gens harcèlent des jeunes et des victimes deviennent très tristes / malades.**	

Sometimes people bully young people and the victims become very sad / ill.

> **Key Point**
>
> Use a variety of structures and phrases in your written and spoken work to 'show what you know' and to make your work more interesting.

How to Avoid Online Problems

on doit…	you must…
on ne doit pas…	you must not…
il faut toujours…	you must always…
il ne faut jamais…	you must never…
…penser à la sécurité.	…think about security.
…protéger ses informations personnelles.	…protect your personal details.
…utiliser des sites sûrs.	…use safe sites.
…entrer en conversation / dialogue avec des personnes qu'on ne connaît pas.	

…enter into conversation with strangers.

> **Key Verbs**
>
> | il y a | there is / there are |
> |---|---|
> | il n'y a pas (de) | there isn't / there aren't |
> | il faut | you must |
> | il ne faut pas | you mustn't |

Using a Variety of Structures Together

À mon avis, **la technologie moderne est essentielle dans la vie actuelle et** je ne peux pas **vivre sans mon portable!** Je pense que **la meilleure chose, c'est que** je peux **facilement communiquer avec toute ma famille et tous mes copains. Cependant,** il faut **toujours penser à la sécurité et** on doit **protéger ses informations personnelles** pour **éviter les problèmes en ligne.**

In my opinion, modern technology is essential for everyday life and I can't live without my mobile! I think that the best thing is that I can communicate easily with all my family and friends. However, we must always think about security and you must protect your personal details to avoid problems online.

> **Quick Test**
>
> 1. Name three different ways of giving your opinion in French.
> 2. Correct the following advice about staying safe online:
>   a) **Il ne faut jamais penser à la sécurité.**
>   b) **On doit partager ses informations personnelles.**
> 3. Translate into English: **Il faut vite contacter quelqu'un en cas d'urgence.**

Media and Technology

1 Unscramble the sentences.

a) SMS   mes   J'envoie   tous   à   amis   des

b) télécharge   de   musique   la   Je   applis   des   et

c) beaucoup   Je   sur   photos   mon   de   prends   portable

d) vais   sur   Je   chaque   sites   mes   préférés   jour

e) recherches   Je   mes   pour   devoirs   des   fais   [5 marks]

2 Read the following sentences aloud.

a) J'utilise mon portable chaque jour.

b) Je tchatte souvent avec mes copains et mes copines.

c) Les applications les plus connues sont internationales.

d) Le musée est ouvert tous les jours sauf le jeudi.

e) Récemment, nous avons reçu une invitation.

f) Il faut toujours penser à la sécurité en ligne.   [6 marks]

3 Decide whether the following sentences are positive or negative. Write **P** for positive or **N** for negative for each sentence.

a) C'est rapide et très pratique.   ....

b) On peut vite communiquer avec les autres.   ....

c) Parfois, il n'y a pas de réseau.   ....

d) La technologie moderne change trop vite.   ....

e) On peut contacter quelqu'un en cas d'urgence.   ....

f) Des inconnus peuvent facilement nous contacter.   ....

g) Les ados passent trop de temps en ligne.   ....   [7 marks]

4 Put these sentences into the past, using the perfect tense. An example has been done for you.

Example: **Je télécharge de la musique. = Hier soir, j'ai téléchargé une émission de musique.**

a) **Je tchatte avec mes copains.**

b) **Nous lisons des articles.**

c) **Ils écrivent des blogs.**

d) **Nous faisons nos devoirs.** [4 marks]

5 Match up the headline with the story theme.

a) **Les musiciens vont arrêter de travailler.**	i) an accident
b) **Plus de mille personnes dans la rue.**	ii) unemployment
c) **Deux jeunes à l'hôpital.**	iii) a strike
d) **Le président va au parlement.**	iv) the environment
e) **Plus de jeunes sans emploi.**	v) a protest
f) **Le vent et le soleil produisent plus d'énergie.**	vi) politics

[6 marks]

6 Match up the English and French adjectives.

a) **inquiétant**	i) available
b) **gratuit**	ii) false
c) **faux**	iii) worrying
d) **sûr**	iv) dangerous
e) **disponible**	v) safe
f) **dangereux**	vi) free (of charge)

[6 marks]

7 Put each of the adjectives in question **6.** into the feminine form. An example has been done for you.

Example: **a) inquiétant = inquiétante** [5 marks]

8 Complete the sentences using your own ideas about technology.

a) **J'utilise** ....

b) **Je trouve ça** .... **parce que** ....

c) **Au collège,** ....

d) **Le week-end ou le soir,** ....

e) **Mon appli préférée** ....

f) **Récemment,** .... [7 marks]

Review Questions

Travel and Tourism

1 Match up the sentence halves.

a) **L'an dernier, je**	i) **reste chez moi.**
b) **L'année dernière, j'ai**	ii) **aller à la plage.**
c) **Normalement, je**	iii) **pas trop le soleil.**
d) **Je préfère**	iv) **passé les vacances au camping.**
e) **Je n'aime**	v) **suis allé en France.**

[5 marks]

2 Read the sentences. Write **P** for a positive opinion, **N** for a negative opinion or **P+N** for a positive and negative opinion.

a) **J'aime bien la côte parce que je me sens toujours plus calme et heureux là-bas.** ....

b) **J'apprécie le beau temps. Travailler en plein soleil est moins agréable.** ....

c) **Je ne peux pas supporter tous les touristes, surtout en été.** ....

d) **J'ai toujours voulu travailler à l'étranger et je ne regrette pas mon choix.** .... [4 marks]

3 Change the following sentences into the tense given in brackets. You will also need to change the time phrase to the word or phrase in brackets.

a) **Pendant mes dernières vacances, j'ai dormi dans un hôtel.**
(normally / present tense)

....

b) **Généralement, je vais en vacances à la montagne pour me relaxer.**
(last year / perfect tense)

....

c) **L'été dernier, j'ai passé quinze jours chez ma tante à la campagne.**
(next year / near future or future tense)

....

d) **Je nage tous les jours dans la mer parce qu'il fait chaud.**
(last year / imperfect tense)

....

[9 marks]

4 Use the vocabulary list on the AQA website to find the French for the following nationalities.

a) British   ....

b) Spanish   ....

c) German   ....

d) American   ....

e) Chinese   ....   [5 marks]

5 Listen to the pronunciations. Write **1**, **2** or **3** for each sentence and explain why.

a) J'adore le temps en automne, même s'il fait du brouillard le matin.   ....

b) L'année dernière, je suis allé(e) à Québec au Canada, avec mon collège, pour faire un échange.   ....

c) Au printemps, le climat est mieux et on peut passer la journée dehors.   ....

d) Bonjour, est-ce que vous avez une chambre pour deux personnes avec vue sur la mer pour cinq nuits, s'il vous plaît?   ....

[4 Marks]

6 Fill in the blanks using the correct word from the box.

à	en	au	dans	sur	en

a) .... **la campagne**   (in the countryside)

b) .... **une île**   (on an island)

c) .... **bateau**   (by boat)

d) .... **les Alpes**   (in the Alps)

e) .... **bord de la mer**   (at the seaside)

f) .... **vacances**   (on holiday)   [6 marks]

Where I Live

You must be able to:

- Describe your house / home
- Talk and write about where you live
- Say what there is nearby.

Where I Live

la maison	house
l'appartement	flat
la ferme	farm
le bâtiment	building
la pièce	room
la salle	room
HT **l'étage**	floor / storey
HT **au premier étage**	on the first floor / upstairs

J'habite dans une maison assez moderne.
I live in a fairly modern house.

Il y a huit pièces chez nous. There are eight rooms in our house.

My House

le bureau	office / study
la chambre	bedroom
la cuisine	kitchen
l'entrée	entrance
la salle à manger	dining room
la salle de bains	bathroom
le salon	lounge / living room
les toilettes	toilet
le jardin	garden

Chez moi, il y a une grande cuisine et un très joli salon.
At my house, there is a big kitchen and a very pretty lounge.

Nous avons un petit jardin derrière la maison.
We have a small garden behind the house.

Au premier étage se trouvent trois chambres et une salle de bains.
On the first floor there are three bedrooms and a bathroom.

La porte d'entrée est bleue et les fenêtres sont grandes et blanches.
The front door is blue and the windows are big and white.

My Bedroom

la fenêtre	window
la porte	door
le mur	wall
la chaise	chair
la table	table
le bureau	desk
le lit	bed

> ### Key Point
>
> Use adjectives to provide detail to your descriptions. Remember that they must agree with the noun to which they refer:
>
> **une grande maison**
> a big house
> **les murs sont blancs**
> the walls are white

> ### Key Point
>
> Notice how we talk about something belonging to someone else in French. Use **de**:
> **la chambre de mon frère**
> my brother's room

> ### Key Point
>
> The word **propre** has two meanings in French. **J'ai ma propre chambre** means 'I have my own room' but **ma chambre est toujours propre** means 'my bedroom is always clean / tidy'.

J'ai ma propre chambre.
I have my own (bed)room.
Je partage une chambre avec ma sœur.
I share a (bed)room with my sister.
Notre chambre est toujours propre.
Our (bed)room is always clean / tidy.
J'aime ma chambre mais la chambre de mes parents est plus grande.
I like my room but my parents' (bed)room is bigger.

My District

le quartier	district / quarter	**derrière**	behind
le coin	corner	**devant**	in front of
la ville	town	**entre**	between
le village	village	**près de**	near
loin (de)	far (from)	HT **proche**	near(by)
HT **la communauté**	community	**community**	
HT **la cité**	housing estate	**la province**	province
HT **la banlieue**	suburbs / outskirts		

J'habite dans le vieux quartier de la ville.
I live in the old district of the town.

HT **J'aime bien y habiter.**	I really like living there.

l'arrêt (d'autobus)	(bus) stop		
la banque	bank		
la bibliothèque	library		
la boulangerie	bakery		
le centre (commercial)	(shopping) centre		
l'église	church	**la gare**	train station
l'hôpital	hospital	**la mosquée**	mosque
la place	square	**la poste**	post office

Près de ma maison, il y a une boulangerie et une poste.
Near my house, there is a bakery and a post office.
Il n'y a pas d'autres magasins. There are no other shops.
Devant l'église, il y a un arrêt d'autobus pour aller en ville.
In front of the church there is a bus stop to go into town.
L'hôpital se trouve entre la gare et la bibliothèque.
The hospital is (situated) between the train station and the library.
On a besoin d'un nouveau centre commercial.
We need a new shopping centre.

Key Point

Use a variety of structures other than **est /sont** (is / are) to describe where you live: **il y a...** (there is… / there are…); **il n'y a pas de**… (there is no… / there isn't a…); **la poste se trouve**... (the post office is (situated)…); **on a besoin de**... (we need…).

Key Sound

The sound **th** is very different to the English sound. The 'h' is silent, so it is just like a 't' sound in English. Listen and repeat: **biblio**th**èque** (library). Now try **disco**th**èque** (nightclub), **sympa**th**ique** (friendly), **th**é (tea).

Quick Test

1. Choose the correct underlined adjective for each noun.
   a) une **petit / petite** maison
   b) un **grand / grande** jardin
   c) une **joli / jolie** cuisine
   d) les murs **blancs / blanches**
   e) les **vieux / vieilles** fenêtres
2. Translate into English:
   Devant la gare se trouve un nouveau centre commercial.
3. Translate into French: I live in a flat. There are five rooms – a lounge, a kitchen, a bathroom and two bedrooms.

Quick Recall Quiz

Key Sound

My Town and Region

You must be able to:

- Describe the town and area where you live
- Discuss the advantages of living in the town or the country
- Talk about amenities and things to do.

Town and Country

Moi, j'habite…	I live…
en ville	in town
à la campagne	in the country
dans le nord / sud de l'Angleterre	in the north / south of England
dans l'est / l'ouest du pays	in the east / west of the country

J'habite dans un petit village qui se trouve dans le nord-ouest.
I live in a little village which is (situated) in the north-west.

Il y a environ mille habitants. There are about a thousand inhabitants.

Nous n'avons pas de voisins tout près.
We don't have any neighbours nearby.

In the Town

J'adore vivre en ville.	I love living in town.
Il y a beaucoup de choses à faire.	There are lots of things to do.
La ville est très vivante!	The town is very lively!
C'est facile d'utiliser les transports.	It's easy to use public transport.
Les rues sont sales.	The roads are dirty.
HT **Il y a trop de bruit / de circulation.**	There is too much noise / traffic.

In the Countryside

Je préfère vivre à la campagne.	I prefer living in the countryside.
La vie là-bas est calme et sûre.	Life there is quiet and safe.
C'est un endroit très propre.	It's a very clean place.
Il y a beaucoup d'espaces verts.	There are lots of green / open spaces.
Il n'y a pas assez d'activités.	There are not enough activities.

On doit prendre la voiture pour voir ses amis.
You have to go by car to see friends.

Je peux voir les avantages et les inconvénients.
I can see the advantages and the disadvantages.

HT **d'un côté / d'un autre côté** on the one hand / on the other hand

Où voudrais-tu habiter à l'avenir? Where would you like to live in the future?

J'ai l'intention d'habiter au centre-ville car on peut facilement aller au cinéma ou aux magasins.
I intend to live in the town centre because you can easily go to the cinema or to the shops.

Je rêve de trouver une maison parfaite. I dream of finding the perfect house.

HT **Si j'étais riche, je voudrais acheter une maison énorme sur la côte avec vue sur la mer.**
If I were rich, I would like to buy a big house on the coast with a sea view.

HT **Ce serait idéal!** It would be ideal!

Key Point

Use a variety of phrases to express your likes, dislikes and preferences. The following are all followed by the infinitive of the verb in French:

j'adore	I love
je préfère	I prefer
je n'aime pas	I don't like
je voudrais	I would like
je rêve de	I dream of
j'ai l'intention de	I intend to

Key Sound

h is never pronounced in French – listen and repeat: **j'h**abite (I live), **h**abiter (to live), les **h**abitants (the residents)

In the Area / Region

le château	castle	**la forêt**	forest	
le marché	market	**le musée**	museum	

Pour les jeunes, il y a beaucoup de clubs et un cinéma moderne.
For young people there are lots of clubs and a modern cinema.

Pour les sportifs, on a un grand stade et une piscine nationale.
For sports people we have a big stadium and a national swimming pool.

HT **Les touristes aiment les lieux naturels comme la forêt et le lac.**
Tourists like the natural places like the forest and the lake.

Le château est célèbre / bien connu. The castle is famous / well known.

Notre région est connue pour sa nourriture / ses fêtes en été.
Our region is known for its food / festivals in the summer.

À Noël, on met un arbre avec beaucoup de lumières sur la place.
At Christmas, we put up a big tree with lots of lights in the square.

Il y a longtemps, au seizième siècle, une bataille a eu lieu ici.
A long time ago, in the 16th century, a battle took place here.

On trouve un bon choix de restaurants au centre-ville.
There is a good choice of restaurants in the town centre.

Au musée, on peut découvrir l'histoire de la région et entrer dans le passé.
At the museum you can discover the history of the area and enter into the past.

Il y a un grand magasin où on peut acheter de beaux vêtements.
There is a department store where you can buy nice clothes.

HT **Allez au marché! Vous pouvez y trouver des produits frais et de bonnes idées cadeaux.**
Go to the market! You can find fresh produce and good ideas for presents.

HT **On peut bénéficier de l'air frais et du beau paysage.**
You can benefit from the fresh air and the lovely scenery.

HT At Higher Tier, use a variety of different structures in your spoken and written work. For example: **être en train de** (to be in the process of); **venir de** (to have just); **cela vaut la peine de** (it is worth).

On est en train de construire un nouveau pont sur la rivière.
They are building a new bridge over the river.

On vient d'ouvrir une belle place qui est toujours vivante et pleine de monde.
They have just opened a beautiful square which is always lively and full of people.

Cela vaut la peine de visiter notre région parce qu'il y a quelque chose pour tout le monde / pour tous les âges!
It's worth visiting our area because there is something for everyone / for all ages!

Key Verbs

on trouve	you find
on peut	you can
on a	we have
il y a	there is / there are

Key Point

You may need to write or talk about different aspects of your town / area, for example attractions for visitors, young people, problems, transport, what it's like at different times of the year etc. Remember to use the imperfect to describe what it used to be like (**il y avait** (there was), **c'était** (it was)) and try to include the future too (**il y aura** (there will be), **on va fêter** (we are going to celebrate)).

Quick Test

1. Translate into English: **Notre ville est connue pour ses beaux espaces verts où on peut jouer ou se relaxer avec ses amis.**
2. Translate into French: I live in a big town which is situated in the south-east of England.

The Environment: Problems and Solutions

Quick Recall Quiz

Key Sounds

You must be able to:

- Talk and write about environmental issues
- Discuss problems and suggest solutions
- Express your opinion about the environment.

Environmental Issues

l'environnement	the environment
le réchauffement de la Terre	global warming
la catastrophe	catastrophe
la crise	crisis
la faute	mistake / error / fault
le souci	worry / concern
grave	serious

Je trouve la situation actuelle affreuse / terrible / inquiétante / triste.
I find the current situation awful / terrible / worrying / sad.

Notre planète / notre monde / la Terre est en danger.
Our planet / our world / the Earth is in danger.

On coupe trop d'arbres / de bois / de forêts.
We're cutting down too many trees / woods / forests.

On jette trop de déchets à la mer / par terre.
We throw too much rubbish / waste into the sea / on the ground.

À mon avis, / je pense que le pire problème, c'est...
In my opinion / I think that the worst problem is...

Les experts / les scientifiques disent que...
Scientists / experts say that...

Les véhicules et les usines sont les causes principales du réchauffement de la Terre.
Vehicles and factories are the main causes of global warming.

Les animaux / les poissons / les fleurs vont mourir.
Animals / fish / flowers are going to die.

Le monde industriel utilise trop d'énergie / de gaz / de ressources.
The industrial world uses too much energy / gas / too many resources.

La pollution détruit l'environnement naturel et change le climat.
Pollution is destroying the natural environment and changing the climate.

HT **Certaines espèces d'animaux sont en train de disparaître.**
Some animal species are disappearing (endangered).

Key Point

Use adverbs to add detail to your comments:

bientôt	soon
déjà	already
immédiatement	immediately
lentement	slowly
probablement	probably
rapidement	quickly / rapidly
récemment	recently
seulement	only
tellement	so much
vite	quickly

Solutions — Useful Verbs

devoir (to have to)	je dois	on doit	nous devons	ils doivent
savoir (to know)	je sais	on sait	nous savons	ils savent
pouvoir (to be able to)	je peux	on peut	nous pouvons	ils peuvent
vouloir (to want)	je veux	on veut	nous voulons	ils veulent

Nous savons que nos habitudes doivent changer.
We know that our habits must change.

Tout le monde peut faire quelque chose pour aider l'environnement.
Everyone can do something to help the environment.

Personnellement, je sais que je dois essayer de recycler plus et que je peux aussi marcher plus au lieu de prendre la voiture. Je veux passer les vacances en Angleterre et réduire les voyages en avion.

Personally, I know I have to try to recycle more and I can also walk more instead of going by car. I want to spend my holidays in England and reduce plane journeys.

Les hommes / femmes politiques peuvent encourager les gens à utiliser l'énergie verte (du vent et du soleil) et ils veulent aussi diminuer le nombre de véhicules dans les centres-villes.

Politicians can encourage people to use green energy (wind / sun) and they also want to reduce the number of vehicles in town centres.

Useful Grammatical Structures

- These structures are very useful for improving your French:
  - **pour** + infinitive…   in order to…
    pour améliorer   in order to improve
    pour protéger   in order to protect
  - with a negative:
    pour ne pas augmenter   in order not to increase
    pour ne pas perdre   in order not to lose
    pour ne plus créer   in order not to create any more / longer
  - **sans** + infinitive   without
    sans détruire   without destroying
    sans polluer   without polluting
  - **en** + present participle   by doing
    en montrant   by showing
    en jetant   by throwing
  - with a negative:
    en ne regrettant pas   by not regretting
    en ne tuant plus   by not killing any more

- Using modal verbs, **pour / sans** + infinitive, **en + -ant**, negatives and opinion phrases together:

  Pour moi, il est évident / clair qu'on doit faire plus pour protéger l'environnement en diminuant la pollution.

  For me it's obvious / clear that we must do more in order to protect the environment by decreasing pollution.

  Je trouve qu'il est essentiel d'encourager le recyclage pour ne plus augmenter les déchets sans créer d'inconvénients pour les gens.

  I think that it is essential to encourage recycling in order not to increase waste any more without creating drawbacks / snags for people.

  Ce qui m'inquiète le plus, c'est l'avenir des animaux et des îles en danger.

  What worries me the most is the future of animals and islands in danger.

> **Quick Test**

1. Put these verbs into the **nous** form: **je dois, je peux, je sais, je veux**
2. Translate into English: **Les scientifiques disent que les véhicules et les usines sont les causes principales du réchauffement de la Terre.**
3. Translate into French: We must protect the environment by decreasing pollution without destroying our industries.

The Environment and Where People Live

1 Draw lines to match up the French and English adverbs.

a) bientôt		**i)** only	
b) déjà		**ii)** quickly	
c) lentement		**iii)** so much	
d) seulement		**iv)** already	
e) tellement		**v)** slowly	
f) vite		**vi)** soon	[6 marks]

2 Read these sentences aloud.

a) **J'habite dans le vieux quartier de la ville.**

b) **Il y a huit pièces chez nous.**

c) **La bibliothèque se trouve entre l'église et la gare.**

d) **Je préfère vivre à la campagne.**

e) **Notre ville est connue pour ses beaux espaces verts.**

f) **L'environnement est en grand danger!** [6 marks]

3 Unjumble the sentences.

a) **Chez a petite une il salon joli un y moi et cuisine**

b) **mon Je chambre partage frère une avec**

c) **centre-ville de trouve un On magasins choix au bon**

d) **Le grand un réchauffement est Terre de problème la actuel** [4 marks]

4 Rewrite these sentences by using the imperative. An example has been done for you.

Example: **Il faut visiter le marché. = Visitez le marché!**

a) **On peut visiter le musée.**

....**!**

b) **On peut aller au stade.**

....!

c) **On doit acheter des produits frais.**

....!

d) **Il faut manger dans des restaurants célèbres.**

....!

e) **On ne doit pas oublier de visiter le château.**

....!

f) **On peut bénéficier de l'air frais.**

....! [6 marks]

5 Match up the halves of the sentences below and then translate them into English.

a) **Au premier étage**   i) **aiment les lieux naturels.**

b) **Mon village**   ii) **se trouvent trois chambres.**

c) **Les touristes**   iii) **il y a beaucoup de clubs.**

d) **L'hôpital**   iv) **se trouve dans l'ouest de l'Angleterre.**

e) **Pour les jeunes,**   v) **se trouve près de chez moi.**   [10 marks]

6 Change the sentences by using the **nous** form of the verb. An example has been done for you.

Example: **On peut aller à l'école en vélo.** = **Nous pouvons aller à l'école en vélo.**

a) **On peut utiliser moins d'énergie.** ....

b) **On doit réduire les déchets.** ....

c) **On sait qu'il faut changer nos habitudes.** ....

d) **On veut aider à améliorer l'environnement.** ....

[4 marks]

Review Questions

Media and Technology

1 Match the French and the English.

a) **de plus en plus**　　　　　　　　i) less and less

b) **de pire en pire**　　　　　　　　ii) more and more

c) **de moins en moins**　　　　　　iii) better and better

d) **de mieux en mieux**　　　　　　iv) worse and worse　　　　　　[4 marks]

2 Translate the following into French. An example has been done for you.

Example: the most important thing = **la chose la plus importante**

a) the most popular app　　　...

b) the most interesting photos　...

c) the biggest demonstration　...

d) the safest sites　　　　　　...

e) the best thing　　　　　　...　[5 marks]

3 Choose the correct verbs from the box to fill the gaps in the sentences below.

nous faisons	je vais passer	j'utilise	j'ai lu	passent	nous avons reçu

a) **Chaque jour,** .... **mon portable pour beaucoup de choses.**

b) **Au collège,** .... **beaucoup de travail sur les ordinateurs.**

c) **Récemment,** .... **un blog au sujet des animaux en danger.**

d) **Les jeunes** .... **trop de temps sur les ordinateurs.**

e) **Hier,** .... **un cadeau gratuit de mon site préféré!**

f) **À l'avenir,** .... **moins de temps en ligne!**　　　[6 marks]

4 Listen to the pronunciations. Write **1**, **2** or **3** for the correct pronunciation and explain why.

a) **La meilleure chose, c'est qu'avec la technologie moderne, on peut vite communiquer.**

....

b) **Pour moi, c'est agréable de tchatter sur les réseaux qui sont disponibles.**

....

c) **Le pire, c'est qu'on peut recevoir des menaces en ligne et se sentir très mal.**

....

d) **Le gouvernement va voter une nouvelle loi sur l'environnement demain.**

....

5 Insert the correct verb forms for each infinitive to complete the table. Two have already been done for you.

Infinitive	Present tense		Perfect tense	
avoir	*j'ai*	nous	j'ai	nous avons ....
recevoir	je	*nous recevons*	j'ai	nous .... reçu
voir	je	nous	j'ai	nous ....
écrire	j'...............	nous	j'...............	nous ....
lire	je	nous	j'...............	nous ....

[18 marks]

Gender, Plurals and Definite, Indefinite and Partitive Articles

You must be able to:

- Use the correct gender of nouns
- Make nouns plural
- Use definite, indefinite and partitive articles.

Gender and Plurals

- All nouns in French are either masculine or feminine.

	Definite articles (the)	Indefinite articles (a / an)
Masculine	**le / l'** (use l' in front of a noun starting with a vowel) **le garçon** the boy **l'arbre** the tree	**un** **un garçon** a boy
Feminine	**la / l'** (use l' in front of a noun starting with a vowel) **la fille** the girl **l'eau** the water	**une** **une fille** a girl
Plural (for both masculine and feminine)	**les** **les garçons** the boys **les filles** the girls	**des** (some) **des garçons** some boys **des filles** some girls

- **le / la** also becomes **l'** in front of most nouns beginning with a silent 'h':
  l'heure hour

Masculine and Feminine Form of a Noun

- To change a noun into the feminine form, follow the rules below:
  - Add **-e**
    un président **une présidente** a president
  - **eur ➜ -rice** and / or **-euse**
    un directeur **une directrice** a director
    un chanteur **une chanteuse** a singer
  - **en ➜ -nne**
    un chien **une chienne** a dog

> **Key Point**
>
> Words ending in **-age**, **-ège**, **-eau**, **-isme** and **-ment** are usually masculine, except **la plage** (beach)
> Words ending in **-ée**, **-té**, **-ie**, **-ine**, **-tion** and **-ence** are usually feminine, except **le musée** (museum), **le lycée** (sixth form)

> **Key Sounds**
>
> **le** and **les** do not sound the same. Don't pronounce the final **-s** in **les**.

> **Key Point**
>
> You often use the definite article in French when in English you don't use it:
> **J'aime les films.**
> I like films.

Plurals

- To change nouns into the plural, follow the rules below:
  - To make most nouns plural, you add **-s**:

    un magasin   a shop   **des magasins**   some shops
  - Add **-x** to masculine nouns ending in **-(e)au** and **-eu**:

    un gâteau   a cake   **des gâteaux**   some cakes
  - No change for nouns ending in **-s** or **-x**:

    un choix   a choice   **des choix**   some choices
  - Most words ending in **-al** become **-aux**:

    un animal   an animal   **des animaux**   animals

Partitive Articles

- The partitive article means 'some'.

Masculine singular	Feminine singular	Masculine or feminine words starting with a vowel	Plural
du	de la	de l'	des
du **travail** (some work)	de la **liberté** (some freedom)	de l'**action** (some action)	des **activités** (some activities)

Key Point

Some nouns do not follow the rules when changing to the feminine:

chef / **cheffe** (chef), **héros** / **héroïne** (hero / heroine), **policier** / **policière** (police officer)

Key Point

Some nouns do not follow the rules when changing to plural, such as:

un œil   an eye
des yeux   eyes

Key Sounds

Liaisons: remember to link **les** and **des** with the noun that follows if it starts with a vowel.
Les amis (the friends) will sound like **les(z)amis**.
Des animaux (some animals) will sound like **des(z)animaux**.

Quick Test

1. Write **le / la** in front of the words. Use the endings of the words to help you work out the gender.
   - a) .... **collège**
   - c) .... **population**
   - b) .... **sécurité**
   - d) .... **réseau**
2. Write the plural form of the following nouns.
   - a) **un pays**   des ....
   - b) **un lieu**   des ....
   - c) **un problème**   des ....
   - d) **un bureau**   des ....
3. Translate into French, using **le / la / les** in front of the nouns:
   - a) I like sport.
   - c) I don't like fruit.
   - b) I love animals.
   - d) I prefer reading.
4. Read the following sentences, paying attention to **le / les** and liaisons with **les / des**.
   - a) **J'ai les yeux marron et les cheveux longs.**
   - b) **J'aime les émissions sur les animaux.**
   - c) **Je déteste le foot et les examens.**

Adjectives and Adverbs

You must be able to:

- Use adjectives correctly: agreements and position
- Use comparative, superlative, possessive and demonstrative adjectives
- Change an adjective into an adverb.

Quick Recall Quiz

Agreement

- Most adjectives change their ending depending on the noun they describe. If the noun they describe is feminine, the adjective will have a feminine ending.

	Masculine singular	Feminine singular	Masculine plural	Feminine plural
No change to adjectives ending in mute **-e**	**possible**	**possible**	**possibles**	**possibles**
Add **-e**	**noir**	**noire**	**noirs**	**noires**
-x ➜ -se	**sérieux**	**sérieuse**	**sérieux**	**sérieuses**
-el ➜ -elle	**industriel**	**industrielle**	**industriels**	**industrielles**
-f ➜ -ve	**positif**	**positive**	**positifs**	**positives**
-er ➜ -ère	**premier**	**première**	**premiers**	**premières**
-en ➜ -enne	**végétarien**	**végétarienne**	**végétariens**	**végétariennes**

> ### Key Point
>
> Some words do not follow these patterns such as:
>
> **faux / fausse** (false), **bon / bonne** (good), **nouveau / nouvelle** (new), **pareil / pareille** (similar), **travailleur / travailleuse** (hard-working), **vieux / vieil / vieille** (old), **blanc / blanche** (white), **frais / fraîche** (fresh), **long / longue** (long)

Position of the Adjectives

- Most adjectives go after the noun they describe:

une ville industrielle	an industrial town
les cheveux courts	short hair

- But some adjectives will go before and they are usually referred to as BAGS adjectives: **B**eauty, **A**ge, **G**ood/Bad and **S**ize.

une belle maison	a beautiful house
un vieux livre	an old book
un bon ami	a good friend
un petit village	a small village

> ### Key Point
>
>
> Some adjectives will have **two masculine forms**. If the following noun starts with a vowel or a silent h, you will then use a different form of the masculine adjective. This is to make it easier to pronounce:
>
> **un vieux train**
> an old train
> **un vieil ami**
> an old friend
> **un beau village**
> a pretty village
> **un bel été**
> a great summer
> **un nouveau livre**
> a new book
> **un nouvel ami**
> a new friend

Comparative Adjectives

plus...que	more...than or -er...than	**Il est plus grand que lui.** He is taller than him.
moins...que	less...than	**Elle est moins sportive que moi.** She is less sporty than me.
aussi...que	as...as	**Il est aussi grand qu'elle.** He is as tall as her.

- Some examples of irregular comparatives: **meilleur(e)(s)** (better) and **pire(s)** (worse)

Superlative Adjectives

le / la / les plus...	the most...	**La plus belle ville.** The most beautiful town.
le / la / les moins...	the least...	**Il est le moins grand.** He is the least tall.

HT **le meilleur / la meilleure / les meilleurs / les meilleures** the best
le pire / la pire / les pires the worst

Possessive Adjectives

	Masculine singular	Feminine singular	Plural
my	**mon**	**ma**	**mes**
your	**ton**	**ta**	**tes**
his / her / its	**son**	**sa**	**ses**
our	**notre**	**notre**	**nos**
your	**votre**	**votre**	**vos**
their	**leur**	**leur**	**leurs**

Demonstrative Adjectives

Masculine singular	Feminine singular	Plural
ce this / that **cet** (if the following noun starts with a vowel or a silent h) this / that	**cette** this / that	**ces** these / those

Adverbs

- Adverbs describe how you do something, for instance 'calmly', 'quickly'.
- Adverbs go after the verb.
- To form an adverb:
  - Add **–ment** to the feminine form of an adjective: **première** (first) ➜ **premièrement** (firstly)
  - Drop **-ant(e) / -ent(e)** from an adjective and add **-amment / -emment**: **courant** (fluent) ➜ **couramment** (fluently) **patient** (patient) ➜ **patiemment** (patiently)

> ### Revise

> ### Key Point
>
> You can create other adjectives by adding **in-** or **im-** meaning 'un-', 'in-' or 'opposite of' (**possible** ➜ **impossible**).

> ### Key Point
>
> Some adjectives will have two meanings, depending on their position:
> **propre** – in front of the noun **propre** means 'own' but after the noun, it means 'clean'.
> **ancien** – in front of the noun **ancien** means 'former' but after the noun, it means 'ancient'.

> ### Key Point
>
> Possessive adjectives agree with the noun that follows.

> ### Key Point
>
> You can create other adverbs by adding **in-** or **im-**:
> **également** (equally) ➜ **inégalement** (unequally)

> ### Quick Test
>
> 1. Change into the feminine form:
>   a) **un homme heureux** – **une femme** ....
>   b) **un livre important** – **une chose** ....
> 2. Translate into French:
>   a) a little park   b) a beautiful modern town
> 3. Form the adverb from the adjective.
>   a) equal = **égal** – equally = ...
>   b) terrible = **terrible** – terribly = ...

The Present Tense

You must be able to:

- Form and use the present tense
- Use reflexive verbs
- Use the present tense with **depuis** and **être en train de** + infinitive
- Use the imperative.

Regular Verbs

- There are three main groups of regular verbs in French.
- Most verbs end in:
  - **-er** like **regarder** – to look at
  - **-ir** like **finir** – to finish
  - **-re** like **attendre** – to wait
- The infinitive is formed from the **stem + infinitive ending**.
- For example, **chant + er** (to sing) is called the infinitive.

Regular Verbs in the Present Tense

- To form the present tense, take off the infinitive ending and add the present tense endings. Each group of verbs will have different endings depending on the person.
- Endings for **–er** verbs:

chanter	to sing
je chante	I sing / am singing
tu chantes	you sing / are singing
il / elle / on chante	he / she / one sings / is singing
nous chantons	we sing / are singing
vous chantez	you sing / are singing
ils / elles chantent	they sing / are singing

- Endings for **-ir** verbs:

finir	to finish
je finis	I finish / am finishing
tu finis	you finish / are finishing
il / elle / on finit	he / she / one finishes / is finishing
nous finissons	we finish / are finishing
vous finissez	you finish / are finishing
ils / elles finissent	they finish / are finishing

- Endings for **-re** verbs:

attendre	to wait
j'attends	I wait / am waiting
tu attends	you wait / are waiting
il / elle / on attend	he / she / one waits / is waiting
nous attendons	we wait / are waiting
vous attendez	you wait / are waiting
ils / elles attendent	they wait / are waiting

>
> ### Key Point
>
> Some verbs change the spelling of their stems. E.g., accents change (**mener** (to lead), **je mène** (I lead)), consonants are doubled (**jeter** (to throw), **je jette** (I throw)) or softened (**manger** (to eat), **nous mangeons** (we eat) and **commencer** (to start), **nous commençons** (we start)).

> ### Key Point
>
> There is only one form of the verbs in the present tense in French: **je joue** means both 'I play' and 'I am playing'.

Reflexive Verbs

- Reflexive verbs include reflexive pronouns (**me, te, se**…).
- **me**, **te**, **se** shorten to **m'**, **t'**, **s'** before a vowel or a silent h.

se laver	to get washed
je me lave	I get / I am getting washed
tu te laves	you get / are getting washed
il / elle / on se lave	he / she / one gets / is getting washed
HT **nous nous lavons**	we get / are getting washed
HT **vous vous lavez**	you get / are getting washed
HT **ils / elles se lavent**	they get / are getting washed

HT depuis

- To say how long you have been doing or have done something, use the present tense + **depuis**:

J'attends depuis 10 minutes.   I have been waiting **for** 10 minutes.

J'habite ici depuis 2005.   I have lived / been living here **since** 2005.

HT être en train de + infinitive

- **être en train de** + infinitive is used to say that you are doing something / are in the middle of doing something:

Je suis en train de manger.

I am eating / I am in the middle of eating.

Nous sommes en train de travailler.

We are working / we are in the middle of working.

The Imperative

- Use the imperative to give instructions or orders.
- Take the **tu** or **vous** form of the verb and drop the pronoun:

Prends ton sac!   Take your bag!

Vas dans ta chambre!   Go to your room!

Fais tes devoirs!   Do your homework!

HT Let's…

sois   be   **soyez**   be

- Use the **nous** form to express 'let's + verb!'

Soyons heureux!   Let's be happy!

Quick Test

1. Fill in with the correct endings of the verbs in the present tense.
   - a) **Je regard**……..:
   - b) **Il fini**……………
   - c) **Nous entend**……………
   - d) **Ils travaill**……………
2. Translate the following verbs into French:
   - a) I am playing.
   - b) She is waiting.
3. What is the English for…?
   - a) **Je visite.**   b) **Nous choisissons.**   c) **Elle change.**
4. What is the French for…? Use the French verbs in brackets to help you.
   - a) I have been working for one hour (**travailler**).
   - b) We have been listening for 5 minutes (**écouter**).

Common Irregular Verbs and Anchor Verbs

You must be able to:

- Form and use the present tense of irregular verbs
- Know and use the anchor verbs
- Use the pattern of the anchor verbs with other verbs
- Use impersonal verbs.

Very High Frequency Verbs

	avoir (to have)	être (to be)	aller (to go)	faire (to do)
je (j')	ai (have)	suis (am)	vais (go)	fais (do)
tu	as (have)	es (are)	vas (go)	fais (do)
il / elle / on	a (has)	est (is)	va (goes)	fait (does)
nous	avons (have)	sommes (are)	allons (go)	faisons (do)
vous	avez (have)	êtes (are)	allez (go)	faites (do)
ils / elles	ont (have)	sont (are)	vont (go)	font (do)

> ### Key Point
>
> There is only one form of the verbs in the present tense in French: **je vais** means both 'I go' and 'I am going'.

High Frequency Verbs

	boire (to drink)	connaître (to know)	courir (to run)	croire (to believe)	écrire (to write)	recevoir (to receive)	rire (to laugh)	suivre (to follow)	voir (to see)
je (j')	bois	connais	cours	crois	écris	reçois	ris	suis	vois
tu	bois	connais	cours	crois	écris	reçois	ris	suis	vois
il / elle / on	boit	connaît	court	croit	écrit	reçoit	rit	suit	voit
HT nous	buvons	connaissons	courons	croyons	écrivons	recevons	rions	suivons	voyons
HT vous	buvez	connaissez	courez	croyez	écrivez	recevez	riez	suivez	voyez
HT ils / elles	boivent	connaissent	courent	croient	écrivent	reçoivent	rient	suivent	voient

Irregular -ir Verbs

- Not all **-ir** verbs follow the same pattern. There are four different patterns and they are referred to as 'anchor verbs':

	choisir (to choose)	partir (to leave)	venir (to come)	ouvrir (to open)
je (j')	choisis	pars	viens	ouvre
tu	choisis	pars	viens	ouvres
il / elle / on	choisit	part	vient	ouvre
nous	choisissons	partons	venons	ouvrons
vous	choisissez	partez	venez	ouvrez
ils / elles	choisissent	partent	viennent	ouvrent

> ### Key Point
>
> Impersonal verbs:
>
> **il y a** meaning 'there is / are'; **il fait** + adjective (e.g. **il fait beau** (the weather is nice), **il fait froid** (it's cold)); **il est** for telling the time; **il faut** meaning 'we must'.

- Examples of verbs that will follow these patterns:
choisir: réagir (to react), **réussir** (to succeed)
partir: sortir (to go out), **dormir** (to sleep)
venir: tenir (to hold), **devenir** (to become)
ouvrir: offrir (to offer), **souffrir** (to suffer)

Irregular -re Verbs

- Not all -re verbs follow the same pattern. There are three different patterns and they are referred to as 'anchor verbs':

	entendre (to hear)	prendre (to take)	traduire (to translate)
je (j')	entends	prends	traduis
tu	entends	prends	traduis
il / elle / on	entend	prend	traduit
nous	entendons	prenons	traduisons
vous	entendez	prenez	traduisez
ils / elles	entendent	prennent	traduisent

- Examples of verbs that will follow these patterns:
entendre: rendre (to return), **vendre** (to sell), **perdre** (to lose)
prendre: comprendre (to understand), **apprendre** (to learn)
traduire: produire (to produce), **réduire** (to reduce)

Modal Verbs

	pouvoir (to be able to)	devoir (to have to)	vouloir (to want)	savoir (to know)
je	peux	dois	veux	sais
tu	peux	dois	veux	sais
il / elle / on	peut	doit	veut	sait
nous	pouvons	devons	voulons	savons
vous	pouvez	devez	voulez	savez
ils / elles	peuvent	doivent	veulent	savent

Quick Test

1. Translate into English:
   a) **Elle a soif.**   c) **Il a chaud.**
   b) **Nous avons peur.** d) **Tu as faim?**
2. What is the French for…?
   a) I want to go there.   c) He has to take.
   b) She can go out.   d) We want to sleep.
3. Pronounce the following words:
   a) **elle peut**   c) **nous entendons**
   b) **ils savent**   d) **vous venez**

Key Point

In some phrases, **avoir** will be used where 'be' + noun / adjective would be used in English:

avoir froid	to be cold
avoir chaud	to be hot
avoir … ans	to be … years old
avoir soif	to be thirsty
avoir faim	to be hungry
avoir peur	to be scared

Key Point

To say that you have just done something, use **venir** in the present tense followed by **de** + infinitive:
Je viens de partir.
I have just left.

Key Point

Modal verbs are followed by an infinitive:
Je veux dormir.
I want to sleep.
Je peux y aller.
I can go (there).

Key Point

savoir   to know how to
Je sais parler français.
I can speak French. (I know how to speak French.)

Grammar 1

1 Change the articles to complete the table. The first row has been done for you.

Indefinite	Definite	Plural indefinite	Plural definite
un problème	le problème	des problèmes	les problèmes
une semaine			
un magasin			
un jeu			
une idée			
un homme			

[15 marks]

2 Decide if the following words are masculine or feminine, then write **le** or **la** in the gaps.

a) .... **société**   c) .... **bateau**   e) .... **moitié**

b) .... **système**   d) .... **plage**   f) .... **population**   [6 marks]

3 Fill in the gaps with the correct partitive article **du / de la / de l'**. Make sure that you identify if the noun is masculine or feminine before choosing the articles.

a) Le matin, je mange .... **pain** et je bois .... **eau**.

b) Je voudrais .... **gâteau** avec .... **glace**.

c) Il y a .... **place** dans le train.

d) Il faut acheter .... **nourriture** pour la fête.

e) J'ai .... **travail** à faire tous les soirs.

f) J'écoute .... **musique** dans ma chambre.   [8 marks]

4 Rewrite the sentences by choosing the correct form of the adjectives.

a) Ma sœur est assez sportive / sportives / sportif.

b) Les maths sont assez difficiles / difficile.

c) Mes amies Lucie et Yasmina sont très sérieux / sérieuses / sérieuse.

d) Il y a de beau / belles / beaux endroits intéressants dans cette région.

e) Ma ville est assez industriel / industrielle / industrielles.   [5 marks]

5 Translate the following sentences into English.

a) Le français est plus intéressant que les maths.

b) Ce film est le meilleur.

c) Je suis plus calme que mon frère.

d) Il est le plus grand de la famille.

e) C'est la ville la plus visitée de France. [5 marks]

6 Change the following adjectives into adverbs. The first one has been done for you.

a) **plein** (full) **pleinement** (fully)

b) **local** (local)...(locally)

c) **spécial** (spécial)...(specially)

d) **normal** (normal)..(normally)

e) **ouvert** (open)...(openly)

f) **égal** (equal)..(equally) [5 marks]

7 Circle all the verbs in the present tense.

| **j'ai mangé** | **je fais** | **je mange** | **il finit** | **nous avons acheté** |

| **elle arrive** | **ils vont partir** | **ils aiment** | **elle pense** | **vous avez eu** |

[6 marks]

8 Translate the following sentences using the verb 'to have' in the present tense.

a) I am hungry. ....

b) She is cold. ....

c) We are hot. ....

d) He is 15. ....

e) They are thirsty. .... [5 marks]

The Environment and Where People Live

1   Choose the correct verb from the box below to complete the sentences.

écoute	habiter	peut	trouve	travaillent	habite	partage

a)   J'.. une vieille maison à la campagne.

b)   Je .... ma chambre avec ma sœur.

c)   Dans ma chambre, j'.. de la musique.

d)   Je voudrais .... à la campagne.

e)   La bibliothèque se .... près de la gare.

f)   On .... faire des promenades dans la forêt.

g)   Mes parents .... en centre-ville.   **[7 marks]**

2   Tick the sentences that suggest living in town is better than living in the countryside.

a)   **La ville est très vivante.**   ☐

b)   **Je voudrais vivre à la campagne.**   ☐

c)   **Il n'y a pas de magasins tout près.**   ☐

d)   **Il est facile d'utiliser les transports publics.**   ☐

e)   **Il y a trop de bruit.**   ☐

f)   **Il y a un bon choix de choses à faire.**   ☐   **[3 marks]**

3   Listen to the pronunciations. Write **1**, **2** or **3** for the correct pronunciation and explain why.

a)   **Dans mon quartier, on trouve un bon choix de magasins.**   ....

b)   **Le château est célèbre et notre région est bien connue pour ses fêtes en été.**   ....

c)   **Le monde industriel utilise trop de ressources qui polluent l'air.**   ....

d) Il est essentiel d'encourager le recyclage pour ne plus augmenter les déchets
sans créer d'inconvénients pour les gens. ....

....

[8 marks]

4 Read the e-mail from Jacques below and decide whether the following activities refer to the past, now or future. Write **P** for past, **N** for now or **F** for future.

Salut!

Moi, j'habite dans une assez grande maison dans une ville qui se trouve dans le sud-ouest de la France. Chez nous il y a neuf pièces et j'ai ma propre chambre. Avant nous habitions dans une maison où j'ai dû partager une chambre avec mon frère. Pas génial! J'aime bien mon quartier – il y a quelques magasins et un parc. Quand j'étais plus jeune, j'aimais jouer au foot au parc et j'allais à la piscine avec ma famille mais je n'aime pas faire cela maintenant – je préfère aller en centre-ville avec mes copains. J'ai l'intention d'acheter une petite maison sur la côte où je peux voir la mer. Maintenant il dois continuer avec mes devoirs!

À bientôt,

Jacques

---

a) sharing a bedroom ....

b) living in a town ....

c) living on the coast ....

d) going into town ....

e) playing football ....   [5 marks]

5 Using the email from Jacques in question **4**, write a response. Include where you live, details about your home, your town or village and your region. Give opinions about your town and reasons why people should visit.   [10 marks]

6 Using the ideas, vocabulary and grammatical structures on pages 90 and 91, write a paragraph on your ideas and concerns about the environment and environmental issues. Try to include as many different structures as you can (e.g. modal verbs, pour + infinitive, sans + infinitive, negatives etc.).   [10 marks]

Perfect and Imperfect Tenses

You must be able to:

- Use the perfect tense with **avoir** and **être**
- Use verbs in the imperfect tense
- Use **après avoir**.

Past Participles

- To form the perfect tense you either need **avoir** and **être** and the **past participle** of the verb.
- To form the **past participle** of regular verbs, you need to follow the following rules:
  - For **-er** verbs, take off **-er** and add **é** (**manger** (to eat) – **mangé**)
  - For **-ir** verbs, take off **-ir** and add **i** (**finir** (to finish) – **fini**)
  - For **-re** verbs, take off **-re** and add **u** (**attendre** (to wait) – **attendu**).

Irregular Past Participles

- There are some irregular past participles that you need to know:

Infinitive	Past participle	Infinitive	Past participle
avoir (to have)	**eu**	**mettre** (to put)	**mis**
boire (to drink)	**bu**	**mourir** (to die)	**mort**
connaître (to know)	**connu**	**ouvrir** (to open)	**ouvert**
courir (to run)	**couru**	**prendre** (to take)	**pris**
devoir (to have to)	**dû**	**pouvoir** (to be able to)	**pu**
dire (to say)	**dit**	**savoir** (to know)	**su**
écrire (to write)	**écrit**	**recevoir** (to receive)	**reçu**
être (to be)	**été**	**venir** (to come)	**venu**
faire (to do)	**fait**	**voir** (to see)	**vu**
lire (to read)	**lu**	**vouloir** (to want)	**voulu**

The Perfect Tense with avoir

- Most verbs will need **avoir** (to have):

avoir (to have)	Past participle	English
j'ai	**mangé**	I ate
tu as	**fini**	you finished
il / elle / on a	**attendu**	he / she / it waited
nous avons	**lu**	we read
vous avez	**vu**	you saw
ils / elles ont	**écrit**	they wrote

The Perfect Tense with être

- Only a small number of verbs will need **être**. These include all reflexive verbs and the following verbs:

Infinitive	Past participle
monter (to go up)	**monté**
rester (to stay)	**resté**
sortir (to go out)	**sorti**
venir (to come)	**venu**
aller (to go)	**allé**
naître (to be born)	**né**

Infinitive	Past participle
tomber (to fall)	**tombé**
revenir (to return)	**revenu**
arriver (to arrive)	**arrivé**
mourir (to die)	**mort**
partir (to leave)	**parti**

être (to be)	Past participle	English
je suis	**allé(e)**	I went
tu es	**sorti(e)**	you went out
il / elle / on est	**venu(e)**	he / she / it came
nous sommes	**tombé(e)s**	we fell
vous êtes	**arrivé(e)(s)**	you arrived
ils / elles sont	**parti(e)s**	they left

The Imperfect

- The imperfect tense is used to express 'used to + verb' (I used to watch) and 'be + ing' (I was watching).
- Here are the imperfect endings for **-er** verbs:

je	**regard**ais (I was looking)	HT **nous**	**regard**ions (we were looking)
tu	**regard**ais (you were looking)	HT **vous**	**regard**iez (you were looking)
il / elle / on	**regard**ait (he / she / it) was looking)	HT **ils / elles**	**regard**aient (they were looking)

Quick Test

1. Do these verbs take **être** or **avoir**?
   a) **avoir**   b) **arriver**   c) **se laver**   d) **croire**
2. Give the past participles of the following verbs.
   a) **vouloir**   b) **boire**   c) **avoir**   d) **devoir**
3. Translate into French:
   a) I went   b) we believed   c) she wrote   d) he returned
4. Translate into English:
   a) **Après avoir lu...**   c) **Après être descendu...**
   b) **Après avoir couru...**   d) **Après m'être lavée...**

Key Point

When using a reflexive verb, you must not forget the reflexive pronoun:
je me suis lavé(e) (I washed myself),
tu t'es lavé(e) (you washed yourself)…

Key Point

When you use verbs with **être**, the past participle needs to agree with the person by adding an extra 'e' and / or an 's'.

Key Point

To say 'after having done / after doing', use **après avoir / être** followed by a past participle:
Après avoir acheté...
After having bought…
Après être parti(e)...
After having left…

Key Verbs

Verbs in the imperfect:
avoir (to have) – **j'avais, tu avais, il / elle avait**
être (to be) – **j'étais, tu étais, il / elle était**
faire (to do) – **je faisais, tu faisais, il / elle faisait**

Key Point

J'étais, tu étais and **il / elle était** also mean 'was / were'.
J'avais, tu avais, il / elle avait also mean 'had'.

Grammar 2

Future and Conditional Tenses and Negatives

Quick Recall Quiz

You must be able to:

- Form and use the near future tense – I am going to…
- Form and use the future tense – I will…
- Form and use the conditional tense – I would…
- Use negatives with all tenses.

The Future Tense

- Using **aller** in the present tense followed by an infinitive is the equivalent of the English 'will + verb' and 'be + going to + verb'.

  Je vais manger   I am going to eat / I will eat

The Conditional Tense

- **Je voudrais** (I would like), **tu voudrais** (you would like), **il / elle voudrait** (he / she would like)

  Je voudrais acheter…   I would like to buy…
  Elle voudrait rester.   She would like to stay.

Regular -er Verbs in the Future Tense

	souhaiter	to wish
je	souhaiterai	I will wish
tu	souhaiteras	you will wish
il / elle / on	souhaitera	he / she / one will wish
nous	souhaiterons	we will wish
vous	souhaiterez	you will wish
ils / elles	souhaiteront	they will wish

Key Point

The future endings are like the verb **avoir** in the present tense (apart from the **nous** and **vous** forms).

Key Point

il y aura means 'there will be'.

Irregular Verbs in the Future Tense

	avoir (to have)	**être** (to be)	**faire** (to do)	**aller** (to go)
je (j')	aurai (I will have)	serai (I will be)	ferai (I will do)	irai (I will go)
tu	auras (you will have)	seras (you will be)	feras (you will do)	iras (you will go)
il / elle / on	aura (he / she / one will have)	sera (he / she / one will be)	fera (he / she / one will do)	ira (he / she / one will go)

Regular -er Verbs in the Conditional Tense

	aider	to help
je (j')	aiderais	I would help
tu	aiderais	you would help
il / elle / on	aiderait	he / she / one would help
nous	aiderions	we would help
vous	aideriez	you would help
ils / elles	aideraient	they would help

110   GCSE French Revision Guide

HT Irregular Verbs in the Conditional Tense

	avoir (to have)	**être** (to be)	**faire** (to do)	**aller** (to go)
je (j')	**aurais** (I would have)	**serais** (I would be)	**ferais** (I would do)	**irais** (I would go)
tu	**aurais** (you would have)	**serais** (you would be)	**ferais** (you would do)	**irais** (you would go)
il / elle / on	**aurait** (he / she / one would have)	**serait** (he / she / one would be)	**ferait** (he / she / one would do)	**irait** (he / she / one would go)

Negatives with All Tenses

- Here is a list of the most common negatives:

ne...pas	not	HT **ne...plus**	no longer
ne...jamais	never	HT **ne...ni...ni**	neither...nor
ne...rien	not...anything	HT **ne...que**	only
ne...personne	not...anybody / nobody	HT **ne...pas encore**	not yet
ne...aucun(e)	not one		

- Negatives go around the verbs:

  Je ne <u>joue</u> plus. I don't play anymore.
  Je ne <u>regarderai</u> rien. I will watch nothing. / I won't watch anything.

- In the perfect tense, the negatives go around the auxiliary:

  Je n'<u>ai</u> pas mangé. I have not eaten.
  Elle n'<u>est</u> jamais allée à Paris. She has never been to Paris.

Key Point

You can also express the future by using the present tense with a future time phrase:

Demain, je vais au cinéma.
Tomorrow, I am going to the cinema.

Key Point

ne will become **n'** in front of a vowel.

Quick Test

1. Say in French that you would like to...
   a) go to the cinema tonight
   b) book a table
   c) see a film
   d) buy a car
2. Fill in the gaps with a verb in the future tense using the infinitives in brackets.
   a) Je _____ contente d'aller au cinéma. (être)
   b) Elle _____ chez sa copine. (aller)
   c) Nous _____ au restaurant. (manger)
   d) Ils _____ dans un magasin. (travailler)

Pronouns and Prepositions

Quick Recall Quiz

You must be able to:

- Use personal pronouns
- Use direct and indirect objects pronouns, on their own and together
- Use prepositions
- Use emphatic pronouns.

Personal Pronouns

je or j'	I
tu	you – one person, informal
il	he
elle	she
on	one, but also used to mean **nous**
nous	we
vous	you, as a group, or one person formal
ils	they – all masculine or masculine and feminine
elles	they – all feminine

Object Pronouns

- An object pronoun replaces the object in a sentence:
  I am watching <u>the film</u>. = I am watching <u>it</u>. (<u>it</u> is the object pronoun, replacing <u>the film</u>)
- There are two types of object pronouns, either direct or indirect:
  - Indirect object pronouns will have a preposition before:
    I give it <u>to her</u>.
  - <u>to her</u> is indirect because there is <u>to</u> in front of <u>her</u>.
  - <u>it</u> is a direct object pronoun because there is no preposition in front of it.

Direct object pronouns		Indirect object pronouns	
me / m'	me	**me / m'**	to me
te / t'	you	**te / t'**	to you
la / l'	her / it	**lui**	to her
le / l'	him / it	**lui**	to him
nous	us	**nous**	to us
vous	you	**vous**	to you
les	them	**leur**	to them

Key Point

Remember that in French all nouns are either masculine or feminine. If you refer to a masculine object you would need to say **il**...:

Il est nouveau.
It is new.
If you refer to a feminine object you would need to say **elle**...:

Elle est nouvelle.
It is new.

Key Point

In front of a vowel, **me**, **te**, **le**, **la** become **m'**, **t'**, **l'**.

Key Point

'to her' and 'to him' are the same word in French (**lui**), but the context will usually help you work out if it is 'to her' or 'to him'.

Key Point

Remember that pronouns go in front of the verbs in French.

Prepositions

- A preposition is a little word that comes before a noun or a verb, such as 'for', 'against', 'next to'.
- Here are some common prepositions:

à	to / at	**contre**	against
dans	in	**derrière**	behind
devant	in front of	**en**	in
entre	between	**pour**	for
sans	without	**de**	of / from
par	by	**avant**	before
après	after	**pendant**	during
depuis	for / since	**jusqu'à**	until

Verbal Phrases with Prepositions

- To express 'by doing', use **en** followed by the present participle form of the verb, which is the stem of the verb plus **-ant**:

en **travaillant**	by working
en **allant**	by going
en **parlant**	by talking

- Irregular present participles:

en **ét**ant	by being
en **ay**ant	by having
en **fais**ant	by doing

- To express 'before doing', use **avant de** followed by an infinitive:

avant de **partir**	before leaving
avant de **regarder**	before watching

Emphatic Pronouns

- Use of emphatic pronouns (**lui**, **elle**, **nous**, **vous**, **eux**, **elles**) after prepositions :

avec lui	with him	**sans eux**	without them
pour eux	for them	**devant lui**	in front of him

Quick Test

1. Replace the nouns with a direct pronoun. The first one has been done for you.
   - a) Je veux <u>la robe</u> = Je <u>la</u> veux
   - b) Je veux les livres = ...
   - c) Je voudrais le chapeau = ...
   - d) Je voudrais les fruits = ...
2. Translate into French:
   - a) before buying
   - b) before going
   - c) before seeing
   - d) before taking
3. What is the English for…?
   - a) sur
   - b) dans
   - c) contre
   - d) devant

Key Point

The object pronoun **en** means 'some'.

J'en ai acheté.
I have bought some.
J'en voudrais.
I would like some.

Key Point

The object pronoun **y** means 'there'.
Some useful phrases:

il y en a
there is / are some
il y en avait
there was / were some
il y en aura
there will be some

Key Point

Some prepositions will contract if they are followed by **le / les**:

à + **le** = **au**
à + **les** = **aux**
de + **le** = **du**
de + **les** = **des**

Key Point

If you use a preposition with a verb, the verb will be in the infinitive form:

pour aller
in order to go
sans penser
without thinking

Asking Questions

You must be able to:

- Form and recognise questions
- Form questions in different ways
- Use a range of question words.

Closed Questions

- A closed question is when the answer is either 'yes' or 'no'.
- There are three ways of asking a question in French:
  1. The question is a statement, and you raise your voice at the end of the sentence. If you want to know if someone likes sport, say 'you like sport?' and raise your voice.
     Tu aimes le sport?   (You like sport?) Do you like sport?
  2. Add **est-ce que** at the start of the sentence.
     Est-ce que tu aimes le sport?   Do you like sport?
  3. Swap the subject and the verb. This is called inversion.
     Aimes-tu le sport?   Do you like sport?

Question Words

qui	who
que	what
quoi	what
où	where
quand	when
pourquoi	why
combien (de)	how much / many
comment	how
quel / quelle / quels / quelles	which
lequel / laquelle / lesquels / lesquelles	which one(s)

> **Key Point**
>
> **Est-ce que?** means 'is it that?'

> **Key Point**
>
> **Tu aimes le sport? Est-ce que tu aimes les sport? Aimes-tu le sport?** all mean 'Do you like sport?'.

> **Key Point**
>
> **quel** and **lequel** agree with the nouns they go with.

Asking a Question with a Question Word

- Question word + **est-ce que** + statement
- If you want to ask someone what they do at the weekend:
  1. Question word = 'what' = **que**
  2. **est-ce que**
  3. 'you do at the weekend' = **tu fais le week-end**
     Qu'est-ce que tu fais le week-end?
     What do you do at the weekend?
- If you want to ask someone where they go on holiday:
  1. Question word = 'where' = **où**
  2. **est-ce que**
  3. 'you go on holiday' = **tu vas en vacances**
     Où est-ce que tu vas en vacances?
     Where do you go on holiday?

Key Point

que will become **qu'** in front of a word starting with a vowel.

Key Point

You can form other question words with a question word and a preposition:

Pour qui?	For whom?
Avec qui?	With whom?
Depuis quand?	
Since when?	

Quick Test

1. What is the French for…?
   a) Where?
   b) At what time?
   c) With whom (who)?
   d) When?
2. Give the two other ways you can ask the following questions.
   a) **Aimes-tu le chocolat?**
   b) **Tu voudrais aller au cinéma?**
3. Write as many questions as you can using the words in the box below.

est-ce que	tu	veux	aller	ce soir
voudrais	où	quand	pourquoi	au restaurant

Grammar 2

1 Change the sentences into the perfect tense. These are regular verbs.

a) **Je regarde un film.** ....

b) **Je mange une glace.** ....

c) **Je choisis un livre.** ....

d) **J'attends ma copine.** .... [4 marks]

2 Choose the correct past participles.

a) **J'ai eu / eue / eus un problème.**

b) **Nous avons prends / pris / prise le train.**

c) **Il a beaucoup rire / ri / rit.**

d) **J'ai faire / fais / fait un voyage.** [4 marks]

3 Match the start and end of the sentences.

a) **Je suis**   i) **parti.**

b) **Nous sommes**   ii) **allé au collège.**

c) **Il est**   iii) **ai reçu la carte.**

d) **J'**   iv) **venues.** [4 marks]

4 Now put the verbs in question **3** in the negative form using **ne... pas**.

....

....

....

....

[4 marks]

5 Translate into English.

a) **Quand j'étais petite** ....

b) **Avant, j'aimais** ....

c) **Avant, je pensais** ....

d) **Quand j'avais dix ans** ....

e) **Avant, j'habitais** .... [5 marks]

6 Translate into French.

a) I am going to go **Je vais** ....

b) I am going to buy ....

c) I am going to eat ....

d) I am not going to be **Je ne vais pas** ....

e) I am not going to play ....

f) I am not going to do .... [6 marks]

7 Fill in the gaps using the verbs from the box.

voudrais	vais	aller	aimerais	allons	va

a) **J'**..**avoir un chien.**

b) **Ils vont** .... **au cinéma demain.**

c) **Je** .... **apprendre l'espagnol.**

d) **Nous** .... **passer une semaine chez mon oncle.**

e) **Elle** .... **écrire un e-mail.**

f) **Je** .... **rencontrer mon acteur préféré.** [6 marks]

Review Questions

Grammar 1

1 Write the following nouns in the plural form.

a) **un film anglais**   **des** ....

b) **une décision importante**   **des** ....

c) **un produit local**   **des** ....

d) **une langue étrangère**   **des** ....

e) **un journal international**   **des** .... [5 marks]

2 Write the feminine form of the following nouns.

a) **un héros**   **une** ....

b) **un policier**   **une** ....

c) **un acteur**   **une** ....

d) **un chanteur**   **une** ....

e) **un artiste**   **une** .... [5 marks]

3 Write the French for the following superlatives in the form indicated in brackets.

a) The best (masculine plural) ....

b) The worst (feminine plural) ....

c) The most beautiful (masculine singular) ....

d) The least expensive (feminine singular) ....

e) The longest (feminine plural) .... [5 marks]

4 Choose the correct possessive articles.

a) **mon / ma / mes ville**

b) **mon / ma / mes collège**

c) **mon / ma / mes avenir**

d) **mon / ma / mes maison**

e) mon / ma / mes chambre

f) mon / ma / mes santé   [6 marks]

5 Write the correct endings in the present tense.

a) Je fin............................. à quinze heure. (finir)

b) Nous habit............................. en ville. (habiter)

c) Ils aim............................. la nourriture française. (aimer)

d) Vous jou............................. au foot? (jouer)

e) J'attend............................. depuis une heure. (attendre)   [5 marks]

6 Complete the table of missing verbs in the present tense.

	avoir (to have)	être (to be)	aller (to go)	faire (to do)
Je (J')				
Tu				
Il / Elle / On				
Nous				
Vous				
Ils / Elles				

[24 marks]

7 Complete the table of modal verbs.

	pouvoir (to be able to)	devoir (to have to)	vouloir (to want)	savoir (to know)
Je				
Tu				
Il/ Elle / On				
Nous				
Vous				
Ils / Elles				

[24 marks]

Review Questions

Grammar 2

1 Write the past participles for the following verbs.

Infinitive	Past participle	Infinitive	Past participle
manger	mangé	écrire	
finir		pouvoir	
répondre		recevoir	
aller		prendre	
boire		voir	

[9 marks]

2 Write the correct form of **être** or **avoir** to complete the verbs in the perfect tense.

a) j'................................... acheté

b) elle .... bu

c) nous .... décidé

d) je .... allé

e) je .... resté

f) nous .... partis

[6 marks]

3 HT Translate into English.

a) **Après avoir vu,...**

b) **Après avoir pris,...**

c) **Après être allé,...**

d) **Après être sorti,...**

e) **Après avoir mangé,...**

f) **Après avoir rencontré,...**

[6 marks]

4 HT Make sentences using the phrases in question **3.**

....

....

....

....

....
....
....

[6 marks]

5 Complete the table.

Je vais aller	Je voudrais aller	HT J'irai
	Je voudrais manger	
Je vais partir		
Je vais choisir		
	Je voudrais passer	
	Je voudrais faire	

[10 marks]

6 Complete the table with either the French or the English translations.

	not	HT	no longer
ne…jamais		ne…ni…ni	
ne…rien		ne…que	

[6 marks]

7 Replace the nouns with a direct pronoun. The first one has been done for you.

a) Je veux <u>la glace</u> = je <u>la</u> veux

b) Je veux les livres = ...

c) Je voudrais le gâteau = ...

d) Je voudrais les fruits = ...

e) J'aime les légumes = ...

f) Je préfère les films américains = ...

[5 marks]

8 Translate into French.

a) In order to have

b) In order to be

c) In order to go

d) In order to do

e) In order to speak

f) In order to be able to

[6 marks]

9 What is the English for?

a) qui   b) quand   c) quel   d) où   e) combien

[5 marks]

Mixed Exam-Style Questions

Speaking

1 **Role-play**

You are talking to your French friend. Your teacher will play the part of your friend and speak first.
You should address your friend as '**tu**'.
When you see this - ? - you will have to ask a question.
In order to score full marks, you must include a verb in your response to each task.

1. Say **one** activity you like to do in your free time.

2. Give **one** opinion about sport.

3. Say where you go at the weekend.

4. Describe your favourite singer.

? **5.** Ask your friend a question about music.

10 marks

2 **Role-play**

You are talking to your Canadian friend. Your teacher will play the part of your friend and speak first.
You should address your friend as '**tu**'.
When you see this - ? - you will have to ask a question.
In order to score full marks, you must include a verb in your response to each task.

1. Describe your favourite celebrity.

2. Say what job they do.

3. Give **one** television programme you like.

? **4.** Ask your friend a question about cinema.

5. Say **one** activity you do online.

10 marks

Reading aloud

Practise saying the following passages aloud **in French**.

Think carefully about the rules you have learnt about French pronunciation.

You may like to try using some of the following strategies:

- underline all the silent letters
- circle all the nasal sounds (e.g. an / en / on)
- show where you need to make a liaison between two words
- practise words individually.

You may also like to use these passages to practise dictation.

3

Au collège, je suis en quatrième.

J'aime bien les cours d'histoire et d'anglais.

Cependant, ma matière préférée, c'est le sport.

Mes profs sont travailleurs et gentils.

Les bâtiments sont assez vieux mais nous avons une nouvelle piscine.

5 marks

4

Il y a cinq personnes dans ma famille.

Je m'entends bien avec mon frère.

Ma sœur est toujours aimable et patiente.

Elle a les yeux bleus et elle est plus grande que moi.

On aime écouter de la musique et jouer aux jeux vidéo.

5 marks

5

Je vais en vacances dans le sud de l'Angleterre.

Je passe deux semaines au bord de la mer.

Il y a beaucoup de choses à faire.

J'aime nager et me relaxer sur la plage.

L'année prochaine, j'espère aller en Belgique.

5 marks

6

J'habite dans un petit village à la campagne.

Je préfère l'air frais et les espaces verts.

Mon meilleur ami n'aime pas vivre ici.

Près de chez moi, il y a une boulangerie et une poste.

Nous avons besoin d'un nouveau centre commercial.

5 marks

7 **Reading aloud**

Read aloud the following text **in French**.

> Chaque jour, j'utilise mon portable.
>
> Je tchatte souvent avec mes copains et mes copines.
>
> Je télécharge de la musique et des émissions.
>
> Il y a beaucoup d'applications pratiques.
>
> Mon frère fait des recherches en ligne.

5 marks

You will then be asked four questions **in French** that relate to the topic of **Media and Technology**.

- Qu'est-ce que tu fais sur Internet?
- Parle-moi de ton appli préférée.
- Quelle est ton opinion sur la technologie?
- Quand utilises-tu la technologie au collège?

10 marks

 8 **Reading aloud**

Read aloud the following text **in French**.

> Il y a toutes sortes d'influenceurs.
>
> Ils communiquent sur les réseaux sociaux.
>
> J'aime les suivre en ligne.
>
> Ma célébrité préférée est actrice.
>
> Elle est très belle et vraiment populaire.

5 marks

You will then be asked four questions **in French** that relate to the topic of **Celebrity Culture**.

- Qu'est-ce que tu fais sur les réseaux sociaux?
- Quelle est ton opinion sur les influenceurs?
- Parle-moi de ta célébrité préférée.
- Quels sont les inconvénients de la célébrité? / Est-ce qu'il y a des inconvénients à être célèbre?

10 marks

9 Photo card

Look at the two photos and talk about the content of these photos. Try to speak for one minute (foundation tier) or one and half minutes (higher tier). You must say at least one thing about each photo.

5 marks

Now answer some questions related to the theme of **Popular Culture**. Here are some examples:

- **Qu'est-ce que tu aimes faire le week-end?**
- **Quelle est ton opinion sur le sport?**
- **Parle-moi d'une visite récente au cinéma.**
- **Décris-moi ta fête préférée.**
- **Que penses-tu des fêtes traditionnelles?**
- **Qu'est-ce que tu veux faire pour célébrer ton prochain anniversaire?**
- **Qui est ton chanteur ou ta chanteuse préféré(e)? Pourquoi?**
- **Quels sont les avantages de la célébrité? / Est-ce qu'il y a des avantages à être célèbre?**

15 marks

10 **Photo card**

Look at the two photos and talk about the content of these photos. Try to speak for one minute (foundation tier) or one and half minutes (higher tier). You must say at least one thing about each photo.

5 marks

Now answer some questions related to the theme of **People and Lifestyle**. Here are some examples:

- **Parle-moi de ton collège.**
- **Quelle est ta matière préférée à l'école? Pourquoi?**
- **Qu'est-ce que tu aimes faire à midi?**
- **Quelle est ton opinion de l'uniforme scolaire?**
- **Qu'est-ce que tu veux faire l'année prochaine (après le collège)?**
- **Décris-moi ton métier idéal.**
- **Parle-moi de tes amis / copains.**
- **Que penses-tu du mariage? Quels sont les avantages d'être marié(e)?**

15 marks

Reading

1 Read what these French teenagers say about where they live.

Benjamin, 14 ans
J'aime ma maison, mais j'habite en ville et il y a trop de bruit.

Killian, 15 ans
Si je veux voir mes amis, je dois prendre le bus.

Lisa, 14 ans
C'est plus propre à la campagne qu'en ville. Ici, les rues sont sales.

Daniel, 15 ans
Par la fenêtre, je vois de beaux arbres et de jolies collines, mais on n'a pas de voisins.

Olivier, 15 ans
J'adore habiter en plein centre-ville parce que c'est très vivant ici.

Marine, 14 ans
Malheureusement, il y a souvent des vols à la petite pâtisserie près de chez moi. C'est dommage parce qu'on peut acheter de très bons gâteaux là-bas!

What do these people think about their area?

Write **P** for a positive opinion

N for a negative opinion

P+N for a positive and negative opinion.

a) Benjamin ☐   **d)** Daniel ☐

b) Killian ☐   **e)** Olivier ☐

c) Lisa ☐   **f)** Marine ☐

g) Read Marine's comment again. What is a '**pâtisserie**'?

A	A restaurant
B	A shop
C	A supermarket

☐

7 marks

Mixed Exam-Style Questions

2 In an online forum, Julie talks about the environment.

> Moi, tous les jours j'essaie de recycler le papier et le plastique chez moi et à l'école; je les mets dans les poubelles correctes. Je sais qu'il n'est pas facile de protéger l'environnement. Par exemple, j'ai essayé d'aller au collège à pied au lieu de prendre le bus mais ça n'a duré que quelques semaines à cause du mauvais temps! Avant, nous avons toujours choisi de partir en vacances en avion mais nous avons décidé qu'à l'avenir nous allons passer les vacances plus près de chez nous et que nous allons prendre le train pour y aller. Je voudrais faire plus pour aider l'environnement et je crois que je peux économiser de l'énergie en éteignant mes appareils électriques quand je ne les utilise pas.

a) What does Julie say about her activities?

Write **P** for an activity in the past

    N for an activity she does now

    F for an activity she wants to do in the future.

i) recycling ☐

ii) walking to school ☐

iii) travelling by plane ☐

iv) saving energy ☐

b) Answer the following questions in English.

i) Where does Julie recycle paper and plastic? (Give **two** details.)

_____

ii) What does she say about future holidays? (Give **two** details.)

_____

iii) How does she think she can help the environment more? (Give **two** details.)

_____ ☐

10 marks

3 You see some headlines in a French newspaper.

A	L'énergie verte: notre avenir!
B	Deux voitures et un autobus en collision en centre-ville!
C	Les portables deviennent de plus en plus chers!
D	Une artiste connue va commencer la fête du village!
E	Les employés de l'usine de notre ville arrêtent de travailler.

Which headline matches each topic?

a) Technology

b) Environment

c) Celebrities

3 marks

4 Translate these sentences into English.

a) Je suis en seconde au collège.

_____

b) Ma matière préférée est l'informatique parce que c'est utile.

_____

c) L'année prochaine, je vais faire un apprentissage.

_____

d) Je m'entends bien avec ma sœur. On ne se dispute jamais.

_____

e) Hier soir, nous avons regardé une émission de sport ensemble dans ma chambre.

10 marks

_____

5 Read what these French teenagers say about their friends and their weekend activities.
Who says what?

Naël: Mon meilleur copain s'appelle Rayan. Nous sommes vraiment sportifs et on joue au foot pour la même équipe tous les samedis. Après, on va en ville et on achète des frites – elles ne sont pas très bonnes pour la santé mais on aime en manger!

Ambre: Le week-end, mes amis et moi se rencontrent au centre-ville. Normalement, on fait les magasins pour trouver de nouveaux vêtements ou des cadeaux. Nous aimons aussi le sport, mais nous ne sommes pas membres d'une équipe.

Elio: J'ai un groupe de bons amis et on fait beaucoup de choses ensemble. Souvent, le week-end, nous faisons du vélo – nous aimons aller à la campagne ou à la plage. Là-bas, on s'amuse bien et parfois on trouve un petit café pour prendre quelque chose.

Write Naël, Ambre or Elio for each answer.

a) Who goes shopping? ....

b) Who plays in a team ? ....

c) Who talks about a particular day of the weekend? ....

d) Who does <u>not</u> mention food and drink? ....

e) Who does <u>not</u> go into town? ....

5 marks

Writing

1 You and your French friends are sharing photos on social media.

What is in this photo?

Write five sentences in French.

☐
10 marks

2 Some French students are coming to visit your area. Write a short description for them.

Write about **50** words in French.

You must write something about each bullet point.

Mention:

- how you spend your free time
- sport in your area
- leisure activities
- shopping
- your school.

☐
10 marks

Mixed Exam-Style Questions

3 Using your knowledge of grammar, complete the following sentences in French.

Choose the correct French words from the three options in the grids.

a)

ont	a	ai

Mon frère _____ **les yeux bleus.**

b)

petites	petit	petite

J'habite dans une _____ **maison.**

c)

nous	elle	vous

Le week-end, _____ **allons à la piscine.**

d)

nouvelle	nouveaux	nouveau

Il y a un _____ **restaurant en ville.**

e)

finissent	finit	finis

Le collège _____ **à trois heures.**

5 marks

4 Translate the following sentences into French.

a) I have a sister.

b) It rains a lot in winter.

c) My school is big and modern.

d) In my opinion, the swimming pool is very nice.

e) Yesterday I went into town by bus.

10 marks

5 HT Translate the following sentences into French.

  a) I must help at home every day.

  b) Next year we will visit France.

  c) It is forbidden to use your mobile in class.

  d) I don't know what I will do as a job in the future.

  e) I have decided to eat less fast food in order to be healthy.

  10 marks

6 You are writing an article about friendship for your French partner school.

Write approximately **90** words in French.

You must write something about each bullet point.

Describe:
- your best friend
- what you have done recently with your friends
- your plans for next weekend.

  15 marks

7 You are writing an e-mail to your Belgian friend about school.
Write approximately **90** words in French.

You must write something about each bullet point.

Describe:
- your favourite subject(s)
- what you did at school yesterday
- your plans for next year.

  15 marks

8 You are e-mailing your French friend about holidays and celebrations.

Write approximately **90** words in French.

You must write something about each bullet point.

Describe:
- your favourite celebration
- a recent family event or holiday
- how you want to celebrate your next birthday.

  15 marks

Mixed Exam-Style Questions

9 HT You are writing a post for a French website. Your post is to promote travel and tourism.

Write approximately **150** words in French.

You must write something about each bullet point.

Describe:

- the positive aspects of travel (and travelling)
- when you spent time away from your home area recently.

25 marks

10 HT You are writing a post for a French website. Your post is to promote health and well-being.

Write approximately **150** words in French.

You must write something about each bullet point.

Describe:

- the importance of a healthy lifestyle
- what you will do in future to improve your health and well-being.

25 marks

Appendix A: French Sound–Symbol Correspondences (SSCs)

French Sound–Symbol Correspondences (SSCs)

The table below specifies key differences in sound-spelling correspondences between French and English. You will need to learn these at GCSE to be able to read out loud (for the Reading Aloud task in Paper 2: Speaking) and transcribe (for the Dictation task in Paper 1: Listening) with sufficient accuracy at this level, along with example words from this Revision Guide, taken from the AQA vocabulary list.

It is not an exhaustive list of the all sound-spelling correspondences in the French language. Where a letter or combination of letters is pronounced (or a sound spelt) in approximately the same way in French as in English, it is not listed.

You will be expected to pronounce words with stress patterns that allow your speech to be clear and comprehensible.

The use of hyphens indicates the position of the letters in a word, when position is relevant to the sound: xx- (at the beginning of a word); -xx- (in the middle of a word); -xx (at the end of a word).

Sound-Symbol Correspondence	Examples
silent final consonant	**blanc, grand, trop, ans, c'est, les yeux**
a	**la table**
i / y	**l'idée, le style**
eu	**les cheveux**
e	**le temps**
au / eau / closed o / ô	**mauvais, l'eau, nos, l'hôpital**
ou	**toujours**
u	**tu utilises**
silent final e	**elle s'appelle**
é (-er, -ez)	**la réponse, marié, demander, répétez**
en / an / em / am	**maintenant, cependant, temps, jambe**
on / om	**content, complet**
ain / in / aim / im	**la main, l'influenceur, faim, impossible**
è / ê / ai	**après, fêter, je vais**
oi / oy	**l'histoire, le voyage**
ch	**chanter, prochain**

Sound-Symbol Correspondence	Examples
ç (and soft 'c')	**le garçon, ce cinéma**
qu	**quand**
j	**je joue**
-tion	**la natation**
-ien	**quotidien**
s-liaison	**nous avons**
t-liaison	**cet homme**
n-liaison	**ton anniversaire**
x-liaison	**deux ans**
h	**j'habite**
un	**un**
-gn-	**la montagne**
r	**rapide**
open eu / œu	**peur, sœur**
open o	**nos notes**
-s-	**la saison**
th	**le thé, sympathique**
-ill- / -ille	**juillet, la famille**
-aill- / ail	**la taille, le travail**

Appendix B: The AQA Specification

The AQA Specification

The AQA GCSE French subject content for teaching from September 2024 onwards and for GCSE exams from 2026 onwards is based on three main components:

1. **Vocabulary lists**
   - At Foundation Tier, the vocabulary list comprises 1,200 lexical items.
   - At Higher Tier, there are a further 500 lexical items (i.e. 1,700 in total).
   - This Revision Guide uses only lexical items / vocabulary found on the AQA vocabulary lists as detailed in Section 3.3 of the AQA 8652 specification.
   - For the full lists provided in Appendices 2 and 3 of the AQA 8652 specification, visit the AQA website.

2. **Grammar requirements**
   - The grammar requirements are set out in two tiers: Foundation Tier and Higher Tier.
   - The requirements set out for Higher Tier include everything specified for Foundation Tier.
   - This Revision Guide uses solely the grammar requirements listed in Section 3.2 of the AQA 8652 specification.
   - For the full list of requirements, visit the AQA website.

3. **Sound-symbol correspondences**
   - French sound-symbol correspondences are required at both Foundation and Higher Tiers and are listed in Appendix A of this Revision Guide (page 135).
   - This Revision Guide provides examples of sound-symbol correspondences on each spread under the 'Key Sounds' heading.
   - The full sound-symbol correspondences can also be found in Appendix 1 of the AQA specification (visit the AQA website).

To enhance teaching and learning, the AQA 8652 specification covers three distinct themes. You will be expected to use the prescribed vocabulary and grammar across a range of contexts and assessment tasks.

Answers

Pages 6–7 Review Questions

1. Les jours de la semaine (Days of the week) – mardi **[1]**; mercredi **[1]**; vendredi **[1]**; dimanche **[1]**
Les mois (Months) – janvier **[1]**; avril **[1]**; juillet **[1]**; août **[1]**
Les saisons (Seasons) – le printemps **[1]**; l'hiver **[1]**
2. Answers will vary. Examples:
   a) Je m'appelle (+ name). **[1]**
   b) J'ai (number for age) ans. **[1]**
   c) Je suis né(e) en (+ year). **[1]**
   d) Je ressemble à ma mère. **[1]**
3. Answers will vary. Examples:
   a) J'habite à (place name) **[1]**
   b) Oui, j'ai …. frère(s) / ….sœur(s) / non, je suis fils / fille unique **[1]**
   c) Oui, j'ai un / une (+ animal) / non, je n'ai pas d'animaux **[1]**
   d) la date de mon anniversaire, c'est le (+ date) **[1]**
4. a) 10, 2, 12 **[1]**; b) 4, 40, 14 **[1]**;
   c) 15, 55, 5 **[1]**; d) 30, 13, 3 **[1]**;
   e) 60, 70, 16 **[1]**; f) 24, 80, 90 **[1]**
5. a) trente-deux **[1]**; b) cinquante-trois **[1]**;
   c) quarante-six **[1]**; d) soixante-cinq **[1]**;
   e) soixante-quatorze **[1]**;
   f) quatre-vingt-treize **[1]**;
   g) quatre-vingt-deux **[1]**
6. a) 8.00 --- Il est huit heures. **[1]**
   b) 8.10 --- Il est huit heures dix. **[1]**
   c) 8.15 --- Il est huit heures et quart. **[1]**
   d) 8.25 --- Il est huit heures vingt-cinq. **[1]**
   e) 8.30 --- Il est huit heures et demie. **[1]**
   f) 8.45 --- Il est neuf heures moins le quart. **[1]**
   g) 8.50 --- Il est neuf heures moins dix. **[1]**
7. a) il fait beau --- it's fine **[1]**
   b) il pleut --- it's raining **[1]**
   c) il fait du soleil --- it's sunny **[1]**
   d) il neige --- it's snowing **[1]**
   e) il fait du brouillard --- it's foggy **[1]**

Pages 8–13 Revise Questions

Page 9 Quick Test
1. Any two from: voici, voilà, je te présente
2. ma sœur; mes parents; mon père
3. grande, jolie, jeune, petite, belle, vieille, gentille
4. I get on very well with my uncle. He is quite old, but he is always happy and nice.
5. Je ne m'entends pas très bien avec ma sœur. Elle est très forte et embêtante. On se dispute toujours.

Page 11 Quick Test
1. positif – all the other adjectives are in the feminine form
2. Nous aimons **la même** musique et **les mêmes** sports. – We like the same music and the same sports.
3. on a; on va; on aime; on fait
4. Answers will vary. Examples:
Nous avons les mêmes passe-temps.; On va en ville ensemble.; On aime les mêmes émissions.; On fait du sport ensemble.

Page 13 Quick Test
1. cette dame (f); ce couple (m); ces filles (pl); cet enfant (word beginning with a vowel)
2. a) My brother has been married for three years.
   b) My sister got married last weekend.
3. a) Mes parents sont mariés depuis vingt ans.
   b) Je voudrais rester célibataire.
4. je ne désire pas; tu ne voudrais pas; je n'ai pas l'intention de; tu ne penses pas

Pages 14–15 Practice Questions

1. a) Ma tante est assez **jeune [1]** et très **jolie [1]**, mais un peu **bavarde [1]**.
   b) Mon beau-père est trop **vieux [1]** et assez **paresseux [1]**.
   c) Mes frères sont **petits [1]**, **beaux [1]** et très **amusants [1]**.
   d) Ma sœur est assez **belle [1]** et un peu plus **grande [1]** que moi.
2. Ma **meilleure [1]** copine s'appelle Yasmine. Elle a les yeux **verts [1]** et les **cheveux [1]** bruns et longs. Elle est un peu **moins [1]** grande que moi. Je la connais **depuis [1]** six ans. On **s'entend [1]** très bien et on ne se dispute **jamais [1]**. Nous **faisons [1]** beaucoup de choses ensemble. J'aime **son [1]** attitude positive – Yasmine est toujours **heureuse [1]**.
3. a) Mon meilleur copain et moi allons en ville tous les week-ends. **[1]**
   b) Ma mère est toujours amusante et heureuse. **[1]**
   c) J'ai les yeux bleus et les cheveux courts et noirs. **[1]**
   d) Mon frère est généreux et gentil mais ma sœur est plutôt embêtante. **[1]**
4. a) Nous **sommes** de bons amis. **[1]**
   b) Elles **ont** les cheveux longs. **[1]**
   c) Il **va** en ville. **[1]**
   d) Je **m'entends** bien avec mon frère. **[1]**
   e) Elle n'**est** pas mariée. **[1]**
5. a) N **[1]**; b) P **[1]**; c) P **[1]**; d) P+N **[1]**
6. a) On **fait** beaucoup de choses ensemble. **[1]**
   b) Nous **aimons** la même équipe de foot. **[1]**
   c) **Nous** avons les mêmes intérêts. **[1]**
   d) On **aime** les mêmes émissions de télé. **[1]**
   e) **On** va au cinéma ensemble. **[1]**
   f) On **écoute** de la musique ensemble. **[1]**
7. Read sentences aloud then listen to sentences to check. **[1 mark for each sentence read correctly]**
8. Answers will vary. Examples:
   a) Je m'entends bien avec **mon père [1]** parce qu'**il est toujours amusant [1]**.
   b) Je me dispute souvent avec **mon frère [1]** car **il est souvent embêtant [1]**.
   c) Mon meilleur copain / Ma meilleure copine a les yeux **bleus [1]** et les cheveux **longs [1]**.

   d) Mon meilleur ami / Ma meilleure amie est toujours **sympa [1]**. Il / Elle n'est jamais en **colère [1]**.
   e) Nous avons **les mêmes intérêts [1]**. On aime **les mêmes sports [1]**. On **sort tous les week-ends [1]** ensemble.

Pages 16–21 Revise Questions

Page 17 Quick Test
1. a) traditionnelle, végétarienne, fraîche
   b) locaux, régionaux
2. I don't have anything for breakfast and I never drink alcohol.
3. Ma famille a mangé dans un restaurant célèbre et le repas était parfait.

Page 19 Quick Test
1. often, sometimes, always, early, late
2. le matin, le samedi, le week-end, à midi
3. Normally I go to bed around 10pm during the week.
4. Samedi dernier, je suis allé(e) en ville avec mes amis.

Page 21 Quick Test
1. I have a headache and my eyes hurt.
2. Je ne fais pas assez d'exercice. Je veux faire des promenades plus souvent.

Pages 22–23 Practice Questions

1. a) Nous aimons manger des produits **locaux [1]** parce qu'ils sont plus **frais [1]** et naturels **[1]**.
   b) Ma famille préfère la cuisine **régionale [1]** avec des plats **traditionnels [1]**.
   c) Je prépare des recettes **végétariennes [1]** pour être en **bonne [1]** santé.
   d) On peut réduire ses **mauvaises [1]** habitudes et mener une vie plus **saine [1]**.
2. Read sentences aloud then listen to sentences to check. **[1 mark for each sentence read correctly]**
3. a) Je me lève à sept heures en semaine. **[1]**
   b) Je prends le petit-déjeuner chez moi avant d'aller au collège. **[1]**
   c) Nous aimons faire du sport pendant la récré. **[1]**
   d) Le week-end je me couche beaucoup plus tard. **[1]**
4. a) Nous avons --- mangé dans un restaurant. **[1]**
   b) Je n'ai --- pas bu d'alcool. **[1]**
   c) Il faut --- éviter le fast-food. **[1]**
   d) Je me --- couche de bonne heure. **[1]**
   e) On doit essayer --- de manger équilibré. **[1]**
5. a) I don't like vegetables very much. **[1]**
   b) I don't have anything for breakfast. **[1]**
   c) I don't drink enough water. **[1]**
   d) He doesn't exercise any more. **[1]**
   e) She never eats meat. **[1]**
   f) We only eat fresh produce. **[1]**

Answers

6.
a) Lundi dernier, **je suis [1]** resté(e) chez moi.
b) J'ai **joué [1]** à des jeux vidéo avec mes copains.
c) Nous **avons [1]** mangé en ville.
d) Nous **sommes [1]** allés au cinéma.
e) Ma sœur a **bu [1]** de l'eau minérale.

7. a) P+N **[1]**; b) P **[1]**; c) P **[1]**; d) N **[1]**

8. Answers will vary. Examples:
a) Généralement, je me lève **vers sept heures du matin [1]** et puis **je me lave [1]**.
b) Avant d'aller au collège, je **prends le petit-déjeuner [1]** ou je bois **du thé [1]**.
c) Souvent, le soir, je mange **du poulet avec des frites [1]** et je bois **de l'eau minérale [1]**.
d) Je n'aime pas **trop la viande [1]**; je préfère **manger des fruits et des légumes [1]**.
e) Pour rester en forme, j'essaie de **manger équilibré et de faire assez d'exercice [1]**.
f) J'ai décidé de **me coucher plus tôt en semaine pour avoir plus d'énergie le lendemain matin [1]**.

Pages 24–25 Review Questions

1.
a) Mon frère **s'appelle** Bruno. **[1]**
b) Mes sœurs **sont** plus grandes que moi. **[1]**
c) Je **m'entends** bien avec mon père. **[1]**
d) Nous **avons** les mêmes intérêts. **[1]**
e) On **va** souvent au cinéma. **[1]**
f) Je **suis** pour le mariage. **[1]**
g) Mon meilleur copain **est** toujours sympa. **[1]**
h) Elle **a** les yeux bleus et les cheveux longs. **[1]**

2.
a) blanche **[1]**
b) bonne **[1]**
c) folle **[1]**
d) longue **[1]**
e) nouvelle **[1]**

3. Answers will vary. Examples:
a) affreux, affreuse, affreux, affreuses heureux, heureuse, heureux, heureuses paresseux, paresseuse, paresseux, paresseuses, sérieux, sérieuse, sérieux, sérieuses **[1]**
b) sportif, sportive, sportifs, sportives vif, vive, vifs, vives, positif, positive, positifs, positives, négatif, négative, négatifs, négatives **[1]**
c) dernier, dernière, derniers, dernières premier, première, premiers, premières entier, entière, entiers, entières régulier, régulière, réguliers, régulières **[1]**

4.
a) 2 [1 = *yeux* and *cheveux*, 3 = *sœur* + some final 's' pronounced] **[2 marks: 1 mark for correct pronunciation and 1 mark for explanation]**
b) 3 [1 = final 's', 2 = parents as in English / é not pronounced] **[2 marks: 1 mark for correct pronunciation and 1 mark for explanation]**

c) 2 [1 = *fille* + *famille*, 3 = *cette*] **[2 marks: 1 mark for correct pronunciation and 1 mark for explanation]**
d) 1 [2 = *copain* + *rester*, 3 = *garçon, célibataire*] **[2 marks: 1 mark for correct pronunciation and 1 mark for explanation]**

5.
a) N **[1]** I often go out with my friends. **[1]**
b) P **[1]** My cousin got married in May. **[1]**
c) N **[1]** We're always arguing. **[1]**
d) F **[1]** I hope to find an ideal partner one of these days! **[1]**
e) F **[1]** I intend to have children. **[1]**
f) N **[1]** We have a lot of fun. **[1]**

6. a) **[1]**; d) **[1]**

7. J'aime bien **ses [1]** cheveux longs et **ses [1]** yeux bleus. Mais ce n'est pas **son [1]** apparence qui est importante pour moi. Il est toujours sympa et j'adore **sa [1]** confiance. Il est très sportif et **son [1]** sport préféré est le foot. **Sa [1]** sœur joue souvent avec nous et j'apprécie **ses [1]** compétences.

Pages 26–31 Revise Questions

Page 27 Quick Test
1. l'histoire, l'informatique, les sciences, les maths, la religion
2. Answers will vary. Examples: Je vais au collège en ville; Je suis en seconde; Il y a environ mille élèves.
3. nous arrivons, nous quittons, nous finissons
4. ils commencent, ils finissent, ils durent

Page 29 Quick Test
1. les devoirs, l'examen, la note, le résultat, le travail scolaire
2. on ne peut pas discuter, on ne doit pas parler, il ne faut pas manger
3. nous **apprenons** beaucoup en classe; je **lis** les textes; on **répond** aux questions
4. At school we work hard (in order) to pass (our) exams.

Page 31 Quick Test
1. Next year I would like to start an apprenticeship.
2. à l'avenir; plus tard (dans la vie); dans cinq ans
3. J'ai l'intention de devenir scientifique. Je vais être (je serai) célèbre.
4. il va aller; elle va voyager; il va faire; elle va travailler
5. il ira; elle voyagera; il fera; elle travaillera

Pages 32–33 Practice Questions

1.
a) J'aime bien la géographie (l'histoire) mais je préfère l'histoire (la géographie). **[1]**
I like geography (history) but I prefer history (geography). **[1]**
b) Je suis assez faible en informatique mais j'adore ça! **[1]**
I am not strong in IT but I love it! **[1]**

c) Ma matière préférée, c'est les maths parce que je suis fort en mathématiques! **[1]**
My favourite subject is maths because I am good at maths! **[1]**
d) J'ai choisi l'allemand et l'espagnol car j'adore les langues. **[1]**
I chose German and Spanish because I love languages. **[1]**
e) Je n'aime pas beaucoup la technologie car je la trouve un peu difficile. **[1]**
I don't like technology very much because I find it a bit difficult. **[1]**

2. Read sentences aloud then listen to sentences to check. **[1 mark for each sentence read correctly]**

3.
a) Les cours **commencent [1]** à huit heures et demie.
b) Nous **avons [1] une récré** à onze heures qui **dure [1]** vingt minutes.
c) En classe, nous **apprenons [1]** beaucoup.
d) Je **réponds [1]** aux questions et **j'écris [1]** les réponses.
e) La journée scolaire **finit [1]** à trois heures et quart.

4.
a) My mother is a teacher. **[1]**
b) I intend to continue my studies. **[1]**
c) I dream of having a varied job. **[1]**
d) I would like to become an artist. **[1]**

5.
a) Mon père est facteur. **[1]**
b) Je vais être médecin. **[1]**
c) Ma sœur veut devenir policière. **[1]**
d) J'ai l'intention de travailler à l'étranger. **[1]**

6. a) P **[1]**; b) P+N **[1]**; c) N **[1]**; d) P **[1]**

7.
a) On doit faire les devoirs. **[1]**
b) Il faut écouter en classe. **[1]**
c) Il ne faut pas arriver en retard. **[1]**
d) On ne peut pas manger en classe. **[1]**
Answers will vary. Examples:
e) On doit porter l'uniforme scolaire. **[1]**
f) Il faut suivre les règles. **[1]**
g) On ne peut pas parler. **[1]**

8. Answers will vary. Examples:
a) L'année prochaine, je vais continuer mes études au lycée. **[1]**
b) Je voudrais travailler en équipe **[1]** mais je ne voudrais pas travailler dans une usine. **[1]**
c) Comme métier, j'ai l'intention de devenir chef(fe) (de cuisine). **[1]**
d) Plus tard dans la vie, j'espère travailler dans un restaurant à l'étranger. **[1]**
e) Dans dix ans, je rêve d'être content(e) et célèbre. **[1]**

Pages 34–35 Review Questions

1.
j'ai faim --- I'm hungry **[1]**
j'ai soif --- I'm thirsty **[1]**
j'ai chaud --- I'm hot **[1]**
j'ai froid --- I'm cold **[1]**
j'ai peur --- I'm frightened **[1]**
j'ai quinze ans --- I'm 15 **[1]**

2. Le week-end **dernier [1]**, nous sommes allés en ville pour **fêter [1]** l'anniversaire de ma sœur. Nous **avons [1]** mangé dans un restaurant **indien [1]** où on peut choisir des plats **spéciaux [1]** des différentes régions. Nous sommes **arrivés [1]** de bonne heure et ma mère a **choisi [1]** une table près de la fenêtre. La **nourriture [1]** était délicieuse et nous nous **sommes [1]** très bien amusés!

3. a) **J'ai mangé** équilibré. **[1]**
   b) **Nous avons mangé** beaucoup de fruits. **[1]**
   c) **J'ai choisi** de faire du sport. **[1]**
   d) **Il a bu** assez d'eau. **[1]**
   e) **Je suis allé(e)** à la piscine. **[1]**

4. a) J'ai mal **à la [1]** tête et j'ai mal **à l'**oreille **[1]**!
   b) Je suis allé **à l'**hôpital **[1]** parce que je suis tombé et que j'avais très mal **au [1]** dos et **à la [1]** jambe.
   c) Je reste **à la [1]** maison et je joue **aux [1]** jeux vidéo.
   d) Le vendredi, je vais **à la [1]** piscine mais mon frère joue **au [1]** foot.

5. a) N **[1]**;   b) P **[1]**;   c) F **[1]**;   d) N **[1]**;
   e) P **[1]**

6. a) They eat well (eat fresh vegetables and drink mineral water). **[1]**
   b) By going on walks with Éric's mother. **[1]**
   c) three times a week **[1]**

Pages 36–40 Revise Questions

Page 37 Quick Test
1. avant; maintenant; à l'avenir
2. 'je joue au foot' = I play / am playing football; 'je jouais au foot' = I used to play / was playing football
3. I used to go to (the) youth club.
4. Je faisais de la natation.
5. I would like to try winter sports.

Page 39 Quick Test
1. a) Je l'aime.
   b) Je ne les aime pas.
2. la pire, la meilleure, la plus populaire
3. I love his / her songs because the lyrics are extraordinary.
4. C'est le meilleur chanteur du monde.

Page 41 Quick Test
1. nous préférons, nous pouvons, nous regardons
2. de plus en plus cher(chère)(s); de moins en moins populaire(s)
3. C'est l'histoire d'un garçon qui sauve la planète.

Pages 42–43 Practice Questions

1. a) Mes parents **préfèrent [1]** les films de guerre, mais ma sœur **préfère [1]** la télé-réalité.
   b) Je **préfère [1]** les sports individuels, mais mes copains **préfèrent [1]** les sports d'équipe.
   c) Ma famille **préfère [1]** écouter de la musique moderne.

2. Je m'intéresse --- aux jeux vidéo. **[1]**
   Je préfère --- regarder les émissions de sport. **[1]**
   J'ai toujours --- joué au foot. **[1]**
   Je suis --- allé au festival de musique. **[1]**

3. Read sentences aloud then listen to sentences to check. **[1 mark for each sentence read correctly]**

4. a) F **[1]**;   b) P **[1]**;   c) N **[1]**;   d) P **[1]**;
   e) P **[1]**;   f) N **[1]**;   g) P **[1]**;   h) F **[1]**

5. a) C'est une chanson **que [1]** j'aime beaucoup.
   b) C'est le dernier film **que [1]** j'ai vu.
   c) C'est l'histoire d'une famille **qui [1]** est en danger.
   d) C'est un groupe **qui [1]** est très populaire.
   e) Ce sont les paroles **que [1]** j'aime le plus.
   f) Ce sont des acteurs **qui [1]** sont très célèbres.

6. a) They're the best group in the world. **[1]**
   b) Films are better on the big screen. **[1]**
   c) Doing sport is more fun. **[1]**
   d) Watching TV is less exciting. **[1]**
   e) It was the most popular song of the year. **[1]**
   f) Tickets are becoming more and more expensive. **[1]**

7. b) Les films sont pires sur grand écran. **[1]**
   c) Faire du sport, c'est moins amusant. **[1]**
   d) Regarder la télé, c'est plus passionnant. **[1]**
   e) C'était la chanson la moins populaire de l'année. **[1]**
   f) Les billets deviennent de moins en moins chers. **[1]**

8. Answers will vary. Examples:
   a) Le week-end ou le soir, j'aime sortir avec mes copains et mes copines. **[1]**
   b) Je n'aime pas rester **[1]** à la maison; je préfère aller en ville. **[1]**
   c) Quand j'étais plus jeune, je nageais à la piscine trois fois par semaine. **[1]**
   d) Pour moi, le sport, c'est important et amusant **[1]** et je fais régulièrement de l'exercice. **[1]**
   e) En ce qui concerne la musique, j'adore toutes sortes de chansons et j'aime danser. **[1]**
   f) Mon groupe / chanteur préféré est très bien connu et célèbre partout dans le monde. **[1]**
   g) À la télé, je regarde les émissions de sport et de télé-réalité – je n'aime pas les séries. **[1]**
   h) À l'avenir, je voudrais essayer les sports d'hiver parce qu'ils me semblent excitants. **[1]**

Pages 44–45 Review Questions

1. a) F kind **[1]**;   b) G useful **[1]**;
   c) B funny **[1]**;   d) I easy **[1]**;
   e) C young **[1]**, H modern **[1]**;
   f) D great **[1]**;   g) E boring **[1]**;
   h) A happy **[1]**

2. a) Ma sœur est forte en histoire. **[1]**
   b) Je suis assez faible en sciences. **[1]**
   c) J'ai choisi l'allemand et le sport. **[1]**
   d) J'aime lire et écrire en classe. **[1]**

3. a) I prefer practical subjects like music and drama. **[1]**
   b) At school, I'm in Year 11. **[1]**
   c) You / we must [it is necessary to] follow the rules and work hard. **[1]**
   d) There are five lessons per day and each lesson lasts an hour. **[1]**

4. a) améliorer – to improve **[1]**
   b) corriger – to correct **[1]**
   c) discuter – to discuss **[1]**
   d) parler – to talk **[1]**
   e) penser – to think **[1]**
   f) préparer – to prepare **[1]**
   g) réussir – to succeed in **[1]**
   h) réussir un examen – to pass an exam **[1]**
   i) apprendre – to learn **[1]**
   j) comprendre – to understand **[1]**
   k) dire – to say **[1]**
   l) écrire – to write **[1]**
   m) lire – to read **[1]**
   n) répondre – to reply **[1]**
   o) suivre – to follow **[1]**
   p) traduire – to translate **[1]**

5. a) 2 [1 = mispronunciation of *préfère*; 3 = anglicised pronunciation of *sciences*] **[2 marks: 1 mark for correct pronunciation and 1 mark for explanation]**
   b) 3 [1 = mispronunciation of *cours* and *finissent*; 2 = mispronunciation of time phrases] **[2 marks: 1 mark for correct pronunciation and 1 mark for explanation]**
   c) 2 [1 = mispronunciation of *faut* and *porter*; 3 = anglicised pronunciation of *règles* and *uniforme*] **[2 marks: 1 mark for correct pronunciation and 1 mark for explanation]**
   d) 1 [2 = mispronunciation of *l'intention* and *boulot*; 3 = mispronunciation of *varié* and *intéressant*] **[2 marks: 1 mark for correct pronunciation and 1 mark for explanation]**

6. L'année prochaine, je vais **passer [1]** mes examens et donc je dois **décider [1]** quoi faire. Moi, je n'ai pas l'intention de **quitter [1]** l'école parce que je veux **continuer [1]** mes études et puis **aller [1]** à l'université. Avant d'y aller, je vais **faire [1]** une année sabbatique. Je vais **voyager [1]** en Asie parce que j'adore la culture asiatique.

7. I'm going to go there **[1]**; I want to become **[1]**; I would like to have **[1]**; I dream of earning **[1]**

Pages 46–50 Revise Questions

Page 47 Quick Test
1. Errors: **Dans** le matin on **passons** notre temps **en** préparer la musique pour le concert.

Answers

Le matin, on passe notre temps à préparer la musique pour le concert.
2. ils aiment, ils pensent, ils sont, ils peuvent
3. For those who like history, traditional festivals are important.
4. Selon certains, il n'est pas nécessaire de préserver la culture régionale.

Page 49 Quick Test
1. 'chez moi' + 'chez nous' (or 'chez soi').
2. 'il y a deux ans' = two years ago; 'dans deux ans' = in two years' time
3. J'ai passé la journée avec ma famille. Nous avons mangé beaucoup et (nous) avons donné des cadeaux.
4. Je vais fêter Pâques avec mes amis. Nous allons manger beaucoup d'œufs en chocolat!

Page 51 Quick Test
1. who?, when?, how?, where?, why?
2. d'abord, plus tard, après, puis / ensuite, enfin
3. **Je suis allé(e)** au mariage de mon frère. **On a mangé** et **dansé**. **C'était** formidable!

Pages 52–53 **Practice Questions**

1. a) --- iv) [1]; b) --- v) [1]; c) --- i) [1]; d) --- vi)[1]; e) --- ii) [1]; f) --- iii) [1]
2. a) N [1]; b) F [1]; c) N [1]; d) P [1]; e) P [1]; f) F [1]; g) P [1]
3. Answers will vary. Examples:
   a) **D'habitude**, nous cherchons les œufs en chocolat dans le jardin. [1]
   b) **À l'Aïd**, je vais voir mes cousins. [1]
   c) **À Pâques**, on passe la journée en famille. [1]
   d) **L'an dernier**, nous avons chanté des chansons traditionnelles. [1]
   e) **Il y a deux ans**, nous avons célébré le mariage de ma sœur. [1]
   f) **Le week-end prochain**, nous allons voir notre groupe préféré au concert. [1]
   g) **La semaine dernière**, je suis resté(e) chez moi. [1]
4. Read sentences aloud then listen to sentences to check. **[1 mark for each sentence read correctly]**
5. a) --- iii) [1]; (The) tourists watch the parades and the fireworks. [1]
   b) --- v) [1]; Lots of people eat special dishes. [1]
   c) --- iv) [1]; Everyone likes giving and receiving presents. [1]
   d) --- i) [1]; We spend the day singing traditional songs. [1]
   e) --- ii) [1]; At the end of the evening we dance in the streets. [1]
6. a) Ils dansent dans les rues. [1]
   b) Ils fêtent l'anniversaire de ma mère. [1]
   c) Ils pensent que c'est important. [1]
   d) Ils disent que c'est nécessaire. [1]
   e) Ils peuvent manger toute la journée! [1]
   f) Ils choisissent de célébrer l'événement en famille. [1]

7. Answers will vary. Examples:
   a) Ma fête préférée, c'est **Noël [1]** parce que **nous passons la journée en famille [1]**.
   b) J'aime surtout **donner [1]** et **recevoir des cadeaux et manger un grand repas en famille [1]**.
   c) L'an dernier pour Noël / l'Aïd, nous **avons fait la fête chez ma tante [1]**.
   d) Pour mon anniversaire, je préfère **aller en ville avec mes amis [1]**.
   e) L'année prochaine, je voudrais **aller au concert pour voir mon groupe préféré [1]**.
   f) En ce qui concerne les fêtes traditionnelles, j'adore **les danses et les chansons [1]**.

Pages 54–55 **Review Questions**

1. a) Nous ador**ons** [1]
   b) Elle écout**e** [1]
   c) Ils téléchar**gent** [1]
   d) Nous chant**ons** [1]
   e) Elles s'intéress**ent** à [1]
   f) Quelle sorte de musique aim**es**-tu? [1]
   g) Quelle sorte de films préfér**ez**-vous? [1]
2. a) Il y a deux ans, **j'allais [1]** au club des jeunes.
   b) En ce moment, **je fais [1]** souvent des promenades à la campagne.
   c) Maintenant, **je vais [1]** au centre sportif tous les samedis.
   d) Quand j'étais plus jeune, **je faisais [1]** de la natation trois fois par semaine.
3. a) C [1]; b) C [1]; c) T [1]; d) T [1]; e) T [1]; f) C [1]; g) T [1]
4. a) (The) special effects are better on the big screen. [1]
   b) Seats are becoming more and more expensive. [1]
   c) You can press pause and restart whenever you like. [1]
   d) You don't have to watch all the adverts. [1]
   e) You can chat a bit, if you want to. [1]
   f) Everyone likes buying popcorn and chocolate at the shop! [1]
   g) For me, the important thing is comfort and you can relax where(ever) you want (to). [1]
5. a) Quand j'avais onze ans, j'allais à la piscine trois fois par semaine. [1]
   b) Ils ont eu beaucoup de succès avec leur musique. [1]
   c) Samedi prochain, je vais voir mon groupe préféré en concert à Paris. [1]
   d) J'ai toujours écouté ses chansons même si mes copains ne les aiment pas. [1]
   e) J'aime mieux regarder les matchs de mon équipe de foot préférée à la télé. [1]
6. a) Il **la** préfère. [1]
   b) Nous **le** regardons en ligne. [1]
   c) Elle **les** adore. [1]
   d) Je ne **les** aime pas. [1]

Pages 56–60 **Revise Questions**

Page 57 Quick Test
1. **leurs** maisons; **leurs** amis; **leur** famille
2. le mode de vie; les entretiens; l'équipe; le personnage; le concours
3. He announced that he was separating from his wife.
4. Elle a toujours voulu devenir chanteuse.

Page 59 Quick Test
1. de plus en plus
2. ils vont; ils ont; ils font
3. He posted videos online and became very popular.
4. Je suis les influenceurs de mode sur les réseaux sociaux.

Page 61 Quick Test
1. la liberté, l'égalité, la vérité, la crise, la menace
2. they express; they talk about; they discuss
3. pour aider; pour améliorer; pour soutenir
4. I would like to spend the day with him and take selfies.

Pages 62–63 **Practice Questions**

1. a) Les célébrités deviennent célèbres à cause des médias. [1]
   Celebrities become famous because of the media. [1]
   b) Les influenceurs en ligne sont de plus en plus nombreux. [1]
   There are more and more online influencers. [1]
   c) Elle a été une inspiration pour les handicapés. [1]
   She has been an inspiration for disabled people. [1]
   d) Je voudrais rencontrer ma célébrité préférée et passer une journée avec elle. [1]
   I would like to meet my favourite celebrity and spend a day with them. [1]
2. Read sentences aloud then listen to sentences to check. **[1 mark for each sentence read correctly]**
3. a) pour aider les jeunes [1]
   b) pour exprimer nos opinions [1]
   c) pour améliorer l'environnement [1]
   d) pour discuter du problème [1]
   e) pour finir l'entretien [1]
   f) pour prendre des selfies [1]
4. a) On aime voir **leurs [1]** grandes maisons.
   b) J'apprécie **leurs [1]** compétences.
   c) Nous discutons **leur [1]** vie personnelle.
   d) Ils ont sorti **leur [1]** nouvelle vidéo.
5. a) Ils ont [1] beaucoup d'argent.
   b) Ils sont [1] très populaires.
   c) Ils font [1] de plus en plus de blogs.
   d) Ils vont [1] gagner le concours.
   e) Ils peuvent [1] parler de la diversité.
   f) Ils discutent [1] des différences.
6. a) P [1]; b) P [1]; c) N [1]; d) P+N [1]
7. a) P [1]; b) F [1]; c) N [1]; d) N [1]; e) F [1]; f) P [1]

8. Answers will vary. Examples:
   a) Mon acteur préféré **est très connu dans le monde entier.** [1]
   b) Je l'aime bien parce qu'il **joue des rôles spectaculaires.** [1]
   c) Pour moi, les influenceurs **deviennent de plus en plus nombreux et peuvent être embêtants.** [1]
   d) Je préfère suivre **le mode de vie et la carrière des personnalités en ligne.** [1]
   e) Je pense que les célébrités **ont beaucoup d'argent et peuvent voyager partout dans le monde quand elles le veulent.** [1]
   f) À l'avenir, je voudrais rencontrer **mon héros et passer la journée avec lui.** [1]

Pages 64–65 Review Questions

1. Au mois de juillet, **je suis allé [1]** au mariage de mon frère. **C'était [1]** une grande fête et l'occasion de **voir [1]** tous les membres de la famille. D'abord, **nous sommes allés [1]** à l'église pour le mariage religieux. Ensuite, **il y avait [1]** une grande réception avec un repas spécial. Plus tard, un groupe **a joué [1]** de la musique et **nous avons dansé [1]** jusqu'à minuit! Tout le monde **était [1]** heureux et joyeux. **J'ai trouvé [1]** l'événement vraiment fantastique!

2. a) 2 [1 = mispronunciation of *soir* and *joyeux*; 3 = incorrect liaison + mispronunciation of *spectacle*] **[2 marks: 1 mark for correct pronunciation and 1 mark for explanation]**
   b) 3 [1 = mispronunciation of 'ent' ending (+ 'ils'?); 2 = mispronunciation of 'o' sounds] **[2 marks: 1 mark for correct pronunciation and 1 mark for explanation]**
   c) 2 [1 = mispronunciation of 'ch' sounds; 3 = incorrect liaison + anglicised pronunciation of *traditionnelles*] **[2 marks: 1 mark for correct pronunciation and 1 mark for explanation]**
   d) 1 [2 = mispronunciation of 'è / ê / ai' sounds; 3 = incorrect liaison + mispronunciation of *famille*] **[2 marks: 1 mark for correct pronunciation and 1 mark for explanation]**

3. a) There are 8 listed in the foundation tier vocabulary: faire, fais, faisais, faisait, faisons, fait, faites, font. There are 5 more listed in the higher tier vocabulary: fera, ferai, ferais, ferait, feras. **[1]**
   b) 4: voir, vois, voit, vu (listed as an auxiliary). **[1]**
   c) Answers will vary. Examples:
      1. avoir: eu, a, ai, as, avais, avait, avez, avoir, avons.
      2. être: été, es, est, étais, était, êtes, être, sont, suis. **[1]**

   d) You can see each entry and learn them as items of vocabulary as well as full verbs. It reminds you of the different spellings. **[1]**

4. Je vais célébrer (je célébrerai) **[1]** mes seize ans, avec tous mes copains. Premièrement, **on va manger (mangera) [1]** au restaurant en ville. **Ma mère va préparer (préparera) [1]** un grand gâteau d'anniversaire pour moi. Après ça, **nous allons voir (nous verrons) [1]** notre groupe préféré en concert. **Ce sera [1]** vraiment excellent – quel bon cadeau!

5. a) P **[1]**; b) P **[1]**; c) P+N **[1]**; d) N **[1]**; e) N **[1]**

6. a) In the afternoon of Bastille Day / 14th July, there are processions in the streets. **[1]**
   b) For those who are interested in history, it is important to preserve (keep) traditions. **[1]**
   c) We went back home to eat a special meal. **[1]**
   d) I'm going to spend the Bank Holiday with my family. **[1]**
   e) My sister's wedding was an unforgettable occasion (event). **[1]**

7. Answers will vary.

Pages 66–71 Revise Questions

Page 67 Quick Test
1. a) Normalement, je passe mes vacances **en** France, **à** la campagne.
   b) L'année dernière, nous sommes allés **à** Québec, **au** Canada.
2. a) L'été dernier, nous **sommes restés** chez nous.
   b) Je **vais passer** mes prochaines vacances en Suisse.

Page 69 Quick Test
1. a) Il faisait chaud et il y avait du soleil.
   b) En vacances, j'aime faire des promenades.
   c) Il y a trois ans, j'ai passé deux semaines en France.
   d) Notre logement était très confortable.
   e) Je voudrais visiter le Maroc.

Page 71 Quick Test
1. a) Good Evening, I have a reservation for a room for six nights.
   b) I've lost my key.
   c) (At) what time does the show start this evening, please?
2. a) Bonjour, je voudrais réserver une chambre pour deux personnes pour deux nuits, s'il vous plaît.
   b) Je voudrais améliorer mon français.

Pages 72–73 Practice Questions

1. a) L'année prochaine, je vais passer mes vacances **au [1]** Maroc. (masculine country) Next year I'm going to spend my holidays in Morocco. **[1]**

   b) J'aimerais bien aller en vacances **dans [1]** les Pyrénées (translate as 'in') **en [1]** France. (feminine country) I would really like to go on holiday to the Pyrenees (mountains) in France. **[1]**
   c) Normalement, nous allons en vacances **en [1]** voiture car mon père aime conduire. (use 'en' with means of transport)
      Normally we go on holiday by car because my father likes driving (to drive). **[1]**
   d) Il y a trois ans, nous avons passé les vacances **en [1]** Belgique. (feminine country)
      Three years ago we spent our / the holidays in Belgium. **[1]**

2. a) Tous les ans, **nous passons [1]** nos vacances au bord de la mer en France.
   b) L'année dernière pendant mes vacances **j'allais [1]** à la plage tous les jours.
   c) Il y a deux ans, **j'ai passé [1]** quinze jours au Sénégal avec ma famille.
   d) Je pense que **je vais passer [1]** mes prochaines vacances dans un camping à la campagne.
   e) Quand j'étais petite, **je passais [1]** mes vacances à la montagne chez ma tante qui habite dans les Alpes.

3. Read sentences aloud then listen to sentences to check. **[1 mark for each sentence read correctly]**

4. a) À l'avenir, je voudrais partir en vacances au Maroc. **[1]**
   b) À la plage, on peut nager dans la mer ou se relaxer. **[1]**
   c) Mon activité préférée pendant les vacances, c'est faire du camping. **[1]**
   d) Je voudrais une chambre pour deux personnes avec vue sur la mer. **[1]**

5. a) Je passe mes vacances en Angleterre. **[1]**
   b) Il y a deux ans, nous sommes allés en Belgique. **[1]**
   c) Il faisait (il y avait) du soleil et (il faisait) chaud. **[1]**
   d) Nous avons voyagé en bateau et en voiture. **[1]**
   e) Je voudrais visiter l'île de la Réunion. **[1]**

6. a) I (have) lost my bag at the airport. **[1]**
   b) It snowed every day. **[1]**
   c) I would like to reserve two seats for the show tomorrow evening. **[1]**
   d) We visited Paris in (the) spring. **[1]**

7. Example answers:
   a) Pendant les vacances, j'aime me lever tard et faire des promenades à la campagne avec mes copains. **[1]**
   b) L'année dernière, j'ai passé les vacances au bord de la mer avec ma famille. **[1]**
   c) Nous avons voyagé en train **[1]** et nous avons dormi dans un camping près de la plage. **[1]**
   d) Tous les jours, je nageais dans la mer et faisais du shopping en centre-ville. **[1]**
   e) En ce qui concerne le temps, il faisait assez beau mais il a plu pendant deux ou trois jours. **[1]**

Answers

f) Plus tard dans la vie, je voudrais passer mes vacances dans un pays chaud, comme le Maroc, par exemple. **[1]**

Pages 74–75 Review Questions

1. a) --- vi) **[1]**; b) --- vii) **[1]**; c) --- viii) **[1]**;
   d) --- x) **[1]**; e) --- iii) **[1]**; f) --- iv) **[1]**;
   g) --- ix) **[1]**; h) --- i **[1]**; j) --- v) **[1]**;
   k) --- ii) **[1]**

2. a) Les influenceurs **sont** **[1]** de plus en plus nombreux.
   b) Ils **ont** **[1]** de plus en plus d'influence.
   c) Ils **donnent** **[1]** leur avis sur les produits.
   d) Ils **font** **[1]** des choses amusantes et **mettent** **[1]** des vidéos en ligne.
   e) À l'avenir, ils **vont** **[1]** devenir encore plus populaires.

3. a) Influencers are becoming more and more numerous. (There are more and more influencers). **[1]**
   b) They have more and more influence. **[1]**
   c) They give their opinion on products. **[1]**
   d) They do funny things and put (the) videos online. **[1]**
   e) In the future, they are going to become even more popular. **[1]**

4. a) 2 [1 = mispronunciation of *célébrités* and *beaucoup*; 3 = mispronunciation of single vowels] **[2 marks: 1 mark for correct pronunciation and 1 mark for explanation]**
   b) 3 [1 = mispronunciation of *influenceurs* and *suis*; 2 = mispronunciation of 'aux' sound in *réseaux sociaux*] **[2 marks: 1 mark for correct pronunciation and 1 mark for explanation]**
   c) 2 [1 = mispronunciation of *peuvent* and *inspirer*; 3 mispronunciation of *personnalités* and *génération*] **[2 marks: 1 mark for correct pronunciation and 1 mark for explanation]**
   d) 1 [2 = mispronunciation of *voudrais* and *préférée*; 3 = mispronunciation of all 'r' sounds] **[2 marks: 1 mark for correct pronunciation and 1 mark for explanation]**

5. a)

Talking About The Past	Talking About Now	Talking About The Future
Il a commencé	s'appelle	Je vais le regarder
(il) a participé	est (connu / populaire / gentil)	je voudrais
	Je l'aime / J'aime	
	j'adore	
	il joue	
	J'attends	

[10 marks : 1 mark for each correct verb]
   b) i) It began in 2009. **[1]** He has been in more than 30 films. **[1]**

   ii) He plays the role of a policeman **[1]** in a small village in the mountains **[1]**
   iii) He would like to meet him **[1]** and spend time with him **[1]**.

6. Answers will vary. See question 5 for ideas.

Pages 76–81 Revise Questions

Page 77 Quick Test
1. a) une grève; b) une manifestation;
   c) la pauvreté; d) le chômage
2. a) la nourriture la plus fraîche; the freshest food
   b) les applis les plus locales; the most local apps
   c) le voyage le plus intéressant; the most interesting journey
   d) l'application la plus amusante; the funniest app.
3. Le château est ouvert tous les jours sauf le mardi.

Page 79 Quick Test
1. a) je (t)chatte; b) je télécharge;
   c) j'envoie; d) je reçois
2. J'utilise un ordinateur au collège et mon portable chez moi tous les jours.
3. Recently, we did some research into the influence of social media on teenagers.

Page 81 Quick Test
1. je pense; à mon avis
2. a) Il faut toujours penser à la sécurité.
   b) On ne doit jamais partager ses informations personnelles.
3. You must contact someone quickly in the case of an emergency.

Pages 82–83 Practice Questions

1. a) J'envoie des SMS à tous mes amis. **[1]**
   b) Je télécharge de la musique et des applis. **[1]**
   c) Je prends beaucoup de photos sur mon portable. **[1]**
   d) Je vais sur mes sites préférés chaque jour. **[1]**
   e) Je fais des recherches pour mes devoirs. **[1]**
2. Read sentences aloud then listen to sentences to check. **[1 mark for each sentence read correctly]**
3. a) P **[1]**; b) P **[1]**; c) N **[1]**; d) N **[1]**;
   e) P **[1]**; f) N **[1]**; g) N **[1]**
4. a) J'ai tchatté avec mes copains. **[1]**
   b) Nous avons lu des articles. **[1]**
   c) Ils ont écrit des blogs. **[1]**
   d) Nous avons fait nos devoirs. **[1]**
5. a) --- iii) **[1]**; b) --- v) **[1]**; c) --- i) **[1]**;
   d) --- vi) **[1]**; e) --- ii) **[1]**; f) --- iv) **[1]**
6. a) --- iii) **[1]**; b) --- vi) **[1]**; c) --- ii) **[1]**;
   d) --- v) **[1]**; e) --- i) **[1]**; f) --- iv) **[1]**
7. b) gratuite **[1]**; c) fausse **[1]**;
   d) sûre **[1]**; e) disponible **[1]**;
   f) dangereuse **[1]**
8. Answers will vary. Examples:
   a) J'utilise les ordinateurs et mon portable tous les jours, chez moi et au collège. **[1]**

   b) Je trouve ça vraiment utile **[1]** parce qu'on peut vite trouver l'information qu'on veut. **[1]**
   c) Au collège, on utilise beaucoup la technologie moderne – par exemple on fait des recherches. **[1]**
   d) Le week-end ou le soir, je joue à des jeux vidéo et je télécharge de la musique ou des applis utiles ou amusantes. **[1]**
   e) Mon appli préférée est TikTok car il y a beaucoup de choses amusantes que j'aime regarder. **[1]**
   f) Récemment, j'ai passé beaucoup de temps sur les réseaux sociaux car je suis des influenceurs. **[1]**

Pages 84–85 Review Questions

1. a) --- v) **[1]**; b) --- iv) **[1]**; c) --- i) **[1]**;
   d) --- ii) **[1]**; e) --- iii) **[1]**
2. a) P **[1]**; b) P+N **[1]**; c) N **[1]**;
   d) P **[1]**
3. a) **Normalement,** **[1]** pendant mes vacances, **je dors** **[1]** dans un hôtel.
   b) **L'année dernière,** **[1]** je suis **allé(e)** **[1]** en vacances à la montagne pour me relaxer.
   c) **L'an prochain,** **[1]** je vais passer **[1]** quinze jours chez ma tante à la campagne.
   d) **L'été dernier,** **[1]** je nageais **[1]** dans la mer tous les jours parce qu'il **faisait** **[1]** chaud.
4. a) britannique **[1]**; b) espagnole **[1]**;
   c) allemand **[1]**; d) américain **[1]**;
   e) chinois **[1]**
5. a) 3 [1 = mispronunciation of *brouillard* and *matin*; 2 = mispronunciation of *temps*] **[2 marks: 1 mark for correct pronunciation and 1 mark for explanation]**
   b) 2 [1 = mispronunciation of *Québec* and *Canada*; 3 = mispronunciation of verb + *échange*] **[2 marks: 1 mark for correct pronunciation and 1 mark for explanation]**
   c) 1 [2 = mispronunciation of *printemps* and *mieux*; 3 = anglicised pronunciation of *dehors* and *climat*] **[2 marks: 1 mark for correct pronunciation and 1 mark for explanation]**
   d) 3 [1 = mispronunciation of *est-ce que vous avez* and *s'il vous plaît*; 2 = mispronunciation of *chambre*] **[2 marks: 1 mark for correct pronunciation and 1 mark for explanation]**
6. a) à la campagne – in the countryside **[1]**
   b) **sur** une île – on an island **[1]**
   c) **en** bateau – by boat **[1]**
   d) **dans** les Alpes – in the Alps **[1]**
   e) **au** bord de la mer – at the seaside **[1]**
   f) **en** vacances – on holiday **[1]**

Pages 86–91 Revise Questions

Page 87 Quick Test
1. a) une **petite** maison; b) un **grand** jardin; c) une **jolie** cuisine; d) les murs

blancs;   **e)** les **vieilles** fenêtres
2. (Situated) In front of the (train) station is a new shopping centre.
3. J'habite dans un appartement. Il y a cinq pièces – un salon, une cuisine, une salle de bains et deux chambres.

Page 89 Quick Test
1. Our town is known for its beautiful green (open) spaces where you can play or relax with (your) friends.
2. J'habite dans une grande ville (qui est) située dans le sud-est de l'Angleterre.

Page 91 Quick Test
1. nous devons, nous pouvons, nous savons, nous voulons
2. Scientists say that vehicles and factories are the main causes of global warming.
3. Nous devons (il faut) protéger l'environnement en réduisant la pollution sans détruire nos industries.

Pages 92-93 Practice Questions

1. **a)** --- vi) **[1]**;   **b)** --- iv) **[1]**;
   c) --- v) **[1]**;   **d)** --- i) **[1]**;
   e) --- iii) **[1]**;   **f)** --- ii) **[1]**
2. Read sentences aloud then listen to sentences to check. **[1 mark for each sentence read correctly]**
3. **a)** Chez moi il y a une petite cuisine et un joli salon. **[1]**
   b) Je partage une chambre avec mon frère. **[1]**
   c) On trouve un bon choix de magasins au centre-ville. **[1]**
   d) Le réchauffement de la Terre est un grand problème actuel. **[1]**
4. **a)** Visitez le musée! **[1]**
   b) Allez au stade! **[1]**
   c) Achetez des produits frais! **[1]**
   d) Mangez dans des restaurants célèbres! **[1]**
   e) N'oubliez pas de voir le château! **[1]**
   f) Bénéficiez de l'air frais. **[1]**
5. **a)** --- ii) **[1]**; On the first floor there are three bedrooms. **[1]**
   b) --- iv) **[1]**; My village is in the west of England. **[1]**
   c) --- i) **[1]**; Tourists love the natural places. **[1]**
   d) --- v) **[1]**; The hospital is near my house. **[1]**
   e) --- iii) **[1]**; For young people, there are lots of clubs. **[1]**
6. **a)** Nous pouvons utiliser moins d'énergie. **[1]**
   b) Nous devons réduire les déchets. **[1]**
   c) Nous savons qu'il faut changer les habitudes. **[1]**
   d) Nous voulons aider à améliorer l'environnement. **[1]**

Pages 94–95 Review Questions

1. **a)** --- ii) **[1]**;   **b)** --- iv) **[1]**;
   c) --- i) **[1]**;   **d)** --- iii) **[1]**

---

2. **a)** l'appli la plus populaire **[1]**
   b) les photos les plus intéressantes **[1]**
   c) la plus grande manifestation **[1]**
   d) les sites les plus sûrs **[1]**
   e) la meilleure chose **[1]**
3. **a)** Chaque jour, **j'utilise [1]** mon portable pour beaucoup de choses.
   b) Au collège, **nous faisons [1]** beaucoup de travail sur les ordinateurs.
   c) Récemment, **j'ai lu [1]** un blog au sujet des animaux en danger.
   d) Les jeunes **passent [1]** trop de temps sur les ordinateurs.
   e) Hier, **nous avons reçu [1]** un cadeau gratuit de mon site préféré!
   f) À l'avenir, **je vais passer [1]** moins de temps en ligne!
4. **a)** 3 [1 = mispronunciation of *meilleure*; 2 = mispronunciation of *technologie moderne*] **[2 marks: 1 mark for correct pronunciation and 1 mark for explanation]**
   b) 2 [1 = mispronunciation of *agréable* and *disponibles*; 3 = mispronunciation of verb + *réseaux*] **[2 marks: 1 mark for correct pronunciation and 1 mark for explanation]**
   c) 1 [2 = mispronunciation of *pire* and *recevoir*; 3 = mispronunciation of *menaces* and *en ligne*] **[2 marks: 1 mark for correct pronunciation and 1 mark for explanation]**
   d) 3 [1 = mispronunciation of *gouvernement* and *l'environnement*; 2 = mispronunciation of *nouvelle loi* and / or *demain*] **[2 marks: 1 mark for correct pronunciation and 1 mark for explanation]**
5.

Infinitive	Present tense		Perfect tense	
avoir	j'ai	nous **avons [1]**	j'ai **eu [1]**	nous avons **eu [1]**
recevoir	je **reçois [1]**	nous recevons	j'ai **reçu [1]**	nous **avons [1]** reçu
voir	je **vois [1]**	nous **voyons [1]**	j'ai **vu [1]**	nous **avons vu [1]**
écrire	j'**écris [1]**	nous **écrivons [1]**	j'**ai** écrit **[1]**	nous **avons écrit [1]**
lire	je **lis [1]**	nous **lisons [1]**	j'**ai lu [1]**	nous **avons lu [1]**

Pages 96–103 Revise Questions

Page 97 Quick Test
1. **a)** le;   **b)** la;   **c)** la;   **d)** le
2. **a)** pays;   **b)** lieux;   **c)** problèmes;
   d) bureaux
3. **a)** J'aime le sport.
   b) J'adore les animaux.
   c) Je n'aime pas les fruits.
   d) Je préfère la lecture.

---

4. **a)** liaisons les(z)yeux
   b) les(z)émissions / les(z)animaux
   c) les(z)examens

Page 99 Quick Test
1. **a)** une femme heureuse
   b) une chose importante
2. **a)** un petit parc
   b) une belle ville moderne
3. **a)** également;   **b)** terriblement

Page 101 Quick Test
1. **a)** Je regard**e**;   **b)** Il fini**t**;
   c) Nous entend**ons**;   **d)** Ils travaill**ent**
2. **a)** Je joue.   **b)** Elle attend.
3. **a)** I visit / I am visiting.
   b) We choose / we are choosing.
   c) She changes / she is changing.
4. **a)** Je travaille depuis une heure.
   b) Nous écoutons depuis 5 minutes.

Page 103 Quick Test
1. **a)** She is thirsty.
   b) We are scared.
   c) He is hot.
   d) Are you hungry?
2. **a)** Je veux y aller.
   b) Elle peut sortir.
   c) Il doit prendre.
   d) Nous voulons dormir.
3. Remember that the final consonants are silent.

Pages 104–105 Practice Questions

1.

Indefinite	Definite	Plural indefinite	Plural definite
une semaine	la semaine	des semaines	les semaines
un magasin	le magasin	des magasins	les magasins
un jeu	le jeu	des jeux	les jeux
une idée	l'idée	des idées	les idées
un homme	l'homme	des hommes	les hommes

[15 marks: 1 mark for each correct answer]
2. **a)** la **[1]**;   **b)** le **[1]**;   **c)** le **[1]**;
   d) la **[1]**;   **e)** la **[1]**;   **f)** la **[1]**
3. **a)** du **[1]**, de l' **[1]**;   **b)** du **[1]**, de la **[1]**;
   c) de la **[1]**;   **d)** de la **[1]**;
   e) du **[1]**;   **f)** de la **[1]**
4. **a)** sportive **[1]**;   **b)** difficiles **[1]**;
   c) sérieuses **[1]**;   **d)** beaux **[1]**;
   e) industrielle **[1]**
5. **a)** French is more interesting than maths. **[1]**
   b) This film is the best. **[1]**
   c) I am calmer than my brother. **[1]**
   d) He is the tallest in the family. **[1]**
   e) It is the most visited town in France. **[1]**
6. **b)** localement **[1]**;   **c)** spécialement **[1]**;
   d) normalement **[1]**;   **e)** ouvertement **[1]**;
   f) également **[1]**
7. je fais **[1]**; je mange **[1]**; il finit **[1]**; elle arrive **[1]**; ils aiment **[1]**; elle pense **[1]**

Answers

8. a) J'ai faim. [1]
    b) Elle a froid. [1]
    c) Nous avons chaud. [1]
    d) Il a 15 ans. [1]
    e) Ils / Elles ont soif. [1]

Pages 106–107 Review Questions

1. a) J'**habite** [1] une vieille maison à la campagne.
    b) Je **partage** [1] ma chambre avec ma sœur.
    c) Dans ma chambre, j'**écoute** [1] de la musique.
    d) Je voudrais **habiter** [1] à la campagne.
    e) La bibliothèque se **trouve** [1] près de la gare.
    f) On **peut** [1] faire des promenades dans la forêt.
    g) Mes parents **travaillent** [1] en centre-ville.
2. a) [1]; d) [1]; f) [1]
3. a) 3 [1 = mispronunciation of *quartier*; 2 = mispronunciation of *choix*] **[2 marks: 1 mark for correct pronunciation and 1 mark for explanation]**
    b) 2 [1 = mispronunciation of *château* and *célèbre*; 3 = mispronunciation of *fêtes* and *été*] **[2 marks: 1 mark for correct pronunciation and 1 mark for explanation]**
    c) 3 [1 = mispronunciation of *trop* and *polluent*; 2 = mispronunciation of *industriel* and *utilise*] **[2 marks: 1 mark for correct pronunciation and 1 mark for explanation]**
    d) 1 [2 = mispronunciation of all *en* / *em* / *an* sounds; 3 = mispronunciation of *inconvénients*] **[2 marks: 1 mark for correct pronunciation and 1 mark for explanation]**
4. a) P [1]; b) N [1]; c) F [1]; d) N [1]; e) P [1]
5. Answers will vary. Example: Bonjour Jacques! Moi aussi, j'habite dans une assez grande maison dans une ville mais ma ville se trouve dans l'ouest de l'Angleterre! Chez nous, il y a huit pièces et je dois partager ma chambre avec mon frère. Tu as de la chance d'avoir ta propre chambre maintenant! J'aime notre maison – elle est assez vielle mais très confortable. Nous avons un petit jardin où je me relaxe quand il fait beau. J'adore mon quartier parce qu'il y a un grand stade de foot près de chez moi où je peux regarder mon équipe tous les samedis! Ma région est connue pour ses fêtes de musique en été. Beaucoup de touristes viennent et on peut y voir les groupes et les artistes célèbres. C'est vraiment super! A bientôt, Chris.
6. Answers will vary. Example: Je m'intéresse à l'environnement et j'essaie de faire de petites choses pour aider notre planète – par exemple je recycle le papier et le plastique chez moi et je vais toujours au collège à pied. Cependant, je trouve la situation actuelle inquiétante. Pour moi, il est évident qu'on doit faire plus pour protéger l'environnement en diminuant la pollution. On sait que le monde industriel utilise trop d'énergie qui détruit l'environnement naturel et change le climat. Je suis sûr que les véhicules et les usines sont les causes principales du réchauffement de la Terre. Ce qui m'inquiète le plus, c'est qu'on continue à couper trop d'arbres, sans penser aux animaux en danger. Il faut vite changer nos habitudes pour ne pas perdre quelques espèces qui sont en train de disparaître.

Pages 108–115 Revise Questions

Page 109 Quick Test
1. a) avoir; b) être; c) être; d) avoir
2. a) voulu; b) bu; c) eu; d) dû
3. a) je suis allé(e)
    b) nous avons cru
    c) elle a écrit
    d) il est revenu
4. a) After having read…
    b) After having run…
    c) After having got off / gone down…
    d) After having washed(myself)…

Page 111 Quick Test
1. a) Je voudrais aller au cinéma.
    b) Je voudrais réserver une table.
    c) Je voudrais voir un film.
    d) Je voudrait acheter une voiture.
2. a) serai; b) ira; c) mangerons; d) travailleront

Page 113 Quick Test
1. b) Je **les** veux
    c) Je **le** veux
    d) Je **les** voudrais
2. a) avant d'acheter
    b) avant d'aller
    c) avant de voir
    d) avant de prendre
3. a) on; b) in; c) against; d) in front of

Page 115 Quick Test
1. a) Où?
    b) À quelle heure?
    c) Avec qui?
    d) Quand?
2. a) Tu aimes le chocolat? Est-ce que tu aimes le chocolat?
    b) Voudrais-tu aller au cinéma? Est-ce que tu voudrais aller au cinéma?
3. Answers will vary. Example answers:
    Tu veux / voudrais aller (au restaurant) (ce soir)?
    Veux / voudrais-tu aller (au restaurant) (ce soir)?
    (Quand) / (Où) / (Pourquoi) est-ce que tu veux / voudrais aller (au restaurant) (ce soir)?

Pages 116–117 Practice Questions

1. a) **J'ai regardé** [1] un film.
    b) **J'ai mangé** [1] une glace.
    c) **J'ai choisi** [1] un livre.
    d) **J'ai attendu** [1] ma copine.
2. a) eu [1]; b) pris [1]; c) ri [1]; d) fait [1]
3. a) --- ii) [1]; b) --- iv) [1]; c) --- i) [1]; d) --- iii) [1]
4. a) Je ne suis pas allé au collège. [1]
    b) Nous ne sommes pas venues. [1]
    c) Il n'est pas parti. [1]
    d) Je n'ai pas reçu la carte. [1]
5. a) When I was little [1]
    b) Before, I used to like [1]
    c) Before, I used to think [1]
    d) When I was 10 [1]
    e) Before, I used to live [1]
6. a) je vais aller [1]
    b) je vais acheter [1]
    c) je vais manger [1]
    d) je ne vais pas être [1]
    e) je ne vais pas jouer [1]
    f) je ne vais pas faire [1]
7. a) J'**aimerais** [1] avoir un chien.
    b) Ils vont **aller** [1] au cinéma demain.
    c) Je **vais / voudrais** [1] apprendre l'espagnol.
    d) Nous **allons** [1] passer une semaine chez mon oncle.
    e) Elle **va** [1] écrire un e-mail.
    f) Je **vais / voudrais** [1] rencontrer mon acteur préféré.

Pages 118–119 Review Questions

1. a) des films anglais [1]
    b) des décisions importantes [1]
    c) des produits locaux [1]
    d) des langues étrangères [1]
    e) des journaux internationaux [1]
2. a) une héroïne [1]
    b) une policière [1]
    c) une actrice [1]
    d) une chanteuse [1]
    e) une artiste [1]
3. a) les meilleurs [1]
    b) les pires [1]
    c) le plus beau [1]
    d) la moins chère [1]
    e) les plus longues [1]
4. a) **ma** [1] ville
    b) **mon** [1] collège
    c) **mon** [1] avenir
    d) **ma** [1] maison
    e) **ma** [1] chambre
    f) **ma** [1] santé
5. a) Je fin**is** [1]
    b) Nous habit**ons** [1]
    c) Ils aim**ent** [1]
    d) Vous jou**ez** [1]
    e) J'attend**s** [1]

6.

	avoir (to have)	être (to be)	aller (to go)	faire (to do)
Je (j')	ai	suis	vais	fais
Tu	as	es	vas	fais
Il / Elle / On	a	est	va	fait
Nous	avons	sommes	allons	faisons
Vous	avez	êtes	allez	faites
Ils / Elles	ont	sont	vont	font

[20 marks: 1 mark for each correct answer)

7.

	pouvoir (to be able to)	devoir (to have to)	vouloir (to want)	savoir (to know)
Je	peux	dois	veux	sais
Tu	peux	dois	veux	sais
Il / Elle / On	peut	doit	veut	sait
Nous	pouvons	devons	voulons	savons
Vous	pouvez	devez	voulez	savez
Ils / Elles	peuvent	doivent	veulent	savent

[20 marks: 1 mark for each correct answer)

Pages 120–121 Review Questions

1.

Infinitive	Past participle	Infinitive	Past participle
manger	mangé	écrire	**écrit**
finir	**fini**	pouvoir	**pu**
répondre	**répondu**	recevoir	**reçu**
aller	**allé**	prendre	**pris**
boire	**bu**	voir	**vu**

[9 marks: 1 mark for each correct answer]

2. **a)** j'**ai [1]** acheté
b) elle **a [1]** bu
c) nous **avons [1]** décidé
d) je **suis [1]** allé
e) je **suis [1]** resté
f) nous **sommes [1]** partis

3. **a)** After having seen,… **[1]**
b) After having taken,… **[1]**
c) After having gone,… **[1]**
d) After having gone out,… **[1]**
e) After having eaten,… **[1]**
f) After having met,… **[1]**

4. Answers will vary. Examples:
a) Après avoir vu le film, il a parlé avec ses frères. **[1]**
b) Après avoir pris son petit-déjeuner, il est allé au collège. **[1]**
c) Après être allé au club des jeunes, il a mangé une pizza avec sa sœur. **[1]**
d) Après être sorti, il a joué au foot au parc. **[1]**

e) Après avoir mangé, il a promené son chien. **[1]**
f) Après avoir rencontré ses copains, il a envoyé un message à ses parents. **[1]**

5.

Je vais aller	Je voudrais aller	J'irai*
Je vais manger	Je voudrais manger	**Je mangerai***
Je vais partir	**Je voudrais partir**	**Je partirai***
Je vais choisir	**Je voudrais choisir**	**Je choisirai***
Je vais passer	Je voudrais passer	**Je passerai***
Je vais faire	Je voudrais faire	**Je ferai***

[10 marks: 1 mark for each correct answer. *indicates higher tier answers]

6.

ne…pas	not	**ne…plus***	no longer*
ne… jamais	**never**	ne…ni…ni*	**neither… nor***
ne…rien	**not… anything**	ne…que*	**only***

[6 marks: 1 mark for each correct answer. *indicates higher tier answers]

7. **b)** je **les [1]** veux
c) je **le [1]** voudrais
d) je **les [1]** voudrais
e) je **les [1]** aime
f) je **les [1]** préfère

8. **a)** pour avoir **[1]**
b) pour être **[1]**
c) pour aller **[1]**
d) pour faire **[1]**
e) pour parler **[1]**
f) pour pouvoir **[1]**

9. **a)** who **[1]**; **b)** when **[1]**; **c)** which **[1]**;
d) where **[1]**; **e)** how much / many **[1]**

Pages 122–134 Mix it Up Questions

Speaking

1. Role-play
1. Je joue au foot.
2. J'aime le sport.
3. Je vais en ville (le week-end).
4. Mon chanteur préféré est très célèbre.
5. Quelle sorte de musique aimes-tu?

> Think about a short sentence for each response and remember to have a verb in your sentence. Look carefully for the question mark sign '?' and prepare a question to ask during your preparation time.

2. Role-play
1. Ma célébrité préférée est grande (et belle).
2. Il est joueur de foot professionnel.
3. J'aime 'The Gladiators' (à la télé).

4. Aimes-tu aller au cinéma?
5. Je suis les influenceurs (en ligne).

> During your preparation time, look carefully at each prompt and think of something you know how to say. You may add detail if you wish but don't make it too complicated.

3.–6. Student to practise dictation.
7. Reading Aloud

> For this type of task, read the passage and look at each individual word. Think about how to pronounce each word so that it sounds French when you read it out loud later. Some of the following strategies might help you:
> - underline all the silent letters
> - circle all the nasal sounds (e.g. an / en / on)
> - think about the French pronunciation of cognates (words that look like English words)
> - show where you need to make a liaison between two words.

Answers will vary. You should say as much as you can in response to each question.

Examples:
- Qu'est-ce que tu fais sur Internet? – Je vais sur mes sites préférés tous les jours. Je suis les influenceurs de mode et de sport. Je m'intéresse aussi à l'environnement et par exemple, la semaine dernière j'ai lu un article sur la santé des animaux en danger et demain je vais faire des recherches pour mes devoirs de sciences.
- Parle-moi de ton appli préférée. – Mon appli préférée s'appelle (TikTok). Je l'aime parce-que je peux regarder des vidéos amusantes et les envoyer à tous mes copains. Hier soir, j'ai …… et demain je vais ……
- Quelle est ton opinion de la technologie? – Je pense que la technologie est très importante et je l'utilise tous les jours dans ma vie quotidienne. Pour moi, c'est un outil nécessaire dans le monde moderne et je ne peux pas vivre sans mon portable! Je pense que la meilleure chose, c'est que je peux facilement communiquer avec toute ma famille et tous mes copains. Cependant il faut toujours penser à la sécurité et on doit protéger ses détails personnels pour éviter les problèmes en ligne.
- Quand utilises-tu la technologie au collège? – Je l'utilise presque tous les jours, dans les cours d'informatique, d'histoire et d'anglais en particulier. A mon avis, c'est plus pratique de répondre aux questions écrites sur l'ordinateur, par exemple, et…

Answers

8. Answers will vary. You should say as much as you can in response to each question.

Examples:

- Qu'est-ce que tu fais sur les réseaux sociaux? – Je passe beaucoup de temps sur les réseaux sociaux. Je tchatte souvent avec mes copains et copines et je leur envoie des messages et des photos. Je regarde aussi des clips sur TikTok et parfois je cherche des idées ou des infos. Hier soir j'ai trouvé de bons vêtements pas chers sur un site et je crois que je vais vendre certains de mes vieux vêtements en ligne à l'avenir.

- Quelle est ton opinion des influenceurs? – Ça dépend. Il y a des influenceurs qui sont très intéressants et donnent beaucoup d'idées pratiques et utiles. Mais à mon avis, d'autres influenceurs sont trop 'célèbres' et font des choses bizarres. Personnellement, je préfère les influenceurs qui partagent leurs expériences (comme Z, par exemple). Cependant, je n'aime pas trop les vidéos 'amusantes' avec de petits enfants.

- Parle-moi de ta célébrité préférée. – Ma célébrité préférée s'appelle Y et elle est connue comme actrice dans le monde entier. J'apprécie sa personnalité et ses compétences dans les rôles qu'elle a joués. (Par exemple…) Je voudrais la rencontrer et lui parler de son nouveau film.

- Quels sont les inconvénients d'être célèbre? – Je crois qu'il y a beaucoup d'avantages d'être célèbre, mais de l'autre côté il y a aussi des inconvénients. Ce qui n'est pas si bien, c'est que leur vie n'est jamais secrète et tout le monde sait tout ce qu'ils font dans la vie. Ça peut être difficile et on peut recevoir des menaces en ligne.

9. Photo card
Answers will vary. You should say as much as you can about both photos and you must say at least one thing about each photo.

Example answers:
Sur la première photo, il y a un homme et une femme. Je pense qu'ils sont des amis ou peut-être un couple. Ils sont contents parce qu'ils rient. Ils sont assis – à l'intérieur et ils regardent quelque chose. Ils mangent du pop-corn et je pense qu'ils sont au cinéma et qu'ils regardent un film amusant. La femme a les cheveux longs et elle porte un T-Shirt blanc et rouge. Derrière la femme et l'homme il y a d'autres personnes… Sur la deuxième photo on voit un groupe de filles qui jouent au foot. Il y a quatre filles sur la photo et elles sont sur un terrain de foot. Elles sont en train de courir. Elles portent des vêtements de sport – deux filles jouent pour l'équipe en rouge et noir et les deux autres filles portent des vêtements verts et jaunes. Je pense que l'équipe en rouge va gagner le match car la fille en avant a le ballon…

Now answer these questions related to the theme of Popular Culture.
Answers will vary. You should say as much as you can in response to each question.

Example answers:

- Qu'est-ce que tu aimes faire le week-end? – Quand j'étais plus jeune, j'aimais faire du sport et je jouais au foot tous les week-ends mais maintenant je préfère aller en ville avec mes copains et copines. Nous faisons beaucoup de choses différentes en ville – par exemple samedi dernier nous sommes allés au cinéma pour voir un film d'action et le week-end prochain nous avons l'intention d'acheter des cadeaux pour Elise parce qu'elle va fêter ses seize ans dans deux semaines. Souvent le dimanche je reste à la maison où je fais mes devoirs avant de sortir avec ma famille.

- Quelle est ton opinion sur le sport? – J'aime bien le sport et je joue au foot au collège tous les mardis. Je suis membre d'un club de foot et j'ai beaucoup de camarades dans mon équipe. Je pense que le sport est bien pour la santé et je me sens bien dans ma peau quand je fais de l'exercice. J'adore aussi regarder le sport à la télé – toutes sortes de sports mais surtout le Tour de France. Je voudrais aller en France pour le regarder plus tard dans la vie.

- Parle-moi d'une visite récente au cinéma. – La dernière fois que je suis allé au cinéma, c'était pour fêter l'anniversaire de mon frère. Après être arrivés, nous avons décidé de voir un film de guerre parce que mon frère aime les effets spéciaux et l'action. Mon père a acheté les billets et mon frère et moi, nous avons choisi des places. Nous nous sommes très bien amusés et le film était superbe. C'était vraiment bien et je voudrais le voir encore.

- Décris-moi ta fête préférée. – Ma fête préférée est Noël, parce que tout le monde est content et heureux et on s'amuse bien. J'adore donner et recevoir les cadeaux mais de l'autre côté je mange trop, ce qui n'est pas si bon pour la santé. L'année dernière, nous avons passé Noël chez ma tante et elle a fait un repas extraordinaire pour toute la famille. C'était vraiment délicieux! À l'avenir, je voudrais voyager à l'étranger et fêter Noël dans un pays froid où il y aurait beaucoup de neige. C'est mon rêve!

- Que penses-tu des fêtes traditionnelles? – Personnellement, je n'aime pas beaucoup les fêtes traditionnelles. Pour ceux qui s'intéressent à l'histoire, par exemple, il est important de préserver la culture régionale, mais moi, je préfère les jours fériés comme le 14 juillet avec les feux d'artifices et les spectacles ou bien les fêtes plus modernes où on souligne l'importance de la vie moderne et la diversité de notre société actuelle. Il y a plus de bruit, de couleurs et de joie, à mon avis.

- Qu'est-ce que tu veux faire pour célébrer ton prochain anniversaire? – Pour mes seize ans, je voudrais faire la fête avec tous mes amis. Mon anniversaire est au mois de juin, alors j'espère qu'il fera du beau temps et qu'on pourra le célébrer dans mon jardin avec de la musique. Je voudrais danser jusqu'à minuit. J'aimerais aller en ville pour voir mon groupe préféré en concert mais je ne sais pas si ce serait possible.

- Qui est ton chanteur ou ta chanteuse préféré(e)? Pourquoi? – La chanteuse que j'aime le plus s'appelle K. Je l'adore parce qu'elle est si originale. Je télécharge ses chansons et j'écoute sa musique sur mon portable tous les jours. Elle est très sympa et gentille. Les paroles de ses chansons sont extraordinaires et elle discute des problèmes d'identité et de l'égalité. Elle est une inspiration pour les jeunes, à mon avis.

- Quels sont les avantages de la célébrité? / Est-ce qu'il y a des avantages à être célèbre? – Il y a beaucoup d'avantages d'être célèbre, selon moi. Par exemple, on est très riche et on peut voyager partout dans le monde. On peut acheter tout ce qu'on veut et je voudrais bien mener la vie d'une célébrité.

In the general conversation, your teacher (as the examiner) will ask you a range of open questions to allow you to talk about yourself and your experiences, preferences, opinions etc. There will not be a set number of questions – the conversation will progress naturally depending on your answers.

10. Photo card

Answers will vary. You should say as much as you can about both photos and you must say at least one thing about each photo. Now answer these questions related to the theme of People and Lifestyle:

- Parle-moi de ton collège. – Mon collège s'appelle D Academy et il est assez grand car il y a environ mille élèves. Les bâtiments au collège ne sont pas si modernes mais j'aime bien y aller parce que les profs sont travailleurs et gentils et la plupart des élèves sont aimables aussi. Nous avons un terrain de sport et beaucoup de place pour se relaxer pendant les récrés.
- Quelle est ta matière préférée à l'école? Pourquoi? – Ma matière préférée, c'est le théâtre, parce que je suis très créatif(ve) et j'aime aussi chanter et danser. Je suis assez fort(e) en langues aussi et j'ai choisi de continuer mes études de français et d'espagnol car à mon avis les langues sont utiles. Cependant je pense que le théâtre est plus amusant et moins difficile que les langues!
- Qu'est-ce que tu aimes faire à midi? – À midi je mange quelque chose et puis je parle avec mes copains et copines. Le mardi je vais au club de musique où on s'amuse toujours bien! La semaine dernière, par exemple, nous avons appris la nouvelle chanson de mon groupe préféré – c'était génial!
- Quelle est ton opinion sur l'uniforme scolaire? – Je n'aime pas trop mon uniforme mais de l'autre côté c'est assez pratique. Tout le monde doit le porter et donc nous portons tous les mêmes vêtements mais ce n'est pas mon choix idéal!
- Qu'est-ce que tu veux faire l'année prochaine (après le collège)? En ce moment je suis en seconde et nous préparons les examens. C'est assez dur et je ne sais pas encore si je vais continuer avec mes études l'année prochaine ou si je vais commencer un apprentissage.
- Décris-moi ton métier idéal. – Comme j'ai dit, j'adore le théâtre et mon rêve est de devenir acteur (actrice) célèbre – ça serait mon métier idéal mais je sais que ce n'est pas facile de trouver un emploi comme ça. Alors, je voudrais aussi utiliser les langues et peut-être travailler à l'étranger. Au moins, je veux trouver un emploi intéressant et varié.

- Parle-moi de tes amis / copains. – J'ai beaucoup de camarades de classe mais mon meilleur ami s'appelle Zack. Il est souvent amusant et il n'est jamais en colère. Il est plus intelligent que moi mais je suis le plus sportif. Nous aimons la même musique et les mêmes jeux vidéo. On s'entend bien et on fait beaucoup de choses ensemble. Par exemple, samedi dernier nous sommes allés au stade pour voir le match de foot de notre équipe préférée.
- Que penses-tu du mariage? Quels sont les avantages d'être marié(e)? – Je n'ai pas d'opinion fixe sur le mariage. En ce moment j'ai l'intention de rester célibataire. Plus tard dans la vie j'espère trouver un partenaire idéal mais je ne sais pas si on va se marier. On dit qu'il y a des avantages d'être marié – par exemple c'est mieux pour les enfants et on a plus de sécurité.

The general conversation questions will try to find out whether you can use past, present and future tenses correctly. Make sure you know all your tenses really well. Also, try to show that you can use other parts of the verb (not just 'je') such as 'on' or 'nous' or by talking about your friends or family as well as yourself.

Reading

1.
- **a)** P+N **[1]**
- **b)** N **[1]**
- **c)** N **[1]**
- **d)** P+N **[1]**
- **e)** P **[1]**
- **f)** N **[1]**
- **g)** B **[1]**

In this type of question, look carefully at each part of each sentence to find all the opinions given by a person. You need to decide whether the opinion is positive or negative. If you find both sorts of opinion, write P+N. Question g) is an example of an 'inference' question. There will be several of these on the Reading paper. You have to work out the meaning of an unknown word by looking at the words around it and finding 'clues'. In this example, Marine talks about a 'pâtisserie' as being 'petite' (small - so unlikely to be a supermarket) and as being somewhere where you can 'acheter' (buy) 'de très bons gâteaux' (really good cakes).

2.
- **a) i)** N **[1]**
  - **ii)** P **[1]**
  - **iii)** P **[1]**
  - **iv)** F **[1]**

For this type of question, look carefully at the verb. This should help you to decide whether it is in the past tense (e.g. 'j'ai essayé), in the present tense (e.g. j'essaie) or in the (near) future tense (e.g. nous allons prendre). There may also be some useful time-phrase indicators – such as 'avant' and 'à l'avenir' in this passage.

2.
- **b) i)** at home **[1]** and at school **[1]**
  - **ii)** (they are going to) spend them closer to home **[1]** and (they will) take the train **[1]**
  - **iii)** by turning off her electrical appliances **[1]** when she's not using them **[1]**

When answering questions in English, make sure that you give enough detail, especially if the answer is worth two marks.

3.
- **a)** C **[1]**
- **b)** A **[1]**
- **c)** D **[1]**

For this type of question, you need to 'match up' words from a headline to decide which topic is being talked about. For example, you will not see the actual word for 'technology', but 'les portables' (mobile phones) should give you the clue.

4.
- **a)** I am in Year 11 **[1]** at school **[1]**.
- **b)** My favourite subject is IT **[1]** because it is useful **[1]**.
- **c)** Next year I'm going to do **[1]** an apprenticeship **[1]**.
- **d)** I get on well with my sister **[1]**. We never argue **[1]**.
- **e)** Last night (yesterday evening) we watched **[1]** a sports programme together in my (bed)room **[1]**.

When you translate into English, stick as closely as possible to the original, but make the English sound natural.

5.
- **a)** Ambre **[1]**
- **b)** Naël **[1]**
- **c)** Naël **[1]**
- **d)** Ambre **[1]**
- **e)** Elio **[1]**

In this type of exercise, you need to read each item carefully and look out for 'distractors'. For example, the word for a team (une équipe) appears twice, but in Ambre's account, it says they like sport but don't play for a team. Look for negatives – both in the question and in the accounts.

Answers

Writing

1. Example answer:

   Il y a quatre personnes.
   Ils mangent.
   Je vois une table.
   Voici un homme.
   Nous sommes au café.

   > This is like the first task on the Foundation Tier writing paper. You can use the same structure to start all of your sentences if you like, or a variety as in the example here. Your sentences don't need to be very long, but they must include a verb.

2. Example answer:

   Le week-end je joue au foot avec mes copains. C'est super.
   J'adore le sport. Nous avons un terrain de sport et un stade.
   Il y a un cinéma en ville. Je regarde les films d'action.
   Je fais du shopping dans le grand centre commercial.
   Mon collège est grand et assez moderne. Les profs sont sympas.

   > For this task, you need to write about 50 words in French. Your sentences can be fairly short, but you must write something about each of the bullet points you are given. If you miss one out, you will lose marks however good your other answers are.

3. a) Mon frère **a** les yeux bleus. **[1]**
   b) J'habite dans une **petite** maison. **[1]**
   c) Le week-end **nous** allons à la piscine. **[1]**
   d) Il y a un **nouveau** restaurant en ville. **[1]**
   e) Le collège **finit** à trois heures. **[1]**

   > In this kind of task, you need to choose the correct word from a choice of three. You will need to use your knowledge of French grammar to select the correct word. In these examples, you are assessed on verbs, personal pronouns and adjectives. Look for 'clues' in the sentence to help you – for example in b) you are given the word 'une' which tells you that 'house' (maison) is feminine. You therefore need to choose the feminine form of the adjective – petite.

4. a) J'ai une sœur. **[2]**
   b) Il pleut beaucoup en hiver. **[2]**
   c) Mon collège est grand et moderne. **[2]**
   d) À mon avis, la piscine est très agréable. **[2]**
   e) Hier je suis allé en ville en autobus. **[2]**

   > At Foundation Tier, you will need to translate 5 sentences into French. Try to make your spelling accurate – if the word is spelt incorrectly, it might not gain the mark. Think carefully about the verb ending and make sure your adjectives agree with the noun they are describing. There will probably be one sentence that uses a past (or future) verb – look out for it!

5. a) Je dois aider à la maison tous les jours. **[2]**
   b) L'année prochaine nous visiterons la France. **[2]**
   c) Il est interdit d'utiliser ton portable en classe. **[2]**
   d) Je ne sais pas ce que je ferai comme métier à l'avenir. **[2]**
   e) J'ai décidé de manger moins de fast-food pour être en forme (en bonne santé). **[2]**

   > At Higher Tier, you also need to translate 5 sentences into French, but they will be longer or more complex. Past and future tenses will be assessed as well as other structures such as modal verbs and constructions with an infinitive (e.g. j'aime visiter). Verbs followed by 'à' or 'de' may also be assessed – look carefully at each sentence and translate precisely and accurately. Don't leave out any words – particularly those 'little' words that you might overlook!

6. Example answer:

   Ma meilleure copine s'appelle Farida. Elle est assez grande avec les cheveux courts et noirs. Nous avons les mêmes passe-temps et nous nous entendons très bien. On ne se dispute jamais! Samedi dernier, je suis allée en ville avec mes amis. D'abord nous avons fait du shopping et après nous avons mangé dans un petit café. J'ai choisi un gâteau et un thé. C'était super! Le week-end prochain, je vais sortir avec ma famille. S'il fait beau, nous allons visiter la côte. J'espère qu'on peut faire une promenade sur la plage!

   > You must write something about each bullet point. Write approximately 90 words in French.

7. Example answer:

   Au collège j'aime bien le sport et la technologie mais ma matière préférée, c'est le théâtre parce que je préfère les matières pratiques et je suis assez fort en théâtre. Hier à l'école j'ai eu un long cours de maths – ce n'était pas si mauvais! Le prof est toujours sympa et nous avons fait des exercices sur l'ordinateur. À midi j'ai rencontré mes copains et nous sommes allés au club de musique. L'année prochaine j'ai l'intention de continuer mes études. Je voudrais aller au lycée et peut-être à l'université, mais mon rêve, c'est de devenir acteur célèbre.

   > There will always be one bullet point asking about a past event and one bullet point asking about the future. This is your chance to show that you can use the perfect (and imperfect) tense(s) for past events / description and the near future tense or a structure like 'je voudrais' or 'j'espère' + infinitive to write about the future.

8. Example answer:

   Ma fête préférée, c'est l'Aïd, parce que tout le monde est content et on s'amuse bien. J'adore donner et recevoir les cadeaux mais nous mangeons trop car mes parents préparent toujours un grand repas spécial! L'été dernier je suis allé(e) au mariage de ma cousine. Après le mariage religieux, nous avons fait la fête dans un grand château. On a dansé et chanté jusqu'au matin! C'était excellent! Je veux célébrer mes seize ans avec mes amis. Nous allons sortir en ville pour voir notre groupe préféré en concert.

   > Try to include a variety of structures, for example a modal verb such as 'je veux' or conjunctions such as 'parce que'. Use adjectives to give more detail and ensure the adjective agrees with the noun it is describing. In the same way, try to use different vocabulary, rather than repeating the same word several times.

9. Example answer:

   Voyager et passer du temps dans une région différente de chez vous peut être une expérience positive pour tout le monde. Les vacances sont bien pour se relaxer ou pour découvrir les sites historiques ou touristiques. Quand on voyage, on a la chance de rencontrer les gens et de se faire de nouveaux amis. Il faut penser aussi à l'environnement. Il vaut mieux prendre le train que l'avion, par exemple, et on ne doit pas détruire les lieux naturels avec les déchets. L'été dernier, j'ai passé des vacances dans le sud-ouest de l'Angleterre avec ma famille. Nous avons fait du camping et c'était vraiment génial. Le camping se trouvait très près de la mer et près de petits magasins où j'allais acheter du pain tous les matins. On a profité du beau temps et nous avons visité un vieux château célèbre. J'ai trouvé la région formidable et j'aimerais y retourner un jour.

You must write something about each bullet point and write about 150 words in French. For one of the bullet points, you will need to write about 'other people' and use the 3rd person – either singular or plural.

10. Example answer:

Être en bonne santé et mener une vie saine est essentiel pour tout le monde si on veut éviter les problèmes ou les maladies. On doit manger équilibré et faire régulièrement de l'exercice parce que c'est mieux pour le corps et pour l'esprit. Pour se sentir bien dans sa peau il vaut la peine de garder la forme et de faire du sport ou une promenade – et en plus, on s'amuse bien en même temps! J'ai toujours essayé de penser à la santé. Par exemple je bois assez d'eau tous les jours et je n'ai jamais mangé trop de fast-food. Cependant, j'ai quelques mauvaises habitudes que je voudrais changer pour améliorer mon style de vie. Je me coucherai plus tôt et je dormirai plus de neuf heures par nuit car je veux être moins fatigué le matin. Je passerai moins de temps devant mon écran avant d'aller au lit et je continuerai à ne pas fumer ou vapoter!

For this type of task, use a range of tenses and structures to 'show what you know'. Try to write longer sentences with some complex language such as comparatives, negatives, pronouns and conjunctions. Use a variety of 'topic-specific' vocabulary but try to stick to the suggested word limit. If you write too much, you could make more mistakes and you want your work to be accurate as well as interesting.

Index

Collins

AQA GCSE 9-1
French

Workbook

Karine Harrington and Stuart Glover

Preparing for the GCSE Exam

Revision That Really Works

Experts have found that there are two techniques that help you to retain and recall information and consistently produce better results in exams compared to other revision techniques.

It really isn't rocket science either – you simply need to:

- **test yourself** on each topic as many times as possible
- **leave a gap** between the test sessions.

Three Essential Revision Tips

1. **Use Your Time Wisely**

   - Allow yourself plenty of time.
   - Try to start revising six months before your exams – it's more effective and less stressful.
   - Don't waste time re-reading the same information over and over again – it's not effective!

2. **Make a Plan**

   - Identify all the topics you need to revise (this Complete Revision & Practice book will help you).
   - Plan at least five sessions for each topic.
   - One hour should be ample time to test yourself on the key ideas for a topic.
   - Spread out the practice sessions for each topic – the optimum time to leave between each session is about one month but, if this isn't possible, just make the gaps as big as realistically possible.

3. **Test Yourself**

   - Methods for testing yourself include: quizzes, practice questions, flashcards, past papers, explaining a topic to someone else, etc.
   - This Complete Revision and Practice book provides seven practice opportunities per topic.
   - Don't worry if you get an answer wrong – provided you check what the correct answer is, you are more likely to get the same or similar questions right in future!

Visit **collins.co.uk/collinsGCSErevision** for more information about the benefits of these revision techniques, and for further guidance on how to plan ahead and make them work for you.

QR Codes

A QR code in this Workbook section links to one or both of the following:
- a video working through the solution to one of the questions on that topic, indicated by the ▶ icon
- audio content to be used with a question, indicated by the ◆ icon.

Contents

Visit our website to download the audio material for the Listening Paper on pages 180–191 of this workbook.

1 These French teenagers are talking about their families. Who says what?

Aimée: Je n'ai pas de frères et sœurs.

Paulin: Je m'entends bien avec ma demi-sœur et mon beau-père.

Farida: J'ai une petite sœur qui a deux ans de moins que moi.

Xavier: Mon frère et ma sœur ont trois ans de plus que moi. Ils ont le même âge.

Amel: Mon frère et moi, nous ne nous disputons jamais. On s'entend très bien.

a) Who is talking about their step-family? _____

b) Who gets on well with their brother? _____

c) Who is older than their sibling? _____

d) Who is an only child? _____

e) Who is younger than their sister? _____ [5 marks]

2 Translate the sentences in question **1** into English.

Aimée: _____

Paulin: _____

Farida: _____

Xavier: _____

Amel: _____

[10 marks]

3 Practise saying the sentences in question **1** aloud. First, underline all the silent letters and circle the nasal sounds (e.g. **an** / **on** / **en**...). Then, practise the sounds [oi], [u] and [j] on their own. Finally, make sure you make the liaison (linking) where the letters have been underlined.

a) Je n'ai pas de frères et sœurs.

b) Je m'entends bien avec ma demi-sœur et mon beau-père.

c) J'ai une petite sœur qui a deu<u>x a</u>ns de moins que moi.

d) Mon frère et ma sœur ont troi<u>s a</u>ns de plus que moi. <u>Ils o</u>nt le même âge.

e) Mon frère et moi, nous ne nous disputons jamais. On s'entend très bien. [5 marks]

4 Complete the following sentences with the correct form of the adjectives.

a) Ma sœur est (embêtant) _____ car elle est très (bavard) _____

b) Mes (petit) _____ frères sont assez (drôle) _____

c) Ma mère est très (actif) _____ et assez (généreux) _____

d) Je pense que mon beau-père est (amusant) _____ et (gentil) _____

e) Ma demi-sœur est très (gentil) _____ et assez (intelligent) _____

[10 marks]

5 Fill in the gaps with the words in the box.

ans	cheveux	qualités	amie	yeux
attitude	bien	bon	taille	copine	moi
mêmes	ami	copain	choses	

a) Mon meilleur _____ s'appelle Marcel et il a quinze _____. On a

les _____ passe-temps.

b) Mon _____ Suriane et moi, on s'entend très _____. Elle a

toujours une _____ positive.

c) J'apprécie vraiment les _____ de mon _____ Victor. C'est un

_____ ami.

d) Le week-end, ma _____ et _____, on fait beaucoup de

_____ ensemble.

e) Mon ami Sylvain a les _____ marron et les _____ courts. Il est

de _____ moyenne.

[15 marks]

6 Translate the sentences into French.

a) My friend Oscar is taller than me.

b) My best friend is 15 years old.

c) My best friend has long hair and she is very kind.

d) I get on well with my friend because we have the same hobbies.

e) I don't get on well with Lena because we don't like the same things. [5 marks]

Healthy Living and Lifestyle

1 Read the prompts and write down sentences to say what the prompts suggest.

a) Say you like French cuisine. ....

b) Say you are a vegetarian. ....

c) Say you drink a lot of water. ....

d) Say what you ate last night. ....

e) Say the type of food you like. ....

[5 marks]

2 Look at the shopping lists, then write **T** for true or **F** for false for the statements below.

Gabriel	Karima	Lucas
légumes verts	pain	vin blanc
vin rouge	gâteau au chocolat	eau
poisson frais	fromage local	fruits frais
frites	fruits	glace à la vanille
poulet	boisson sans alcool	

a) Karima wants to buy alcohol. ....

b) Gabriel wants any kind of wine. ....

c) Lucas doesn't want frozen fruit. ....

d) Gabriel wants frozen fish. ....

e) Karima wants a particular type of cheese. ....

f) Lucas needs vanilla ice cream. ....

[6 marks]

3 Read the text below. Write **P** for food Loïc ate in the past, **N** for food he eats now and **F** for food he wants to eat more of in the future.

Salut, moi c'est Loïc! Maintenant, je mange beaucoup de fruits frais et de légumes verts et je bois beaucoup plus d'eau. Je trouve que c'est mieux pour la santé. Avant, j'aimais manger beaucoup de glaces ou de gâteaux. Le gâteau au chocolat était mon dessert préféré. J'aime faire des gâteaux aux fruits mais c'est seulement pour des occasions spéciales. Je voudrais manger plus de produits locaux et régionaux, comme du fromage, des fruits, de la viande et des légumes.

a) fresh fruit ....

d) chocolate cake ....

b) local cheese ....

e) regional food ....

c) ice cream ....

f) fruit cakes ....

[6 marks]

4 Look at the words below and say them aloud. Pay attention to the sounds / letters that have been underlined. Some letters will be silent.

a) le c<u>œu</u>r   c) la p<u>eau</u>   e) le <u>s</u>a<u>ng</u>   g) le cor<u>ps</u>   i) le pie<u>d</u>

b) la <u>s</u>a<u>n</u>té   d) le do<u>s</u>   f) le taba<u>c</u>   h) l'orei<u>lle</u>   j) la <u>j</u>a<u>m</u>be

[10 marks]

5 Match the beginnings and endings to form sentences. Then translate the sentences into English.

a) J'ai mal au   i)   jambe.

b) Elle a mal à   ii) la tête.

c) Il a mal à l'   iii) dos.

d) Je me suis cassé la   iv) à la main.

e) Je me suis coupé   v)   oreille.

a) ....

b) ....

c) ....

d) ....

e) ....

[10 marks]

6 Read the following sentences. What are they?

A   Il faut éviter de boire de l'alcool et de fumer!

B   Hier, je me suis fait mal au dos.

C   Demain, j'ai rendez-vous chez mon médecin.

D   Je ne mange ni viande ni poisson.

E   Je vais me coucher tôt tous les soirs.

a) A healthy routine   ....

b) An appointment   ....

c) A health advice   ....

d) An injury   ....

e) A type of diet   ....

[5 marks]

Education and Work

1 Make a list of 10 school subjects. Write them in French and English. Make sure you write **le**, **la** or **les** in front of the subjects in French.

	French	English		French	English
1			6		
2			7		
3			8		
4			9		
5			10		

[10 marks]

2 Read the sentences and write **P** if the opinion is positive, **N** if the opinion is negative and **P+N** if the opinion is positive and negative.

a) Ma matière préférée, c'est le français, car je trouve cette matière géniale et très utile.

b) Je suis assez faible en sciences car je trouve cette matière assez difficile.

c) J'aime bien le sport mais de temps en temps, c'est assez dur car je ne suis pas très sportive.

d) Mon meilleur ami est très fort en espagnol. Il est le meilleur de notre classe!

e) Ma sœur est très forte en français mais assez faible en physique.

[5 marks]

3 Read the sentences. Who says what?

Axelle: Ma matière préférée est l'histoire mais je n'aime pas les maths. Je trouve les cours de maths très longs et ennuyeux. Je ne comprends rien aux exercices. On a beaucoup de devoirs mais je pense qu'ils sont importants.

Karim: Les bâtiments de mon collège sont assez modernes et nous avons une nouvelle bibliothèque. J'aime bien mon collège car les profs sont sympas. En plus, on n'a pas beaucoup de travail à la maison!

Tessa: Les devoirs sont difficiles et je pense que mes professeurs ne sont pas gentils. Ils sont trop stricts et ils nous donnent beaucoup de devoirs à faire.

a) Who has a negative opinion of their teachers?

b) Who has a positive opinion of their school?

c) Who finds some lessons boring?

d) Who doesn't like homework?

[4 marks]

4 Practise saying the sentences in question **3** aloud. First practise the following words on their own.

a) l'histoire   c) longs   e) importants   g) la bibliothèque   i) gentils

b) les maths   d) ennuyeux   f) mon collège   h) beaucoup   j) trop

[9 marks]

5 Make five sentences using the vocabulary below. Then, translate your sentences into English.

Plus tard,	je voudrais	continuer mes études.
L'année prochaine,	je rêve de	faire un apprentissage.
À l'avenir,	je vais	voyager.
Dans deux ans,	je veux	faire un stage.
Dans 10 ans,	j'ai l'intention de	prendre une année sabbatique.
Après mes examens,	j'espère	aller à l'université.
Un jour,		devenir [....]
Bientôt,		être bénévole.
		travailler comme [...]
		trouver un travail.
		me marier.

[10 marks]

6 Read the text and answer the questions in English.

Je m'appelle Alina. J'ai toujours aimé étudier et j'ai bien aimé mes années au collège. Je suis actuellement en seconde et je trouve que le lycée est un peu plus difficile. Avant, mes matières préférées étaient l'anglais et le français, mais maintenant je préfère les sciences et la géographie. En effet, plus tard, j'aimerais voyager et travailler à l'étranger. Je voudrais faire des études pour apprendre plus sur l'environnement et peut-être travailler pour une entreprise qui protège l'environnement.

a) What does Alina think of her time in secondary school?

b) What year is she in now?

c) What subjects does she like now? Give **two** details.

d) Where would she like to work later?

e) What type of studies would she like to do?

[6 marks]

Free-time Activities

1 These French teenagers are talking about their hobbies. Who says what?

Arthur: Avant, j'allais à la piscine tous les jours mais maintenant je fais du vélo.

Pauline: Je suis très active et je suis membre du club des jeunes de ma ville. On fait beaucoup de choses avec notre club!

Farid: Je fais beaucoup de compétitions de natation.

Léna: Je ne suis pas sportive. Je préfère regarder le sport à la télé!

Hector: Moi, je préfère les sports d'équipe. C'est mieux que de jouer seul!

a) Who does a lot with other young people? ....

b) Who swims? ....

c) Who does not do any sport? ....

d) Who likes being with other people when playing a sport? ....

e) Who likes cycling? ....

[5 marks]

2 Practise saying the following cognates aloud. Make sure that they sound French, not English!

a) le foot   c) le centre sportif   e) le parc   g) la participation   i) le succès

b) l'exercice   d) le club   f) dangereux   h) populaire   j) les sports individuels

[10 marks]

3 Read the sentences and write **P** if the sentence is in the past, **N** if the sentence is in the present (now) or **F** if the sentence is in the future.

a) Tous les week-ends, je fais beaucoup d'activités avec mon club. ....

b) Hier, j'ai participé à une compétition de tennis. ....

c) Je voudrais essayer un sport extrême. ....

d) Avant, j'aimais faire du vélo. ....

e) Quand j'étais petite, je jouais au foot. .... [5 marks]

4 Read the sentences and write **P** if the sentence is positive, **N** if it is negative or **P+N** if it is positive and negative.

a) Les paroles de la chanson sont très intéressantes.

b) Je n'aime pas le rythme de cette chanson.

c) Le concert a eu beaucoup de succès.

d) Le festival de musique est très populaire.

e) Chanter ne m'intéresse pas du tout.

[5 marks]

5 Translate the following sentences into French.

a) Yesterday, I watched a concert.

b) Last weekend, I downloaded a song.

c) I liked the festival.

d) I played with my group last Monday.

e) I listened to music this morning before school.

[5 marks]

6 Translate the following words into English.

a) une émission

b) une série

c) l'écran

d) la télé-réalité

e) l'histoire

f) en ligne

g) célèbre

h) nouveau / nouvelle

[8 marks]

7 Fill in the gaps to complete the text with some of the words from question **6**.

Ma _____ préférée est l' _____ d'un groupe d'ados.

Je la regarde tous les jours _____

L'actrice principale est américaine et elle est très _____ Elle chante aussi.

C'est comme de _____ car dans chaque épisode on suit les
ados dans leur vie de tous les jours.

[5 marks]

Customs, Festivals and Celebrations

1 Match the French to the English.

a) **passer du temps**

b) **fêter**

c) **recevoir**

d) **l'anniversaire**

e) **la naissance**

f) **le mariage**

g) **le jour férié**

h) **la fête des Mères**

i) Mother's Day

ii) birthday

iii) bank holiday

iv) to spend time

v) wedding

vi) to celebrate

vii) birth

viii) to receive

[8 marks]

2 Read the following sentences. What are they?

A **J'aimerais passer mon anniversaire avec mes amis.**

B **Ma famille a toujours fêté les anniversaires avec un gâteau au chocolat!**

C **Vous êtes invités à notre mariage!**

D **L'année prochaine, on va fêter les 50 ans de ma mère.**

E **Il y aura de la musique française.**

F **La cérémonie va être à l'église de mon village.**

a) an invite

b) a music festival

c) a birthday wish

d) a religious event

e) a future family event

f) a family tradition

[6 marks]

3 Read the text below. Write **P** for what Alice did in the past, **N** for events that she does now and **F** for what she will do in the future.

Tous les ans, je passe mon anniversaire avec ma famille. Normalement, on mange à la maison, on joue à des jeux, on chante et on danse. L'année dernière, c'était différent. J'ai célébré mes 14 ans au restaurant. Mon oncle et ma tante qui habitent en Italie sont venus. J'étais très contente. Pour mes 15 ans, l'année prochaine, je pense fêter mon anniversaire avec mes amis aussi. J'aimerais manger mon gâteau sur la plage.

a) Birthday with family

b) Birthday with friends

c) Playing games for her birthday

d) Eating at the restaurant

e) Celebrating her 14th birthday

f) Eating cake on the beach

[6 marks]

4 Read the sentences and write **P** if the sentence is positive, **N** if it is negative or **P+N** if it is positive and negative.

a) **Je trouve les repas de famille très ennuyeux.**

b) **Le spectacle de musique était vraiment formidable mais un peu long.**

c) **Je n'aime pas fêter mon anniversaire avec ma famille.**

d) **Au défilé, il y avait trop de monde et trop de bruit. J'ai été très déçu.**

e) **À mon avis, les traditions sont très importantes.**

[5 marks]

5 Read the following sentences aloud, paying attention to the underlined sounds / letters.

a) **J'aim<u>e</u> être avec ma fam<u>ille</u>.**

b) **Je re<u>ç</u>oi<u>s</u> beaucou<u>p</u> de cadeau<u>x</u>.**

c) **Le festiv<u>al</u> étai<u>t</u> vraim<u>ent</u> <u>int</u>éress<u>ant</u>.**

d) **Nou<u>s</u> <u>a</u>im<u>ons</u> fêter le<u>s</u> <u>a</u>nniversaire<u>s</u> au restau<u>r</u>ant.**

e) **Je p<u>en</u>se <u>qu</u>e le<u>s</u> fête<u>s</u> tradi<u>ti</u>onnelle<u>s</u> <u>s</u>ont trè<u>s</u> <u>im</u>port<u>an</u>tes.**

[5 marks]

6 Look at the sentences in question **5** and find…

a) Two words that have a silent final consonant.

b) Two words that contain the same sound.

c) Two words that have a silent final [s].

d) Two words that contain a silent [e].

e) One example of a 'liaison'.

[9 marks]

Celebrity Culture

1 Make a list of 10 words linked to the topic of the internet.

....

....

....

....

....

[10 marks]

2 Fill in the gaps with vowels to complete the words. Then translate the words into English.

a) la m...d...　　..

b) la s...nt...　　..

c) la d...v...rs...t...　　..

d) l'...nfl... ... nc...　　..

e) la l...b...rt...　　..

f) les h...nd...c...p...s　　..

g) l'...g...l...t...　　..

h) la d...ff...r...nc...　　..

[16 marks]

3 Match the beginnings to the endings to form sentences.

a) Les réseaux sociaux

b) Je suis beaucoup

c) J'ai décidé de

d) J'aime lire les blogs de

e) Beaucoup de célébrités

i) d'influenceurs de mode.

ii) mes influenceuses préférées.

iii) sont importants pour les ados.

iv) parlent de problèmes de société.

v) commencer un blog.

[5 marks]

4 Translate the sentences from question **3** into English.

a) ....

b) ....

c) ....

d) ....

e) ....

[5 marks]

▶ **5** Read what each teenager says about the internet. Who says what?

Marion	Maximilien	Rania	Fariq
Je passe beaucoup de temps sur les réseaux sociaux. Je sais que je dois réduire le temps que je passe devant un écran mais c'est difficile car les réseaux sociaux sont importants pour les ados. De plus en plus d'ados ne peuvent pas vivre sans les réseaux sociaux!	Les influenceurs peuvent avoir une bonne influence sur nous car certains influenceurs font des choses formidables pour notre société, comme parler des problèmes de notre société.	Les réseaux sociaux peuvent être un bon moyen de parler de certains problèmes comme les différences, la discrimination, l'égalité et le racisme. Il est possible de poster des messages pour défendre nos idées. Certains blogs sont excellents pour cette cause.	Internet a beaucoup d'avantages mais je pense qu'il y a aussi beaucoup de dangers. Il est facile de dire qu'avec Internet on peut changer le monde mais malheureusement Internet peut causer des problèmes très graves.

a) The internet can be good and bad. ....

b) Some influencers can have a positive influence on us. ....

c) They should spend less time on the Internet. ....

d) Social networks can be useful. ....

e) Teenagers rely too much on social networks. .... [5 marks]

6 Read the texts in question **5** again and find the French for the following phrases.

a) I spend a lot of time ....

b) I know that… ....

c) to live without ....

d) great things for our society ....

e) a good way to talk ....

f) It is possible to… ....

g) to defend our ideas ....

h) a lot of advantages ....

i) it is easy to ....

j) can cause problems ....

[10 marks]

7 Look at Marion's text in question **5** and read it aloud. Before you read it aloud, try to annotate it to help you pronounce the words. For example, cross out the letters you won't say and underline the nasal sounds (**en / an / in / on**…). [3 marks]

Travel and Tourism

1 Make a list of places of interest you can visit whilst on holiday. Write six places in French and their English translation.

....

....

....

....

....

....

[12 marks]

2 Match the countries to the people.

A England	**C** Morocco
B Belgium	**D** Switzerland

Lydie: L'année dernière, je suis allée en Suisse avec ma famille ....

Marcel: Un jour, je voudrais aller en Belgique. ....

Erika: Nous avons passé une semaine au Maroc et c'était génial. ....

Mohammed: Avant, je passais mes vacances en Angleterre. ....

[4 marks]

3 These people are complaining about their last holidays. What are they complaining about and why? Complete the table below.

A Le restaurant était fermé le soir.

B La nourriture était froide.

C Notre chambre était trop petite et très sale.

D L'eau de la piscine était trop chaude et il y avait trop de monde.

E La nuit, il y avait trop de bruit sur la plage de l'hôtel.

	What?	Why?
A		
B		
C		
D		
E		

[10 marks]

4 Problems on holiday. What are these comment headlines describing? Match the headlines with the issue.

A **Nous avons attendu trois heures à l'aéroport!**

B **Ils ont cassé la fenêtre et ils ont volé notre argent.**

C **Trop de monde, trop petit, trop de bruit et très sale!**

D **Nos sacs ne sont pas arrivés! Nous avons dû acheter de nouveaux vêtements!**

E **Trop de déchets sur la plage et dans la mer.**

a) A robbery _____

b) Lost bags _____

c) Pollution _____

d) Bad hotel _____

e) A delay _____

[5 marks]

5 Read the sentences and write **P** if the sentence is in the past, **N** if it is in the present (now) or **F** if it is in the future.

a) **Un jour, je voudrais passer mes vacances à la Réunion.** _____

b) **Quand j'étais petite, j'allais souvent en vacances chez ma grand-mère à la campagne.** _____

c) **Normalement, nous allons en vacances dans un pays où on parle espagnol.** _____

d) **Cet été, on va rester chez nous car notre famille vient nous voir.** _____

e) **L'hiver prochain, nous allons aller à la montagne pour faire du ski.** _____

[5 marks]

6 Read the following sentences aloud.

a) **L'hôtel est situé près de la plage.**

b) **Il y a quarante chambres avec vue sur la mer.**

c) **Le restaurant a un grand choix de nourriture de différents pays.**

d) **La piscine est ouverte tous les jours de neuf heures à vingt heures.**

e) **L'été, les animaux ne sont pas acceptés dans notre hôtel.** [5 marks]

7 Read the text again in question **6** and complete the sentences, according to the meaning of the text.

a) The _____ is not far from the hotel.

b) The hotel has _____ rooms.

c) The food is very _____

d) The swimming pool is open _____ from _____ to _____

e) Pets are _____ in _____ [8 marks]

Media and Technology

1 These people are talking about how they use technology. Who says what?

Roselyne: Je passe deux ou trois heures par jour sur Internet pour faire mes devoirs.

Émeric: Moi, j'aime bien les réseaux sociaux pour rester en contact avec ma famille.

Marceline: Internet est vraiment formidable pour regarder des films et jouer à des jeux.

Youssef: Je suis mes célébrités préférées sur les réseaux sociaux.

Claire: Pour moi, Internet, c'est principalement pour acheter des choses. Je n'aime pas aller dans les magasins alors je fais mon shopping en ligne!

Who uses technology to…

a) stay in touch with people? ....

b) follow people? ....

c) buy things? ....

d) do some work? ....

e) watch something and play games? .... [5 marks]

2 Unjumble the sentences.

a) **vidéos / télécharge / je / beaucoup de**

b) **toujours / portable / suis / je / mon / sur**

c) **des / les / passe / heures / sociaux / sur / réseaux / je**

d) **des / partage / photos / je / avec / amis / mes**

e) **influenceurs / la / vie / des / suis / je** [5 marks]

3 Say the following words aloud, focussing on the underlined letters.

a) l'éc<u>ran</u>   d) <u>In</u>ternet

b) mon port<u>able</u>   e) les infl<u>ue</u>nceurs

c) <u>un o</u>rdinateur   f) j'<u>u</u>tilise [6 marks]

4 Read the sentences and write **P** if the sentence is positive or **N** if it is negative.

a) **À mon avis, Internet est formidable. On peut tout faire et tout trouver! Je ne voudrais pas vivre sans Internet!** ....

b) **Les réseaux sociaux posent des problèmes et ils sont un danger.** ....

c) **Les applis sont très utiles. Il y a des applis pour tout! Moi, j'ai beaucoup d'applis sur mon portable.** ....

d) **Internet est un outil nécessaire dans le monde moderne.** ....

e) **Je télécharge de la musique sur mon portable. C'est rapide et gratuit!**

[5 marks]

5 Match the beginnings and endings to form sentences. Then translate the sentences into English.

a) Hier, j'ai

b) Le week-end dernier,

c) Hier soir, j'ai téléchargé

d) Récemment, j'ai écrit

e) J'ai regardé

i) des chansons.

ii) un blog sur mon sport préféré.

iii) partagé des photos.

iv) j'ai fait des courses en ligne.

v) une émission.

a) _____

b) _____

c) _____

d) _____

e) _____

[10 marks]

6 Fill in the gaps with a word from the box.

| parle | lis | devoirs | suivre | temps |
| messages | courses | peut |

a) J'envoie tous les jours des _____

b) Je _____ avec mes copains et ma famille.

c) Je fais des _____ en ligne.

d) Je _____ mes messages.

e) Je fais des recherches pour mes _____

f) On _____ communiquer facilement.

g) Beaucoup d'ados passent trop de _____ sur leur portable.

h) On peut _____ beaucoup de personnes comme des influenceurs ou des célébrités.

[8 marks]

7 Answer the following sentences with your own opinions.

a) Qu'est-ce que tu penses d'Internet?

_____

b) Qu'est-ce que tu fais sur les réseaux sociaux?

_____

c) Quelle est ton appli préférée et pourquoi?

_____

d) Qu'est-ce que tu as fait récemment sur Internet?

_____

[4 marks]

The Environment and Where People Live

1 Write the French for the following words.

building	a)	garden	f)
house	b)	kitchen	g)
flat	c)	window	h)
room	d)	door	i)
office	e)	bed	j)

[10 marks]

2 Translate the following sentences into English.

a) J'habite en ville.

_____

b) Je voudrais vivre à la campagne.

_____

c) Il y a un centre commercial et une piscine.

_____

d) Il n'y a pas assez de magasins.

_____

e) Mon village est très calme.

_____

[5 marks]

3 Read the sentences in question **2** aloud.   [5 marks]

4 Read what people say about where they live.

Kylian: Où j'habite, il y a des problèmes dans le centre-ville. Le week-end, il y a vraiment trop de gens dans les rues!

Mélinda: Dans mon quartier, il y a trop de bruit. Les restaurants sont ouverts jusqu'à minuit! C'est tard!

Georges: Je voudrais vivre à la campagne dans une grande ferme, loin du bruit, loin des gens. Je préfère le calme!

Caroline: Les transports sont fréquents, on a un grand choix de magasins et de restaurants et les parcs sont propres. C'est formidable!

a) Who is happy about the facilities where they live?   _____

b) Who would like to live somewhere quieter?   _____

c) Who says that sometimes the streets are too busy?   _____

d) Who says it is too noisy where they live?   _____

e) Who says restaurants are open late?   _____

[5 marks]

5 Say the following words aloud, paying attention to the underlined letters.

a) L'environnem<u>ent</u>

b) Les déche<u>ts</u>

c) Une catastro<u>ph</u>e

d) La situa<u>tion</u>

e) Le <u>pr</u>oblème

f) Le m<u>on</u>de

g) Le d<u>an</u>ger

h) La c<u>au</u>se

[8 marks]

6 Read the sentences and write **P** if the sentence is positive or **N** if it is negative.

a) On jette trop de déchets à la mer. ....

b) On utilise trop d'énergie. ....

c) Je recycle tous les jours. ....

d) Notre monde est en danger. ....

e) La situation actuelle est triste. .... [5 marks]

7 Translate the following sentences into French.

a) I have to recycle more and pollute less.

....

b) It is important to use public transport.

....

c) We must not throw rubbish on the ground.

....

d) We must not destroy our environment.

....

e) We have to change!

....

[5 marks]

Grammar 1

Gender, Plurals and Definite, Indefinite and Partitive Articles

1 Write **un** or **une** for each word.

a) .... maison

b) .... médecin

c) .... fille

d) .... père

e) .... camping

f) .... jour

g) .... famille

h) .... chien

i) .... heure

j) .... année   [10 marks]

2 Write the words in question **1** in the plural form, starting with **des**.

a) ....

b) ....

c) ....

d) ....

e) ....

f) ....

g) ....

h) ....

i) ....

j) ....   [10 marks]

3 Fill in the gaps with **le**, **la**, **l'** or **les**.

a) .... Canada

b) .... beau-père

c) .... copain

d) .... copines

e) .... hiver

f) .... enfants

g) .... parents

h) .... légumes

i) .... Angleterre

j) .... France   [10 marks]

4 Write these words in the plural form.

a) un bateau   des ....

b) un bras   des ....

c) un chapeau   des ....

d) un cheval   des ....

e) un repas   des ....

f) un journal   des ....

g) une table   des ....

h) un taux   des ....

i) un château   des ....

j) un animal   des ....

[10 marks]

5 Fill in the gaps with an appropriate article.

J'habite dans .... grande ville dans .... nord de .... Angleterre avec .... parents,

.... petite sœur et .... deux frères. Nous avons aussi .... petit chien qui s'appelle Léo

et .... poissons. Nous habitons dans .... grand appartement dans .... centre-ville, près

de .... hôpital et .... magasins.

[12 marks]

Adjectives and Adverbs

6 Write the following adjectives in the feminine form.

a) Mon frère est grand.   Ma sœur est _____.

b) Mon sac est gris.   Ma table est _____.

c) Mon vélo est rouge.   Ma voiture est _____.

d) Mon frère est sympa.   Ma sœur est _____.

e) Mon chapeau est cher.   Ma robe est _____.

f) Mon père est petit.   Ma mère est _____.

g) Mon cousin est brun.   Ma cousine est _____.

h) Mon manteau est blanc.   Ma robe est _____.

i) Mon beau-père est actif.   Ma belle-mère est _____.

j) Mon appartement est beau.   Ma maison est _____.   [10 marks]

7 Fill in the appropriate comparatives.

a) Je suis _____ grande _____ ma sœur. (taller than)

b) Ma sœur est _____ gentille _____ moi. (as nice as)

c) Mon frère court _____ vite _____ moi. (faster)

d) Le français est _____ intéressant _____ l'espagnol. (more interesting than)

e) La Belgique est _____ belle _____ la Suisse. (more beautiful than)   [10 marks]

8 Fill in the gaps with an adjective from the box below with the correct endings.

végétarien	petit	paresseux	grand	le meilleur
	plus âgé	sportif	noir	

Salut! Je m'appelle Lisa et j'ai deux _____ (little) **sœurs. Maria est très** _____ (tall)

et elle a les cheveux _____ (black). **Nous sommes très** _____ (sporty) **mais parfois**

un peu _____ (lazy). **Nous sommes toutes les trois** _____ (vegetarian). **J'ai aussi un**

demi-frère qui est _____ (older than) **nous. Maria est la** _____ (tallest) **et Sophia est**

la _____ (smallest). **Je suis** _____ (the best).   [10 marks]

9 Transform the following adjectives into adverbs. Add **-ment,** meaning 'ly' as in 'quick**ly**'. An example has been done for you.

Example: **calme** = <u>calme</u>ment (calmly)

	Adjectives	French Adverbs	English Adverbs
a)	possible		possibly
b)	simple		simply
c)	juste		rightly
d)	libre		freely
e)	faible		weakly

[5 marks]

Grammar 1

The Present Tense

1 Use the endings in the box below to complete the verbs in the present tense.

e	ent	s	s	e	t	ons	s	ez	ent	ez	issons

		parler	finir	attendre
Je	parl_____	fini_____	attends
Tu	parles	fini_____	attend_____
Il / Elle / On	parl_____	fini_____	attend_____
Nous	parl_____	fin_____	attendons
Vous	parlez	finiss_____	attend_____
Ils / Elles	parl_____	finissent	attend_____

[12 marks]

2 Match up the beginnings and endings to complete the sentences.

a) Tu   i) détestent les chiens.

b) Je   ii) finit tous les jours son travail à 17h00.

c) Ma mère   iii) aimes les animaux?

d) Mes parents   iv) finis l'école à 15h30.

e) Nous   v) habitons en ville.   [5 marks]

3 Circle the correct form of the verbs in each sentence.

a) Je manges / manger / mange beaucoup de légumes.

b) Elle regarder / regarde / regardent tous les soirs la télé.

c) Nous passons / passez / passe nos vacances à la montagne.

d) Le collège finir / finit / finis à 15h30.

e) Nous nous entendez / entendons / entendent bien.   [5 marks]

▶ 4 Fill in the gaps with the correct endings of the verbs in brackets.

Normalement, nous pass _____ (passer) nos vacances en France, au bord de la mer.

Parfois, s'il pleut, on rest _____ (rester) à la maison de vacances. Ma mère et ma sœur

ador _____ (adorer) passer les vacances en France car elles parl _____

(parler) français.

[4 marks]

5 Translate the following sentences into French.

a) I am working (**travailler**).   Je _____

b) She is looking for (**chercher**).   Elle _____

c) We use (**utiliser**).   Nous _____

d) He prepares (**préparer**).   Il _____

[4 marks]

Common Irregular Verbs and Anchor Verbs

6 Use the words in the box to translate the phrases below into French.

je	tu	il	elle	nous	vous	ils
elles		suis	sommes	est	sont	ai
	a	as	avons	ont		

a) she has _____

b) we are _____

c) she is _____

d) they (all girls) have _____

e) I am _____

f) we have _____

g) they (boys and girls) are _____

h) he has _____

i) I have _____

j) you (informal) have _____ [10 marks]

7 Complete the sentences with the correct form of **avoir**.

a) I am 14 and my sister is 16.   **J'** _____ **quatorze ans et ma sœur** _____ **seize ans.**

b) My friend is the same age as me.   **Mon copain** _____ **le même âge que moi.**

c) Are you thirsty?   **Tu** _____ **soif?**

d) I am very hungry.   **J'** _____ **très faim.**

e) Are you hot or cold?   **Tu** _____ **chaud ou tu** _____ **froid?**   [7 marks]

8 Say each sentence in question **7** aloud.   [5 marks]

9 Translate into English.

a) **Je fais** _____

b) **Elle fait** _____

c) **Nous allons** _____

d) **Ils vont** _____

e) **Je vais** _____   [5 marks]

10 Make five sentences using the verbs in the box below. Then translate the sentences into English. An example has been done for you.

Example: **Je peux acheter**   I can buy

je peux	elle veut	je veux	je dois	il doit
aller	aider	arrêter	acheter	

_____

_____

_____

_____

_____

[10 marks]

Grammar 2

Perfect and Imperfect Tenses

1 Circle the verbs in the perfect tense.

je vais	je fais	je suis allé	nous avons rencontré	nous allons
je mange	elle a mangé	j'ai préparé	il doit	il a acheté

[5 marks]

2 Match the beginnings and endings. Then translate into English.

a) J'ai   i) a regardé.   ....

b) Tu   ii) passé.   ....

c) Elle   iii) avez choisi.   ....

d) Nous avons   iv) as essayé.   ....

e) Vous   v) décidé.   ....

f) Ils   vi) ont participé.   ....

[12 marks]

3 Fill in the gaps with the correct past participles from the box below.

lu	bu	vu	fait	pris	reçu

a) J'ai ....   I took

b) Elle a ....   She did

c) Nous avons ....   We saw

d) Il a ....   He drank

e) J'ai ....   I received   [5 marks]

4 Fill in the gaps with a verb in the imperfect tense from the box below. Then translate the sentences into English.

faisait	étais	avais	regardais	était	jouais

a) Quand j'................ petite, je .... beaucoup la télé.

....

b) Quand j'................ 10 ans, je .... au tennis.

....

c) Avant, mon frère .... moins timide.

....

d) Avant, ma sœur .... de la gymnastique.

....

[10 marks]

Future and Conditional Tenses and Negatives

5 Translate the sentences into French using the verbs in the box below.

je vais	elle va	nous allons	je voudrais		elle voudrait
aller	réserver	passer	travailler	être	avoir

a) I am going to go _____

b) I would like to spend _____

c) She would like to be _____

d) She is going to have _____

e) I would like to book _____

f) We are going to work _____

g) She would like to go _____

h) I am going to be _____ [8 marks]

6 Choose the correct form of the verbs to complete the sentences.

a) **Demain, je vais aller / je suis allé / je vais allé au cinéma.**

b) **La semaine prochaine, je voudrais rester / je rester / je suis resté chez moi.**

c) **Un jour, je vais avoir / j'ai / je vas avoir un chien.**

d) **Ce soir, je vais regarde / je voudrais regardé / je voudrais regarder un film.**

e) **Dimanche prochain, je voudrait voir / je vais vu / je vais voir mes copains.**

[5 marks]

7 Continue the sentences with your own ideas.

a) **Ce soir, je vais** _____

b) **Demain, je voudrais** _____

c) **Le week-end prochain, nous allons** _____

d) **Lundi prochain, je vais** _____

e) **Un jour, je voudrais** _____

[5 marks]

8 Match the French to the English.

a) **ne…pas**   i) nothing

b) **ne…rien**   ii) nobody

c) **ne…personne**   iii) not

d) **ne…jamais**   iv) never   [4 marks]

Grammar 2

Pronouns and Prepositions

1 Rewrite the sentences, changing the underlined words into pronouns from the box below.

il	ils	elles	nous	elle

a) Je pense que <u>ma sœur</u> est gentille.

b) <u>Mon collège</u> est très grand.

c) <u>Mes parents</u> travaillent dans la police.

d) <u>Mes copines</u> sont en vacances.

e) <u>Ma mère et moi</u> aimons faire du vélo.

[5 marks]

2 Choose the correct pronoun to match the English translation.

a) Je ne **la / les** regarde jamais.   I never watch them.

b) Je ne **l' / les** aime pas.   I don't like it.

c) Je voudrais **la / les** prendre.   I would like to take it.

d) Je ne **la / le** connais pas.   I don't know her.

e) Il faut **les / la** respecter.   We must respect them.

[5 marks]

3 Write the English for the following prepositions.

a) devant _____   d) pour _____

b) entre _____   e) après _____

c) dans _____   f) avant _____

[6 marks]

4 Choose the correct preposition for each sentence.

a) J'habite **dans / à / en** France.

b) Mon collège est **sans / dans / entre** le parc et la gare.

c) **Contre / Après / Derrière** les vacances, je vais aller **pour / à / par** l'université.

d) **En / Pour / Dans** mon anniversaire, je veux aller au restaurant.

[5 marks]

Asking Questions

5 Fill in the table with the English translations.

qui		pourquoi	
que		combien (de)	
quoi		comment	
où		quel / quelle / quels / quelles	
quand		lequel / laquelle / lesquels / lesquelles	

[10 marks]

6 Translate the following sentences into English.

a) **Qu'est-ce que tu aimes?**

b) **Où est-ce que tu voudrais aller?**

c) **Qui est-ce que tu voudrais rencontrer?**

d) **Comment est-ce que tu aimes passer ton week-end?**

e) **Pourquoi est-ce que tu aimes...?**

[5 marks]

7 Look at the table below. Make up six questions using a word from each column. You may need to complete the questions by adding something after the last verb. Write the English translation as well. An example has been done for you.

Example: **Où est-ce que tu vas aller [demain]...?** Where are you going to go tomorrow?

Où	est-ce que	tu	vas	aller...
Quand			voudrais	regarder...
Pourquoi			aimes	faire...
Qu'			préfères	passer...

[12 marks]

Collins

GCSE
French

H

Higher Tier Paper 1 Listening

Time allowed: 45 minutes

(including 5 minutes' reading time before the test and 2 minutes' checking time at the end of the test)

Instructions

- Download the audio material to use with this test from **www.collins.co.uk/collinsgcserevision**
- Use black ink or black ball-point pen.
- You must **not** use a dictionary.

Information

- The marks for questions are shown in brackets.
- The maximum mark for this paper is 50.

Advice

For each item, you should do the following:

- Listen carefully to the recording. Read the questions again.
- Listen again to the recording. Then answer the questions.
- You may write at any point during the test.
- In **Section A**, answer the questions in **English**. In **Section B**, which is dictation, write in **French**.
- Answer all questions in the spaces provided.
- Write down all the information you are asked to give.
- You have 5 minutes to read through the question paper before the test begins. You may make notes during this time.

Name: ....

Section A   Listening comprehension

Home regions

You hear some French students talking about their area.

What is the opinion of the students on the following aspects?

Write **P** for a **positive** opinion.

N for a **negative** opinion.

P+N for a **positive** and **negative** opinion.

0 1	The streets		[1 mark]
0 2	The town		[1 mark]
0 3	The countryside		[1 mark]
0 4	The region		[1 mark]

A famous actor

You hear this podcast about Lucas, a Canadian actor.

Choose the correct answer and write the letter in each box.

Answer both parts of question 5.

`0 5` · `1` Lucas…

A	started acting aged 10.
B	is famous worldwide.
C	has been an actor for 10 years.

[1 mark]

`0 5` · `2` At school, Lucas…

A	had bad grades in geography.
B	was good at all his subjects.
C	got good marks in only one subject.

[1 mark]

Answer both parts of question 6.

`0 6` · `1` Lucas studied drama…

A	after he left school.
B	at school.
C	instead of doing languages.

[1 mark]

0 6 · 2 Lucas…

A	is going to marry a TV personality.
B	has just got married.
C	is going to get married in Spain.

[1 mark]

0 7 Lucas is going to…

A	take part in a sporting event.
B	come to Europe for the first time
C	go to his brother's wedding.

[1 mark]

Practice Exam Paper 1: Listening

A new shopping centre

You hear this information about a new shopping centre.

Write **A** if only statement **A** is correct.

B if only statement **B** is correct.

A+B if both statements **A** and **B** are correct.

Write the correct letter(s) in each box.

Answer both parts of question 8.

`0 8 · 1` The new shopping centre is open…

A	after midday.
B	before midday.

[1 mark]

`0 8 · 2` There will be…

A	free gifts.
B	reduced prices.

[1 mark]

`0 9` The offer is limited to…

A	certain age groups.
B	a certain day.

[1 mark]

A French school

Your French friend, Ahmed, is talking about his school.

Choose the correct answer and write the letter in each box.

Answer both parts of question 10.

`1 0` · `1` Ahmed thinks that his school…

A	starts too early.
B	is boring.
C	starts very late.

[1 mark]

`1 0` · `2` His journey to school…

A	is really interesting.
B	takes over an hour.
C	often makes him late.

[1 mark]

Answer both parts of question 11.

`1 1` · `1` This morning Ahmed has…

A	had breakfast.
B	a test in IT.
C	a computer problem.

[1 mark]

`1 1` · `2` He finds history…

A	useful.
B	interesting.
C	of no use.

[1 mark]

Practice Exam Paper 1: Listening

Healthy lifestyles

You hear this interview with Marthe, a Belgian doctor.

Answer the questions in **English**.

1 2   What **two** pieces of advice does Marthe give to stay fit?   [2 marks]

1. ....

2. ....

Answer question 13.

1 3   What **two** suggestions does Marthe make?   [2 marks]

1. ....

2. ....

Choose the correct answer and write the letter in the box.

1 4   What is the most important thing to stay healthy according to Marthe?

A	Keep active.
B	Follow a diet.
C	Don't smoke.

[1 mark]

A famous sportsman

You hear this podcast about Franck, a famous French sportsman, and his life.

Choose the correct answer and write the letter in each box.

1 5 · 1 Before he was 15, Franck…

A	was very sporty.
B	didn't do any sport.
C	did a lot of cycling.

[1 mark]

1 5 · 2 According to Franck, cycling is…

A	a great way to make friends.
B	not fun.
C	very tiring.

[1 mark]

Answer both parts of question 16.

1 6 · 1 What did Franck do last year? [1 mark]

_____

1 6 · 2 Where does Franck relax? [1 mark]

_____

Choose the correct answer and write the letter in the box.

1 7 Franck will soon…

A	visit a lot of schools.
B	talk to school children.
C	go to a hot country.

[1 mark]

Future plans

Sami and Marion are talking about their future plans.

A	They don't want to get married.
B	They want a well-paid job.
C	They want to work abroad.
D	They want to follow their parents' example.
E	They think their future will be sad.
F	They want a job which makes them happy.

Which are the **two** correct plans for each person?

Write the correct letters in the boxes.

```
1 8                                                    [2 marks]
```

```
1 9                                                    [2 marks]
```

Life in Senegal

Listen to Myriam talking about life in her country.

Choose the **two** correct statements.

Write the letters in the boxes.

A	Unemployment is a problem in Senegal.
B	Myriam has been ill recently.
C	Homelessness is common in Senegal.
D	Myriam's family has food and money problems.

```
2 0                                                    [2 marks]
```

The environment

Listen to this podcast about environmental issues.

Choose the **two** correct statements.

Write the letters in the boxes.

A	Young people aren't interested in environmental issues.
B	Older people are more worried about the environment.
C	Well over half the people over 60 years of age don't think recycling is important.
D	Teenagers think that nature is important.

2 1

[2 marks]

A radio programme

Listen to this radio broadcast.

Choose the correct answer and write the correct letter in each box.

2 2 . 1 Tomorrow hospitals will…

A	close.
B	only deal with emergencies.
C	continue as normal.

[1 mark]

2 2 . 2 There will be…

A	more than a thousand protesters.
B	government representatives on the streets in Paris.
C	a protest against capital punishment.

[1 mark]

Technology

Listen to Éric and Alicia discussing technology.

Choose the correct answer and write the letter in each box.

2 3 · 1 Éric's uncle…

A	was careless online.
B	has been accused of identity theft.
C	warned Éric about the dangers of the Internet.

[1 mark]

2 3 · 2 Alicia…

A	has been bullied at school.
B	has a family member who went on a social network.
C	says that her sister thinks that the Internet is safe.

[1 mark]

2 4 · 1 Alicia…

A	stays in touch with friends abroad.
B	buys clothes online.
C	thinks it's cheaper to shop online.

[1 mark]

2 4 · 2 Yesterday Éric…

A	had problems online.
B	bought a gift online.
C	chatted to his friend online.

[1 mark]

Section B   Dictation

You will now hear 5 short sentences.

Listen carefully and using your knowledge of French sounds, write down in **French** exactly what you hear for each sentence.

You will hear each sentence **three** times: the first time as a full sentence, the second time in short sections and the third time again as a full sentence.

Use your knowledge of French sounds and grammar to make sure that what you have written makes sense. Check carefully that your spelling is accurate.

[10 marks]

Sentence 1

Sentence 2

Sentence 3

Sentence 4

Sentence 5

YOU NOW HAVE TWO MINUTES TO CHECK YOUR WORK

END OF QUESTIONS

Collins

GCSE
French

Higher Tier Paper 2 Speaking

H

Candidate's material – Role-play

Candidate s material – Reading aloud text

Candidate's material – Photo card

Time allowed: 10–12 minutes

(+ 15 minutes' supervised preparation time)

Instructions

- During the preparation time, you are required to prepare **one** Role-play card, one Reading aloud task and **one** Photo card.
- You must **not** use a dictionary, including during the preparation time.

Information

The test will last a maximum of 12 minutes and will consist of three parts:

Part 1: a Role-play card (approximately 1–1.5 minutes).

Part 2: a Reading aloud text and short conversation based on the topic of the text (approximately 3–3.5 minutes).

Part 3: discussion of a Photo card containing two photos (approximately 6–7 minutes).

Name: ....

Part 1: Role-play

Prepare your <u>spoken</u> answers to this Role-play.

Instructions to candidates

You are talking to your French friend.

Your teacher will play the part of your friend and will speak first.

You should address your friend as *tu*.

When you see this – **?** – you will have to ask a question.

In order to score full marks, you must include at least one verb in your response to each task.

1. Describe your school. (Give **two** details.)
2. Say something about your teachers. (Give **two** details.)
3. Describe a recent school visit. (Give **two** details.)
4. Give **one** disadvantage about the Internet.
5. Ask your friend a question about social networks.

Practice Exam Paper 2: Speaking

Part 2: Reading aloud

When your teacher asks you, read aloud the following text **in French**.

> Hier, je suis allé en ville en train, avec mes copains.
>
> Mon meilleur ami a choisi un cadeau pour son oncle.
>
> J'aime télécharger de la musique sur Internet.
>
> Quand je suis libre, je fais du vélo ou je nage à la piscine.
>
> Pour moi, le sport est vraiment important.

You will then be asked four questions **in French** that relate to the topic of **Free-time activities**.

In order to score the highest marks, you must try to **answer all four questions as fully as you can**.

- Qu'est-ce que tu aimes acheter?
- Que penses-tu de la musique?
- Parle-moi de ton film préféré.
- Est-ce qu'il y a des avantages à faire du sport?

Part 3: Photo card

- During your preparation time, look at the two photos. You may make as many notes as you wish on an Additional Answer Sheet and use these notes during the test.
- Your teacher will ask you to talk about the content of these photos. The recommended time is approximately **one and a half minutes. You must say at least one thing about each photo.**
- After you have spoken about the content of the photos, your teacher will then ask you questions related to **any** of the topics within the theme of **People and lifestyle**.

Photo 1

Photo 2

Collins

GCSE
French
Higher Tier Paper 3 Reading

H

Time allowed: 1 hour

Instructions

- You must **not** use a dictionary.
- Use black ink or black ball-point pen.
- Answer all questions.
- You must answer the questions in the space provided.
- In **Section A**, answer the questions in **English**.
  In **Section B**, translate the sentences into **English**.

Information

- The marks for questions are shown in brackets.
- The maximum mark for this paper is 50.

Name: _____

Section A   Reading comprehension

Magazine headlines

You see these headlines in a French magazine.

A	Concert gratuit au parc demain
B	La grève des facteurs va causer des problèmes
C	Changement de climat: la Terre en danger
D	Le coût de la vie augmente
E	Vents difficiles au sud du pays demain

Which headline matches each event?

Write the correct letter in each box.

0 1 A damaging strike   [1 mark]

0 2 Increased costs   [1 mark]

0 3 Bad weather forecast   [1 mark]

Family life

You see a French website where people are talking about their families.

Chloé: Ma belle-mère est vraiment gentille mais je ne m'entends pas bien avec mon père.

Dominique: Ma petite sœur est très embêtante et elle parle tout le temps.

Jules: Ma famille est parfaite. Mes parents sont sympas, mon frère est génial et ma sœur m'aide toujours avec mes devoirs.

Karine: Mes parents sont ennuyeux et un peu trop bavards.

Luc: Je trouve mon frère très paresseux. Il ne fait rien à la maison.

What do these people think about their family?

Write **P** for a **positive** opinion.

N for a **negative** opinion.

P+N for a **positive** and **negative** opinion.

Write the correct answer in each box.

| 0 4 | Chloé | | [1 mark] |

| 0 5 | Dominique | | [1 mark] |

| 0 6 | Jules | | [1 mark] |

| 0 7 | Karine | | [1 mark] |

| 0 8 | Luc | | [1 mark] |

A teenager's life

Read Élodie's blog

> J'habite dans une petite ville dans le sud du pays. J'aime bien vivre ici car il y a beaucoup à faire pour les jeunes. Le seul inconvénient, c'est qu'il ne fait pas souvent chaud.
>
> Je sors souvent avec mes copains et hier, on est allés au centre commercial. J'ai acheté de nouveaux vêtements et ma meilleure amie a choisi un livre intéressant à la bibliothèque. Avant de rentrer, j'ai acheté des fraises puis je les ai mangées.

Answer the following questions in **English**.

0 9   Give **one** advantage and **one** disadvantage of Élodie's town.

Advantage ....

Disadvantage ....

[2 marks]

1 0   What did Élodie buy?

....

[1 mark]

1 1   What did her best friend do?

....

[1 mark]

1 2   Read the last sentence again. What would you do with **des fraises**?

Write the correct letter in the box.

A	drink them
B	wear them
C	eat them

[1 mark]

A famous singer

Read this online report about Memo, a French singer.

> **Demain soir, Memo chantera au Stade de France mais il ne reste plus de billets. Memo a commencé à chanter en ligne il y a deux ans et maintenant il est connu partout en France. Il vient d'écrire une chanson sur le chômage et il va bientôt jouer le rôle d'un jeune acteur dans une émission de télé.**

What does the article say about these events?

Write **P** for something that happened **in the past**.

N for something that is happening **now**.

F for something that will happen **in the future**.

Write the correct letter in each box.

| 1 3 | Memo's concert at the stadium | | [1 mark] |

| 1 4 | Memo's online singing | | [1 mark] |

| 1 5 | Being well known in France | | [1 mark] |

| 1 6 | Writing a song about unemployment | | [1 mark] |

| 1 7 | Appearing in a TV programme | | [1 mark] |

Environmental issues

You read this online forum.

People are discussing environmental issues.

Ahmed: Je pense qu'il faut essayer de réduire la circulation, surtout dans les grandes villes, parce qu'il est important d'arrêter non seulement la pollution, mais aussi le bruit.

Bruno: Pour moi, on doit absolument continuer de tout recycler: le bois, le verre, les boîtes et les journaux! Si on ne fait rien, on risque de détruire notre planète.

Caroline: Je crois qu'il est essentiel de ne pas faire construire de nouveaux bâtiments à la campagne car la nature est importante pour tout le monde.

Who expresses which opinions?

Write **A** for **Ahmed**.

      B for **Bruno**.

      C for **Caroline**.

Write the correct letter in each box.

| 1 8 | Don't do more building | | [1 mark] |

| 1 9 | Recycle everything | | [1 mark] |

| 2 0 | Stop noise | | [1 mark] |

| 2 1 | Reduce traffic | | [1 mark] |

| 2 2 | If we don't do anything | | [1 mark] |

Practice Exam Paper 3: Reading

A local festival

You read this article about a local festival.

> À partir du 30 avril, au Stade de France, il y aura un concert de musique populaire qui durera trois jours. Plus de 50 groupes vont y participer et il ne reste plus de billets. On pourra aussi acheter des vêtements, des cadeaux et des articles comme des instruments de musique et des livres. Ceux qui habitent près du stade commencent à s'inquiéter à cause du bruit, non seulement de la musique mais aussi des gens qui iront au concert.

Complete these sentences. Write the letter for the correct option in each box.

2 3 The concert will last…

A	until 30 April.
B	3 days.
C	50 minutes.

[1 mark]

2 4 The tickets…

A	have sold out.
B	are free.
C	cost 50 euros.

[1 mark]

2 5 At the concert you will be able to…

A	buy food and drink.
B	hear more than 50 groups.
C	play musical instruments.

[1 mark]

2 6 The people living near the stadium are…

A	noisy.
B	helping out at the event.
C	worried.

[1 mark]

Practice Exam Paper 3: Reading

A town that has changed

Ahmed has written this blog about his town.

> Quand j'avais cinq ans, ma ville, qui est située dans le sud-ouest de la France, était moins propre et il y avait beaucoup de déchets dans les rues. Heureusement, on a essayé d'améliorer ma région et maintenant j'aime bien le centre-ville. Le soir, on peut y marcher sans avoir peur, car dans le passé, il y avait de la violence. Plus tard dans la vie, j'aimerais vivre sur la côte car la mer me plaît beaucoup.

Answer the following questions in **English**.

2 7 What was Ahmed's town like when he was 5 years old? Give **two** details.

1. ....

2. ....

[2 marks]

2 8 Why does Ahmed like the town centre nowadays?

....

[1 mark]

2 9 Where would Ahmed like to live in the future?

....

[1 mark]

Two students

You read these posts on a French website.

Je me sens vraiment seule au lycée. J'avais beaucoup de copines mais il y a six mois, j'ai mis une photo sur un réseau social et ma vie a changé. Je souriais toujours, j'étais ouverte et contente. Maintenant, personne ne me parle, je n'ai plus de bonnes notes et je ne m'entends pas bien avec ma famille. (Lydie)

Moi, j'ai des problèmes au lycée. Je suis forte dans toutes les matières et on me dit que je réussirai aux examens, mais je suis toujours très triste parce que je n'ai pas d'amis. J'étudie tout le temps et je ne sors jamais. Je m'entends bien avec mes profs et mes parents mais je suis fille unique, alors je n'ai pas beaucoup de contacts sociaux chez moi. (Manon)

Who do the following statements refer to?

Write **M** for **Manon**.

     L for **Lyd**ie.

     M+L for **Manon** and **Lydie**.

Write the correct answer in each box.

3 0 Who has no friends?   [1 mark]

3 1 Who used to be happy?   [1 mark]

3 2 Who gets good marks in school?   [1 mark]

3 3 Who doesn't get on with her family?   [1 mark]

Practice Exam Paper 3: Reading

Changing hobbies

Read Pascal's blog.

> Avant, je faisais beaucoup d'activités sportives et on me disait que je serais peut-être joueur de sport professionnel. Je n'aimais pas lire car je pensais que c'était ennuyeux et que je n'avais pas le temps. En plus, je jouais beaucoup sur mon ordinateur et je passais des heures devant un écran, mais récemment, j'ai lu un roman qui m'a vraiment touché. Le roman raconte l'histoire d'un homme qui n'avait pas d'argent et qui a essayé d'améliorer sa vie. Après avoir lu le livre, j'ai voulu trouver d'autres livres du même auteur. Malheureusement, je suis un peu <u>frustré</u> car je ne peux pas en trouver.

Answer the question in **English**.

3 4 Why didn't Pascal (use to) read much?

....

....

[2 marks]

Complete these sentences. Write the letter for the correct option in each box.

3 5 The man in the novel...

A	succeeded in turning his life around.
B	was poor.
C	was an author.

[1 mark]

3 6 After reading the novel, Pascal…

A	wanted to write a book.
B	didn't read again.
C	wanted to read more books.

[1 mark]

3 7 Read the last sentence again. Which is the best translation for **frustré**?

A	frustrated
B	happy
C	nervous

[1 mark]

Section B   Translation into English

3 8   Translate these sentences into **English**.

Je vis à l'étranger depuis quatre ans.

[2 marks]

On dit que je passe trop de temps en ligne.

[2 marks]

Je vais essayer de boire moins de café.

[2 marks]

Si je travaille dur, je trouverai un bon boulot.

[2 marks]

Après être rentrée chez elle, elle a commencé à parler à son beau-père.

[2 marks]

END OF QUESTIONS

Collins

GCSE
French

Higher Tier Paper 4 Writing

Time allowed: 1 hour 15 minutes

Instructions

- Use black ink or black ball-point pen.
- You must answer **three** questions.
- In **Section A**, you must answer Question 1.
- In **Section B**, you must answer **either** Question 2.1 **or** Question 2.2. You must only answer **one** of these questions.
- In **Section C**, you must answer **either** Question 3.1 **or** Question 3.2. You must only answer **one** of these questions.
- Answer all questions in French.
- Answer the questions in the spaces provided.

Information

- The marks for questions are shown in brackets.
- The maximum mark for this paper is 50.
- You must **not** use a dictionary during this test.
- In order to score the highest marks for Question 2.1/Question 2.2, you must write something about each bullet point.
- In order to score the highest marks in Question 3.1/Question 3.2, you must write something about both bullet points.

Name:

Practice Exam Paper 4: Writing

Section A   Translation into French

0 1   Translate these sentences into **French**.   **[10 marks]**

I like to go to the beach with my friends in summer.

_____

_____

Next week, my brother will be fourteen.

_____

_____

Unfortunately it rains a lot in England.

_____

_____

I will not eat meat in the future.

_____

_____

I have decided to play football in order to be in good health.

_____

_____

Section B   Answer **either** Question 2.1 **or** Question 2.2

You must only answer **one** of these questions.

Either Question 2.1

0 2 . 1 You are emailing your Canadian friend about holidays.

Write approximately **90** words in **French**.

You must write something about each bullet point.

Describe:

- your favourite holiday destination
- a recent holiday
- where you will go next year.

[15 marks]

Or Question 2.2

0 2 . 2 You are writing an article about free time activities for a French school's magazine.

Write approximately **90** words in **French**.

You must write something about each bullet point.

Describe:

- your favourite free time activity
- a recent event
- what you plan to do with friends next weekend.

[15 marks]

Section C   Answer **either** Question 3.1 **or** Question 3.2

You must only answer **one** of these questions.

Either Question 3.1

0 3 · 1 You are writing an article about schools.

Your article is for a social media post.

Write approximately **150** words in **French**.

You must write something about both bullet points.

Describe:

- why your school is a good school
- your education plans for the future.

[25 marks]

Or Question 3.2

0 3 · 2 You are writing a post for a French website.

Your post is about the environment.

Write approximately **150** words in **French**.

You must write something about both bullet points.

Describe:

- the importance of protecting the planet
- what you have done to help the environment.

[25 marks]

END OF QUESTIONS

Answers

People and Lifestyle

Pages 154–155: Identity and Relationships with Others

1. a) Paulin [1]
   b) Amel [1]
   c) Farida [1]
   d) Aimée [1]
   e) Xavier [1]

2. **Aimée:** I don't have / any brother and sisters. [2]
   Paulin: I get on well with / my step-sister and my step-dad. [2]
   Farida: I have a little sister who / is two years younger than me. [2]
   Xavier: My brother and my sister / are 3 years older than me. They are the same age. [2]
   Amel: My brother and I never argue. / We get on very well. [2]

3. a) Je n'ai pas de frères et sœurs.
   b) Je m'entends bien avec ma demi-sœur et mon beau-père.
   c) J'ai une petite sœur qui a deux ans de moins que moi.
   d) Mon frère et ma sœur ont trois ans de plus que moi. Ils ont le même âge.
   e) Mon frère et moi, nous ne nous disputons jamais. On s'entend très bien.

   Read sentences aloud then listen to sentences to check. (1 mark for each sentence read correctly)

4. a) embêtante [1]; bavarde [1]
   b) petits [1]; drôles [1]
   c) active [1]; généreuse [1]
   d) amusant [1]; gentil [1]
   e) gentille [1]; intelligente [1]

5. a) ami [1]; ans [1]; mêmes [1]
   b) amie [1]; bien [1]; attitude [1]
   c) qualités [1]; copain [1]; bon [1]
   d) copine [1]; moi [1]; choses [1]
   e) yeux [1]; cheveux [1]; taille [1]

6. a) Mon ami / copain Oscar est plus grand que moi. [1]
   b) Ma meilleure amie / copine / Mon meilleur ami / copain a 15 ans. [1]
   c) Ma meilleure amie / copine a les cheveux longs et elle est très gentille. [1]
   d) Je m'entends bien avec ma copine / mon amie / mon copain / ami parce que nous avons les mêmes passe-temps. [1]
   e) Je ne m'entends pas bien avec Lena parce que nous n'aimons pas les mêmes choses. [1]

Pages 156–157: Healthy Living and Lifestyle

1. a) J'aime la cuisine française. [1]
   b) Je suis végétarien / ne. [1]
   c) Je bois beaucoup d'eau. [1]
   d) J'ai mangé du poulet. [1]
   e) J'aime la cuisine / nourriture chinoise. [1]

2. a) F [1]; b) F [1]; c) T [1]; d) F [1]; e) T [1]; f) T [1]

3. a) N [1]; b) F [1]; c) P [1]; d) P [1]; e) F [1]; f) N [1]

4. Read words aloud then listen to words to check. (1 mark for each word read correctly)

5. a) --- iii) [1] My back hurts. [1]
   b) --- ii) [1] Her head hurts. [1]
   c) --- v) [1] His ear hurts. [1]
   d) --- i) [1] I have broken my leg. [1]
   e) --- iv) [1] I have cut my hand. [1]

6. a) E [1]; b) C [1]; c) A [1]; d) B [1]; e) D [1]

Pages 158–159: Education and Work

1. Answers will vary. (1 mark per correct answer)

2. a) P [1]; b) N [1]; c) P+N [1]; d) P [1]; e) P+N [1]

3. a) Tessa [1]; b) Karim [1]; c) Axelle [1]; d) Tessa [1]

4. Read words aloud then read sentences aloud. Listen to sentences to check. (1 mark for each sentence read correctly)

5. Answers will vary. (5 marks for making sentences and 5 marks for translating into English)

6. a) She liked it. [1]
   b) in year 11 [1]
   c) science [1] and geography [1]
   d) abroad [1]
   e) about the environment [1]

Popular Culture

Pages 160–161: Free-time Activities

1. a) Pauline [1]
   b) Farid [1]
   c) Léna [1]
   d) Hector [1]
   e) Arthur [1]

2. Read words aloud then listen to words to check. (1 mark for each word read correctly)

3. a) N [1]; b) P [1]; c) F [1]; d) P [1]; e) P [1]

4. a) P [1]; b) N [1]; c) P [1]; d) P [1]; e) N [1]

5. a) Hier, j'ai regardé un concert. [1]
   b) Le week-end dernier, j'ai téléchargé une chanson. [1]
   c) J'ai aimé le festival. [1]
   d) Lundi dernier, j'ai joué avec mon groupe. [1]
   e) Ce matin, avant le collège, j'ai écouté de la musique. [1]

6. a) a programme [1]
   b) a series [1]
   c) screen [1]
   d) reality tv [1]
   e) the story [1]
   f) online [1]
   g) famous [1]
   h) new [1]

7. Ma **série** [1] préférée est l' **histoire** [1] d'un groupe d'ados.
   Je la regarde tous les jours **en ligne** [1].
   L'actrice principale est américaine et elle est très **célèbre** [1]. Elle chante aussi.
   C'est comme de **la télé-réalité** [1], car dans chaque épisode on suit les ados dans leur vie de tous les jours.

Pages 162–163: Customs, Festivals and Celebrations

1. a) --- iv) [1]; b) --- vi) [1]; c) --- viii) [1]; d) --- ii) [1];
   e) --- vii) [1]; f) --- v) [1]; g) --- iii) [1]; h) --- i) [1]

2. a) C [1]; b) E [1]; c) A [1]; d) F [1]; e) D [1]; f) B [1]

3. a) N [1]; b) F [1]; c) N [1]; d) P [1]; e) P [1]; f) F [1]

4. a) N [1]; b) P+N [1]; c) N [1]; d) N [1]; e) P [1]

5. Read sentences aloud then listen to sentences to check.
   (1 mark for each sentence read correctly)

6. a) beaucoup [1]; cadeaux [1]
   b) restaurant [1]; intéressant [1]
   c) aimons [1]; anniversaires [1]
   d) j'aime [1]; pense [1]
   e) nous aimons / les anniversaires [1]

Pages 164–165: Celebrity Culture

1. Answers will vary. (1 mark for each correct answer)

2. a) la mode [1] fashion [1]
   b) la santé [1] health [1]
   c) la diversité [1] diversity [1]
   d) l'influence [1] influence [1]
   e) la liberté [1] freedom [1]
   f) les handicapés [1] disabled people [1]
   g) l'égalité [1] equality [1]
   h) la différence [1] difference [1]

3. a) --- iii) [1]; b) --- i) [1]; c) --- v) [1]; d) --- ii) [1]; e) --- iv) [1]

4. a) Social media are important for teenagers. [1]
   b) I follow many fashion influencers. [1]
   c) I have decided to start a blog. [1]
   d) I enjoy reading the blogs of my favourite
      influencers. [1]
   e) Many celebrities talk about problems in our
      society. [1]

5. a) Fariq [1]
   b) Maximilien [1]
   c) Marion [1]
   d) Rania [1]
   e) Marion [1]

6. a) Je passe beaucoup de temps [1]
   b) Je sais que… [1]
   c) vivre sans [1]
   d) des choses formidables pour notre société [1]
   e) un bon moyen de parler [1]
   f) Il est possible de… [1]
   g) pour défendre nos idées [1]
   h) beaucoup d'avantages [1]
   i) il est facile de [1]
   j) peut causer des problèmes [1]

7. Read text aloud then listen to text to check.
   (1 mark for each sentence read correctly)

Communication and the World Around Us

Pages 166–167: Travel and Tourism

1. Answers will vary. (1 mark for each correct answer)

2. Lydie: D [1]
   Marcel: B [1]
   Erika: C [1]
   Mohammed: A [1]

3.

	What?		Why?	
A	Restaurant	[1]	Closed in the evening	[1]
B	Food	[1]	Cold	[1]
C	Bedroom	[1]	Too small / very dirty	[1]
D	Pool	[1]	Too hot / too crowded	[1]
E	Beach	[1]	Too noisy	[1]

4. a) B [1]; b) D [1]; c) E [1]; d) C [1]; e) A [1]

5. a) F [1]; b) P [1]; c) N [1]; d) F [1]; e) F [1]

6. Read sentences aloud then listen to sentences to check.
   (1 mark for each sentence read correctly)

7. a) beach [1]
   b) 40 [1]
   c) varied [1]
   d) every day [1]; 9am [1]–8pm [1]
   e) not allowed [1]; summer [1]

Pages 168–169: Media and Technology

1. a) Émeric [1]
   b) Youssef [1]
   c) Claire [1]
   d) Roselyne [1]
   e) Marceline [1]

2. a) Je télécharge beaucoup de vidéos. [1]
   b) Je suis toujours sur mon portable. [1]
   c) Je passe des heures sur les réseaux sociaux. [1]
   d) Je partage des photos avec mes amis. [1]
   e) Je suis la vie des influenceurs. [1]

3. Read words aloud then listen to words to check.
   (1 mark for each word read correctly)

4. a) P [1]; b) N [1]; c) P [1]; d) P [1]; e) P [1]

5. a) --- iii) [1]; Yesterday, I shared some photos. [1]
   b) --- iv) [1]; Last weekend, I did some online
      shopping. [1]
   c) --- i) [1]; Last night, I downloaded some songs. [1]
   d) --- ii) [1]; Recently, I wrote a blog about my
      favourite sport. [1]
   e) --- v) [1]; I watched a show. [1]

6. a) messages [1]
   b) parle [1]
   c) courses [1]
   d) lis [1]
   e) devoirs [1]
   f) peut [1]
   g) temps [1]
   h) suivre [1]

7. Answers will vary. (1 mark for each answer)

Pages 170–171: The Environment and Where People Live

1.

building	a) le bâtiment	[1]	garden	f) le jardin	[1]
house	b) la maison	[1]	kitchen	g) la cuisine	[1]
flat	c) l'appartement	[1]	window	h) la fenêtre	[1]
room	d) la salle	[1]	door	i) la porte	[1]
office	e) le bureau	[1]	bed	j) le lit	[1]

2. a) I live in town. [1]
   b) I would like to live in the countryside. [1]
   c) There is a shopping centre and a swimming pool. [1]
   d) There aren't enough shops. [1]
   e) My village is very quiet. [1]

3. Read sentences aloud then listen to sentences to check. (1 mark for each sentence read correctly)

4. a) Caroline [1]
   b) Georges [1]
   c) Kylian [1]
   d) Melinda [1]
   e) Melinda [1]

5. Read words aloud then listen to words to check. (1 mark for each word read correctly)

6. a) N [1]; b) N [1]; c) P [1]; d) N [1]; e) N [1]

7. a) Je dois recycler plus et polluer moins. [1]
   b) Il est important d'utiliser les transports publics. [1]
   c) Il ne faut pas jeter les déchets par terre. [1]
   d) Il ne faut pas détruire notre environnement. [1]
   e) On doit changer! [1]

Grammar 1

Pages 172–173

1. a) une [1]; b) un [1]; c) une [1]; d) un [1]; e) un [1];
   f) un [1]; g) une [1]; h) un [1]; i) une [1]; j) une [1]

2. a) des maisons [1]
   b) des médecins [1]
   c) des filles [1]
   d) des pères [1]
   e) des campings [1]
   f) des jours [1]
   g) des familles [1]
   h) des chiens [1]
   i) des heures [1]
   j) des années [1]

3. a) le [1]; b) le [1]; c) le [1]; d) les [1]; e) l' [1];
   f) les [1]; g) les [1]; h) les [1]; i) l' [1]; j) la [1]

4. a) des bateaux [1]
   b) des bras [1]
   c) des chapeaux [1]
   d) des chevaux [1]
   e) des repas [1]
   f) des journaux [1]
   g) des tables [1]
   h) des taux [1]
   i) des châteaux [1]
   j) des animaux [1]

5. J'habite dans une **[1]** grande ville dans le **[1]** nord de l'Angleterre **[1]** avec mes **[1]** parents, ma **[1]** petite sœur et mes **[1]** deux frères. Nous avons aussi un **[1]** petit chien qui s'appelle Léo et des **[1]** poissons. Nous habitons dans un **[1]** grand appartement dans le **[1]** centre-ville, près de l'hôpital **[1]** et des **[1]** magasins.

6. a) Ma sœur est **grande**. [1]
   b) Ma table est **grise**. [1]
   c) Ma voiture est **rouge**. [1]
   d) Ma sœur est **sympa**. [1]
   e) Ma robe est **chère**. [1]
   f) Ma mère est **petite**. [1]
   g) Ma cousine est **brune**. [1]

h) Ma robe est **blanche**. [1]
i) Ma belle-mère est **active**. [1]
j) Ma maison est **belle**. [1]

7. a) Je suis **plus [1]** grande **que [1]** ma sœur.
   b) Ma sœur est **aussi [1]** gentille **que [1]** moi.
   c) Mon frère court **plus [1]** vite **que [1]** moi.
   d) Le français est **plus [1]** intéressant **que [1]** l'espagnol.
   e) La Belgique est **plus [1]** belle **que [1]** la Suisse.

8. Salut! Je m'appelle Lisa et j'ai deux **petites [1]** (little) sœurs. Maria est très **grande [1]** (tall) et elle a les cheveux **noirs [1]** (black). Nous sommes très **sportives [1]** (sporty) mais parfois un peu **paresseuses [1]** (lazy). Nous sommes toutes les trois **végétariennes [1]** (vegetarian). J'ai aussi un demi-frère qui est **plus âgé que [1]** (older than) nous. Maria est la **plus grande [1]** (tallest) et Sophia est la **plus petite [1]** (smallest). Je suis **la meilleure [1]** (the best).

9.

	Adjectives	French Adverbs	English Adverbs
a)	possible	**possiblement [1]**	possibly
b)	simple	**simplement [1]**	simply
c)	juste	**justement [1]**	rightly
d)	libre	**librement [1]**	freely
e)	faible	**faiblement [1]**	weakly

Pages 174–175

1.

	parler		finir		attendre	
Je / J'	parl**e**	**[1]**	fini**s**	**[1]**	attends	
Tu	parles		finis	**[1]**	attend**s**	**[1]**
Il / Elle / On	parl**e**	**[1]**	finit	**[1]**	attend	
Nous	parl**ons**	**[1]**	fin**issons**	**[1]**	attendons	
Vous	parlez		fin**issez**	**[1]**	attend**ez**	**[1]**
Ils / Elles	parl**ent**	**[1]**	finissent		attendent	**[1]**

2. a) --- iii) [1]
   b) --- iv) [1]
   c) --- ii) [1]
   d) --- i) [1]
   e) --- v) [1]

3. a) Je **mange** beaucoup de légumes. [1]
   b) Elle **regarde** tous les soirs la télé. [1]
   c) Nous **passons** nos vacances à la montagne. [1]
   d) Le collège **finit** à 15h30. [1]
   e) Nous nous **entendons** bien. [1]

4. Normalement, nous pass**ons [1]** (passer) nos vacances en France, au bord de la mer. Parfois, s'il pleut, on reste **[1]** (rester) à la maison de vacances. Ma mère et ma sœur ador**ent [1]** (adorer) passer les vacances en France car elles parl**ent [1]** (parler) français.

5. a) Je **travaille**. [1]
   b) Elle **cherche**. [1]
   c) Nous **utilisons**. [1]
   d) Il **prépare**. [1]

6. a) elle a [1]
   b) nous sommes [1]
   c) elle est [1]
   d) elles ont [1]
   e) je suis [1]

f) nous avons [1]
g) ils sont [1]
h) il a [1]
i) j'ai [1]
j) tu as [1]

7. **a)** J'**ai** [1] quatorze ans et ma sœur **a** [1] seize ans.
   b) Mon copain **a** [1] le même âge que moi.
   c) Tu **as** [1] soif?
   d) J'**ai** [1] très faim.
   e) Tu **as** [1] chaud ou tu **as** [1] froid?

8. Read sentences aloud then listen to sentences to check. (1 mark for each sentence read correctly)

9. **a)** I do / I am doing [1]
   b) She does / she is doing [1]
   c) We go / we are going [1]
   d) They go / are going [1]
   e) I go / am going [1]

10. Answers will vary. (5 marks for making five sentences and 5 marks for translating into English)

Grammar 2

Pages 176–177

1. je suis allé [1]; nous avons rencontré [1]; elle a mangé [1]; j'ai préparé [1]; il a acheté [1]

2. **a)** --- ii) / v) [1]; I spent / decided [1]
   b) --- iv) [1]; You tried [1]
   c) --- i) [1]; She looked [1]
   d) --- ii) / v) [1]; We spent / decided [1]
   e) --- iii) [1]; You chose [1]
   f) --- vi) [1]; They participated / took part [1]

3. **a)** J'ai **pris** [1]
   b) Elle a **fait** [1]
   c) Nous avons **vu** [1]
   d) Il a **bu** [1]
   e) J'ai **reçu** [1]

4. **a)** Quand j'**étais** [1] petite, je **regardais** [1] beaucoup la télé.
      When I was little, I used to watch TV a lot. [1]
   b) Quand j'**avais** [1] 10 ans, je **jouais** [1] au tennis.
      When I was 10 years old, I used to play tennis. [1]
   c) Avant, mon frère **était** [1] moins timide.
      Before, my brother was less shy. [1]
   d) Avant, ma sœur **faisait** [1] de la gymnastique.
      Before, my sister used to do gymnastics. [1]

5. **a)** je vais aller [1]
   b) je voudrais passer [1]
   c) elle voudrait être [1]
   d) elle va avoir [1]
   e) je voudrais réserver [1]
   f) nous allons travailler [1]
   g) elle voudrait aller [1]
   h) je vais être [1]

6. **a)** Demain, **je vais aller** [1] au cinéma.
   b) La semaine prochaine, **je voudrais rester** [1] chez moi.
   c) Un jour, **je vais avoir** [1] un chien.
   d) Ce soir, **je voudrais regarder** [1] un film.
   e) Dimanche prochain, **je vais voir** [1] mes copains.

7. Answers will vary. (1 mark for each correct sentence)

8. **a)** --- iii) [1]
   b) --- i) [1]
   c) --- ii) [1]
   d) --- iv) [1]

Pages 178–179

1. **a)** Je pense qu'**elle** [1] est gentille.
   b) **Il** [1] est très grand.
   c) **Ils** [1] travaillent dans la police.
   d) **Elles** [1] sont en vacances.
   e) **Nous** [1] aimons faire du vélo.

2. **a)** Je ne **les** [1] regarde jamais.
   b) Je ne **l'**aime [1] pas.
   c) Je voudrais **la** [1] prendre.
   d) Je ne **la** [1] connais pas.
   e) Il faut **les** [1] respecter.

3. **a)** in front of [1]
   b) between [1]
   c) in [1]
   d) for [1]
   e) after [1]
   f) before [1]

4. **a)** J'habite **en** [1] France.
   b) Mon collège est **entre** [1] le parc et la gare.
   c) **Après** [1] les vacances, je vais aller **à** [1] l'université.
   d) **Pour** [1] mon anniversaire, je veux aller au restaurant.

5.

qui	who [1]	pourquoi	why [1]
que	what [1]	combien (de)	how many / much [1]
quoi	what [1]	comment	how [1]
où	where [1]	quel / quelle / quels / quelles	which [1]
quand	when [1]	lequel / laquelle / lesquels / lesquelles	which one(s) [1]

6. **a)** What do you like? [1]
   b) Where would you like to go? [1]
   c) Who would you like to meet? [1]
   d) How do you like to spend your weekend? [1]
   e) Why do you like…? [1]

7. Answers will vary. (1 mark for each correct sentence)

Pages 180–191

Higher Tier Paper 1 Listening – Mark Scheme

Section A Listening comprehension

01. N [1]
02. P+N [1]
03. N [1]
04. P [1]
05.1 C [1]
05.2 C [1]
06.1 A [1]
06.2 B [1]
07. B [1]
08.1 A [1]
08.2 A [1]
09. A+B [1]
10.1 A [1]
10.2 B [1]

11.1 B [1]

11.2 C [1]

12. Avoid eating too much red meat [1] and (try to) stop vaping [1].

13. Try a new sport [1] and exercise twice a week [1].

14. B [1]

15.1 B [1]

15.2 A [1]

16.1 Won his second Tour de France. [1]

16.2 Far away from people [1]

17. C [1]

18. B and C in either order [2]

19. A and F in either order [2]

20. A and D in either order [2]

21. C and D in either order [2]

22.1 B [1]

22.2 A [1]

23.1 A [1]

23.2 B [1]

24.1 C [1]

24.2 B [1]

Section B Dictation

Sentence 1: Ma mère / est timide. [2]

Sentence 2: J'aime manger / des fraises. [2]

Sentence 3: On doit / toujours / faire de son mieux. [2]

Sentence 4: Hier, je suis allé / à la mairie. [2]

Sentence 5: À l'avenir / je travaillerai / dans une bibliothèque. [2]

Pages 192–195

Higher Tier Paper 2 Speaking – Mark Scheme

Part 1: Role-play

Teacher script and sample answers:
1 Ton école, elle est comment?
 Mon école est grande. Il y a cinq bâtiments.
2 Parle-moi de tes professeurs.
 Mon prof de français est gentil mais je déteste mon prof de maths.
3 Où es-tu allé récemment avec ton collège?
 Je suis allé au musée et c'était excellent.
4 Que penses-tu d'Internet?
 Internet est très dangereux.
5 D'accord! (Then respond appropriately to the question asked.)
 Tu aimes les réseaux sociaux?

Part 2: Reading aloud

Sample answers:
1 J'aime acheter des livres car j'adore lire. J'aime aussi acheter des cadeaux pour mes amis.
2 J'adore la musique et je télécharge souvent des chansons. Mon chanteur préféré est Stormzy.
3 Je préfère les films comiques parce que j'adore rire. Mon film préféré s'appelle Up!
4 Le sport est important car c'est bon pour la santé. Il faut faire beaucoup d'exercice.

Part 3: Photo card

Sample answer:
Sur la première photo, il y a quatre personnes qui marchent à la campagne. Je crois que c'est une famille.

Je pense qu'il fait assez froid car les parents et les deux enfants portent des vêtements chauds. Sur la deuxième photo, il y a deux jeunes gens près d'une grande rivière. Ils prennent un selfie et ils sourient. Derrière les deux personnes, il y a des bâtiments et des bateaux.

Teacher script:
Theme: Communication and the world around us
The candidate is given a card containing two photos from the same topic and makes notes on them in the preparation period.
You ask the candidate to talk about the photos. At Higher tier, the recommended time is approximately **one and a half minutes**. The candidate must say at least one thing about each photo. You then have an unprepared conversation which is recommended to last between **four and a half and five and a half minutes.**
Candidates may use any notes they have made during the preparation time.
You begin by asking the candidate to tell you about the photos.

• Parle-moi des photos.

When the candidate has finished talking about the photos for approximately one and a half minutes, you have a conversation within the theme of **Communication and the world around us**. This can include **any or all** of the prescribed topics:

• Travel and tourism including places of interest
• Media and technology
• The environment and where people live

At Higher tier, Part 3 of the test is recommended to last in total **between six and seven minutes.**
This includes the description of the photos and the unprepared conversation.

Pages 196–208

Higher Tier Paper 3 Reading – Mark Scheme

Section A Reading comprehension

01. B [1]

02. D [1]

03. E [1]

04. P+N [1]

05. N [1]

06. P [1]

07. N [1]

08. N [1]

09. Lots to do for young people [1]; hot weather is very rare [1]

10. new clothes [1]

11. chose a library book [1]

12. C [1]

13. F [1]

14. P [1]

15. N [1]

16. P [1]

17. F [1]

18. C [1]

19. B [1]

20. A [1]

21. A [1]

22. B [1]

23. B   [1]
24. A   [1]
25. B   [1]
26. C   [1]
27. less clean [1]; there was rubbish in streets [1]
28. you / one can walk at night without fear   [1]
29. on the coast   [1]
30. M+L   [1]
31. L   [1]
32. M   [1]
33. L   [1]
34. found it boring [1] and didn't have the time [1]
35. B   [1]
36. C   [1]
37. A   [1]

Section B Translation into English

I have lived abroad for 4 years.   [2]
People / they say that I spend too much time online.   [2]
I'm going to try to / and drink less coffee.   [2]
If I work hard, I'll find a good job.   [2]
After returning home, she started talking to her step-father.   [2]

Pages 209–214

Higher Tier Paper 4 Writing – Mark Scheme

Section A Translation into French

01 L'été, j'aime aller à la plage avec mes amis. [2]
   La semaine prochaine, mon frère aura quatorze ans. [2]
   Malheureusement, il pleut beaucoup en Angleterre. [2]
   À l'avenir, je ne mangerai pas de viande. [2]
   J'ai décidé de jouer au football pour être en bonne santé. [2]

Section B

02.1   Sample answer:
     Quand je vais en vacances, j'adore aller en France car en général il fait beau et chaud. J'aime bien parler avec les gens et essayer la nourriture de la région.
     L'année dernière, avec mes copains, je suis allé au bord de la mer dans le sud de l'Angleterre et je me suis très bien amusé. On est allés à la plage et il a fait beau, alors on a nagé dans la mer et c'était vraiment génial.
     L'année prochaine, j'irai au Canada avec ma famille. On va aller voir mon oncle qui habite là-bas. Je voudrais visiter Montréal. Je ferai des achats. J'achèterai des cadeaux pour mes amis. Ce sera super.

02.2   Sample answer:
     Quand je suis libre, j'adore jouer au foot avec mes copains car c'est un sport passionnant qui est bon pour la santé. Je joue pour une équipe locale et c'est amusant.
     Le mois dernier, j'ai fait du vélo avec mon meilleur copain, à la campagne. C'était vraiment génial et nous avons passé une excellente journée. Ma mère nous avait préparé un repas que nous avons mangé dans un joli champ.
     Le week-end prochain, je vais aller en ville avec mes amis et nous allons voir un film comique au cinéma. J'espère qu'on s'amusera bien.

Section C

03.1   Sample answer:
     Mon collège est vraiment excellent parce que les bâtiments sont modernes et que je m'entends très bien avec tous mes professeurs. Ils sont travailleurs et gentils et ils me respectent. Je travaille dur et ils m'aident beaucoup si j'ai un problème avec mes devoirs. Les règles du collège ne sont pas trop strictes et je les trouve justes.
     L'année prochaine, j'ai l'intention de rester dans la même école. J'aimerais étudier l'anglais, le français et l'histoire car je suis fort en langues et je m'intéresse au passé. Plus tard, j'irai à l'université: je voudrais étudier les langues. Si je travaille beaucoup et que j'ai de la chance, je réussirai.

03.2   Sample answer:
     À mon avis, il faut protéger notre planète car c'est vraiment important. Je m'intéresse à l'environnement et je crois qu'on doit arrêter la pollution qui menace la Terre. Si on ne réagit pas, on risque de ne pas continuer de vivre. C'est très dangereux. Mes amis pensent qu'il faut faire plus et dans notre région, nous avons créé un club où on peut discuter les problèmes du monde.
     Récemment, j'ai commencé à tout recycler: le verre, le plastique, le métal et le papier. Je pense que cela est nécessaire car je voudrais habiter un monde propre où on peut vivre longtemps. J'ai aussi décidé de prendre le bus ou le train pour les voyages assez longs et d'aller en ville à pied ou à vélo.

Collins

GCSE
FRENCH

H

Higher Tier Paper 1 Listening Test Transcript

Section A		Listening comprehension

01	F1	Dans ma ville, les rues ne sont pas propres. Il faut les nettoyer chaque jour et c'es nul.
02	F2	J'habite dans une ville où il y a beaucoup d'excellents magasins mais il y a aussi beaucoup de pollution.
03	M1	J'habite dans un petit village à la campagne. Il n'y a rien à faire et je trouve ça difficile.
04	M2	Ma région est parfaite et il fait toujours beau. J'ai vraiment de la chance d'y vivre.
05	M1	Lucas est né au Canada. Il est acteur depuis dix ans et il est célèbre partout dans le monde francophone. Quand il était plus jeune, il rêvait de réussir dans la vie mais à l'école, il n'avait pas de bonnes notes sauf en géographie où il était fort.
06	M1	Après avoir quitté l'école, Lucas a commencé à étudier le théâtre. Il a aussi essayé d'améliorer ses compétences en langues. Il a appris l'espagnol et il le parle très bien. Il vient de se marier avec une star de la télévision qui ne parle que l'espagnol!
07	M1	Le mois prochain, pour la première fois, il va venir en Europe car son frère participera à un concours sportif et Lucas voudrait le voir.

08	F1	Le nouveau centre commercial ouvrira ses portes demain après-midi. Il y aura des produits gratuits mais pas de prix réduits.
09	F1	Le lendemain, si vous avez moins de seize ans, vous pourrez recevoir une glace gratuite.
10	M2	Le matin, on commence vraiment trop tôt car le voyage jusqu'au collège dure plus d'une heure et je n'aime pas ça. C'est vraiment ennuyeux.
11	M2	Ce matin, j'ai un contrôle en informatique et après le déjeuner, on a un cours d'histoire, une matière inutile à mon avis.
12	M1	Alors, Marthe, vous avez des conseils pour garder la forme?
	F2	Il faut éviter de manger trop de viande rouge et si vous vapotez, cela vaut la peine d'essayer d'arrêter, car c'est mauvais pour la santé.
13	M1	C'est intéressant, ça. Le sport, c'est une bonne idée pour améliorer sa santé?
	F2	Certainement. Pourquoi ne pas essayer une nouvelle activité sportive ou de faire de l'exercice deux fois par semaine?
14	M1	Que faites-vous pour rester en forme, Marthe?
	F2	Moi je fais beaucoup de choses. Je suis très active et je n'ai jamais fumé, mais pour moi, le plus important, c'est de suivre un régime qui me permet d'être en bonne santé.
15	M3	Tout le monde pense que j'ai toujours été sportif, mais ce n'est pas vrai. J'ai commencé à faire du vélo dans un club à l'âge de quinze ans. Avant, je ne faisais pas du tout de sport. Le vélo, c'était non seulement amusant mais surtout un bon moyen de se faire de nouveaux amis.
16	M3	Aujourd'hui, je suis un sportif célèbre et j'ai participé à cinq Tours de France. L'année dernière, j'ai gagné mon deuxième tour et c'était passionnant. Maintenant, comme je suis très connu, j'aime bien me relaxer loin des gens.
17	M3	Cette année, j'ai passé des heures à parler de mon sport aux enfants de beaucoup d'écoles et je vais bientôt aller en vacances dans un pays chaud.

18	M1	J'ai toujours aimé voyager, alors plus tard dans la vie, j'aimerais habiter ailleurs, dans un pays différent. J'ai aussi l'intention de trouver un travail très bien payé parce qu'un jour j'espère me marier et avoir des enfants.
19	F1	Pour moi, l'argent n'est pas important, donc quand je choisirai un emploi, être heureuse sera la chose la plus importante. Je ne voudrais pas me marier car mes parents se sont séparés il y a quelques années et ils sont toujours tristes.
20	F3	J'habite à la campagne, au Sénégal. Dans mon pays, le chômage est un problème grave et ma famille a des problèmes pour se nourrir. Récemment, mon père est tombé malade, et nous n'avons pas assez d'argent pour vivre.
21	F1	Quand on parle de l'environnement, il y a une grande différence entre les générations. En général, les jeunes sont plus conscients des problèmes et ils essayent d'améliorer la situation, mais trois quarts des plus de soixante ans disent que recycler n'est pas important. Les adolescents pensent qu'il faut préserver la nature.
22	M2	Demain, il y aura une grève des médecins à Paris. Les hôpitaux ne seront pas fermés, mais on n'admettra que les cas urgents. Plus de mille employés vont manifester contre le gouvernement dans les rues de la capitale.
23	M1	Je trouve Internet vraiment dangereux. La semaine dernière, on a volé l'identité de mon oncle qui a laissé ses informations personnelles en ligne.
	F1	Je suis d'accord. Ma sœur a été harcelée, après avoir passé des heures sur un réseau social.
	M1	Quel dommage!
24	F1	Il y a aussi des choses positives.
	M1	Ah oui, je peux communiquer facilement avec mes copains qui vivent à l'étranger.
	F1	C'est génial. Moi, j'aime faire des achats en ligne car c'est moins cher, mais je n'achète jamais de vêtements sur Internet.
	M1	Hier, je cherchais un petit cadeau pour mon meilleur ami en ligne et j'en ai trouvé un sans problèmes.

Section B   Dictation

Sentence 1   **F1**   Ma mère / est timide.

Sentence 2   **M1**   J'aime manger / des fraises.

Sentence 3   **F2**   On doit / toujours / faire de son mieux.

Sentence 4   **M2**   Hier, je suis allé / à la mairie.

Sentence 5   **M2**   À l'avenir / je travaillerai / dans une bibliothèque.

END OF TEST